DIVE SUᴗᴗᴇх

A DIVER GUIDE

Kendall McDonald

Underwater World Publications

Above: The bell from the *Blanefield,* recovered by
Michael Keane (Site **270**).
Title page: The slipway at Newhaven Marina.
Front cover: The 12-pounder gun on the wreck of
HMS *Northcoates* (Site **99**).

Editorial production by Martyn Yeo

Map artwork by Design IT, Liphook, Hampshire

Produced by Diver Magazine

Published by Underwater World Publications Ltd,
55 High Street, Teddington, Middlesex, TW11 8HA

First published 1985
Second edition 1989
Reprinted 1995
Third edition 1999
Reprinted 2003

© Underwater World Publications Ltd 1999

ISBN 0 946020 28 0

Printed in the United Arab Emirates by Emirates Printing Press,
PO Box 5106, Al Quoz, Dubai

Contents

Divers loading into an RIB at Newhaven Marina.

Preface

The enormous amount of diving information that you now have in front of you could not have been brought together without the help of the leading Sussex divers and experts. All gave freely of their time and knowledge, and every reader of this book will want to thank them.

Some contributors ranged along great stretches of the Sussex coast, while others concentrated on their own special patch. I have attributed their information to certain areas, but this is not to say that they did not help in other areas too.

- Major Hume Wallace for Bracklesham Bay, Selsey and the Mixon. The late Alexander McKee for Chichester Harbour and Bracklesham standing stones.

- John Messent and Geoff Bowden for more Mixon material.

- Malcolm Tipping and the divers of Chichester BSAC for Selsey and the offshore wrecks.

- North Sea divers Derek Allchurch and Pip Maidment for their home patch of the Owers and round about. Mike Maloney for more Owers diving.

- Eric Smith, Dave Barnard, Mick Veal and Steve Westall of the Sussex Spearfishing Club for the Mulberries and inshore sites from Selsey to Beachy Head.

- Terry Barwick and Newham BSAC for Littlehampton wrecks and inshore sites.

- Ray Lee and Trevor Francis for a vast input from their great knowledge of wrecks out of Littlehampton.

- Peter Van Der Boon for Shoreham diving and a mass of detail about wrecks offshore.

- Mike Davies for more Shoreham material.

- Kevin Gillespie, Dave Willis, Jim Cole, Mike Campbell and the divers of the Sussex Diving Club BSAC for Brighton inshore sites and many deep-water wrecks.

- Jim Hollingsworth for Brighton dive-boat expertise.
- Doug Barnard for Peacehaven and for Newhaven and Seaford and his discoveries there.
- Peter Bailey, Curator of Newhaven Museum, for massive help with local wrecks.
- Fred Baldwin, Bob Bearchall, Alan Loader, Brian Coleman, Roger Tudor and the divers of Bromley BSAC for more Seaford and Seven Sisters material.
- Patricia Berry of Seaford's Martello Museum for local wrecks and their history.
- Barry Blackwell, John Edmonds and the divers of Eastbourne BSAC for their detail from Beachy Head to the Royal Sovereign Light Tower and beyond.
- Ed Cumming and the divers of Chelmsford BSAC for The Bottle Wreck and Bexhill wreck diving detail.
- Peter Marsden for the *Amsterdam* and other Sussex historical wrecks.
- Geoff Parsons and John Short for their Hastings and other wreck expertise.
- Tony Marshall, Harry Kennard and Malcolm Inch for the wrecks off Rye.
- Ian O'Riley and the Argonaut Wreck Exploration Group for more Rye diving.
- Richard Larn for his research on Sussex offshore wrecks.
- Erling Skjold for extra information about the Norwegian wrecks in this book.
- Lieutenant-Commander J.D. Pugh, RN, and Mr Eric Lang, formerly of the Wrecks Section of the Hydrographic Department of the Ministry of Defence, for much wreck detail.
- Tim Bennetto of the Brighton dive boat *Spartacus* for great detail about wrecks in his area.
- Paul Brown of Hastings for local wreck and shore dive detail.
- Michael Keane of South London for the *Blanefield* and Beachy Head.
- Ross McNeill for details of lost aircraft.

Though the above named are those who made major contributions to the content of this book there are scores of others who gave me small, but no less vital, information, and I am most grateful for their help too.

Writing this book made my own diving much more interesting and exciting. I hope that when you Dive Sussex it will do the same for you.

KENDALL McDONALD

Acknowledgements

Of the colour illustrations in this book, the bell on page ii was taken by Michael Keane and the porthole cover on page 81 by Bob Gibson. The underwater photographs on the front cover and on pages 38 and 76 were taken by Brian Humphreys. The remaining colour photographs are by Roy Smallpage.

These organisations gave the publishers kind permission to reproduce the following black-and-white illustrations: Imperial War Museum (pages 53, 60 and 75), National Maritime Museum (pages 78, 83, 167 and 171), Newhaven Local and Maritime Museum (page 139), Royal Air Force Museum (page 117), Royal Navy Submarine Museum (page 28) and World Ship Society (pages 80 and 82). The photograph on page 153 was taken by R. Nisbet, the photograph on 157 by T. Connolly and the photograph on page 189 by Ian O'Riley. All the other black-and-white illustrations are from the author's collection.

The Diver's Code of Conduct (Appendix 2) has been included with the kind permission of the BSAC.

Littlehampton Harbour, on the River Arun. The concrete slipway can be seen in the background.

How to use this Guide

The coastline of Sussex is divided from west to east into eight areas. Each area has a chapter to itself containing not only a guide to diving, spot by spot, wreck by wreck, but also back-up information of vital importance to divers. This includes launch sites, parking places, route details, contact telephone numbers, Admiralty chart numbers and Ordnance Survey maps. Appendix 1 gives details of dive boats, air supplies, dive shops and BSAC branches to contact for local help.

Depths given are in metres; distances in yards and miles. Dimensions of ships are in feet and tonnages are gross. Admiralty charts are the metric versions. Ordnance Survey maps are the Landranger 1:50,000 series. Positions are shown in degrees, minutes and seconds – a conversion table to their decimal equivalents for GPS use is printed on page 198.

Practically all Sussex diving is boat diving. In this guide boat diving should be taken to cover inflatables and hard boats, although not all the boat-diving sites can be reached safely by inflatables. In the same way, the few shore dive sites are intended only for the strong swimmer on the calmest of calm days.

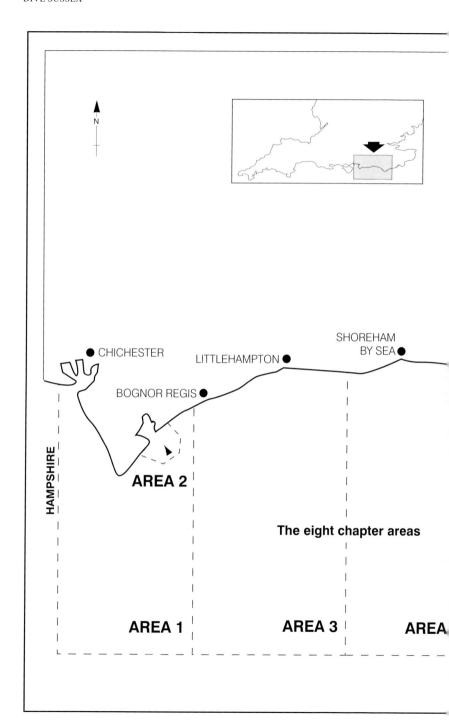

CHICHESTER ●

LITTLEHAMPTON ●

SHOREHAM
BY SEA ●

BOGNOR REGIS ●

HAMPSHIRE

AREA 2

The eight chapter areas

AREA 1

AREA 3

AREA

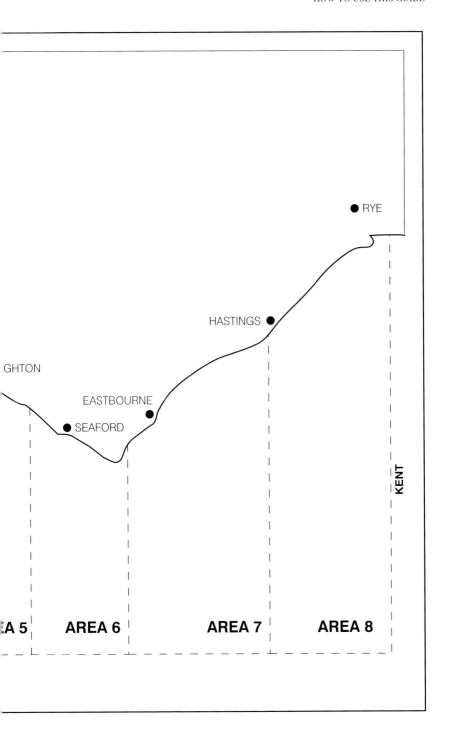

RYE

HASTINGS

GHTON

EASTBOURNE

SEAFORD

KENT

A 5   AREA 6   AREA 7   AREA 8

Undercliff Walk at Saltdean, looking towards Brighton. This is a suitable launch site for inflatables.

About Sussex

The Sussex coastline has more relatively modern wrecks lying off it than almost any other slice of Britain's coastline. This profusion of diveable wrecks provides today's sport divers with some sensational sites, many of which are the result of the activities of German U-boats in both World Wars. In fact, many divers think only of those torpedoed ships and other wrecks when talking of diving in Sussex, but there is much, much more to it than that. For those who know – and those who will know after reading this book – there are reefs of hard-rock and chalk; there are walls and holes, whirlpools and great rifts in the sea bed; there are chasms, canyons, cliffs, deserts, banks, boulders; and everywhere, or nearly everywhere, there is prolific marine life.

The county was divided in 1974 into West Sussex and East Sussex. West Sussex has Chichester as its administrative centre and consists of 779 square miles, which 658,562 people call home. East Sussex is slightly smaller, with an area of 693 square miles, but the population, at 652,568, is almost the same. The administrative centre is Lewes.

The coastline of West Sussex begins just east of Emsworth on the banks of Chichester Harbour, finishing at Portslade-by-Sea. The East Sussex coast runs from Portslade to Broomhill Sands, to the east of Rye.

From the point of view of development, East Sussex must be said to have come off better as far as her coastline is concerned, with little building in the east before Hastings, then the magnificent protected Seven Sisters cliffs from Beachy Head to Seaford Head. From the air, West Sussex looks like one long strip of coastal towns, but on the ground Pagham Harbour and East Head give some relief.

Erosion has always been a problem along the Sussex coast – the old wooden groynes sticking out into the sea from beach after beach are testament to that. But erosion does not stop when the great chalk cliffs are reached. Beachy Head, where the cliffs reach 534ft, faces south and is exposed to south-westerly gales. These undercut the chalk fast enough to ensure that regular falls keep the cliffs vertical. Here, it is interesting to note that erosion at one time left seven towers of chalk standing out from the cliffs near Beachy Head. These were called the Seven Charleses, but erosion got them too, the last one toppling in 1853.

The Seven Sisters cliffs run from Beachy Head to Seaford Head.

Erosion is also the reason for the massive coastal defence works at Peacehaven, which give divers at least one magnificent launching site in the area.

Brighton, too, has always suffered from erosion. The old town of Brighthelmstone was built on the foreshore beneath the cliffs and was a fishing port of some note in Norman days. Erosion destroyed Brighthelmstone, and by 1803 the first concrete sea walls were being built to keep out the sea.

Access by road

This is easy. Too easy, you may think, if you get stuck in a traffic jam on a hot summer's day. The secret of getting to the Sussex coast comfortably is now, as it always has been, to make an early start. The average day tripper is not very good at getting up early, so take advantage of it!

If heading for the eastern end of East Sussex from London or the North you should use the A21 Sevenoaks by-pass (which links up with the M25) to Hastings. For Eastbourne, use the A26, changing to the A22 just after Uckfield. Or stay on the A26 to Lewes and then cut across on the A27. Divers heading for Seaford can take winding back roads off the A27 through Alfriston (beware jams on summer weekends) or the A26 for Newhaven before branching off for Seaford.

If heading for Brighton, only use the M25 if necessary to get yourself onto the M23. Then take the Brighton road straight into the town.

If aiming for Littlehampton, use the M23 in its entirety, but shortly after the end of the motorway turn off for Handcross, then take the A272 at Cowfold to get onto the A24. This is the Worthing road, which you should leave at the Findon roundabout, taking the A280 and going on through Angmering to Littlehampton.

The road that links most of Sussex together from east to west is the A27 trunk road. This runs parallel to the coast from Eastbourne to Emsworth, and it is the quickest way – except at the very height of the tourist season when most roads are choked – to travel along from one diving site to another.

For Bognor Regis, take the A29 (which joins the A24 from Dorking).

For Selsey, unless you want to do a great deal of winding about from Bognor, the best plan is to get onto the A27 ring-road round Chichester, then take the B2145 (which can, however, be very slow in season).

Divers who make these runs regularly usually work out alternative routes to these main-road approaches for when day-trippers pour into the resorts. Many of these alternative routes use minor roads, so a large-scale motoring map is a must. Some roads used by these back-road drivers are very small and often very hilly, so seek advice or check them out before towing a boat down them!

Wrecks

To say that Sussex is a wreck diver's idea of paradise is not far short of the truth. U-boats in both World Wars have laid down a carpet of wrecks along the shipping lanes. E-boats in World War Two added to those numbers by catching smaller craft inshore. And aircraft bombed others to the sea bed.

Apart from the violence of their sinking, the most damage done to these sunken wrecks has been by wire sweep or explosive dispersal to make the way safe for other shipping. As the sea bed is, in most places, of sand, shingle or mud, Sussex wrecks are generally better preserved than those that have fallen on rocky ground in other parts of Britain.

Such a soft sea bed is not always a blessing, however. In some areas, early wrecks have now disappeared into the sea bed for ever, while in others there is a great deal of movement of the sea bed, which means that wrecks may be covered for years and then just as suddenly reappear again. There is a classic example of this in a 14-gun brig near Brighton that has recently appeared – or at least the keel, ribs and guns have – to the amazement of divers who had travelled that same ground the previous year and seen nothing. The yielding quality of patches of clay found inshore – and its ability to swallow ships – is perhaps best demonstrated by the Dutch East Indiaman *Amsterdam*, which is largely under the beach at Hastings.

Although over 300 wreck sites are pinpointed in this book, these are only some of the vast number of wrecks that have taken place along this dangerous coast over the centuries. In olden times there was little shelter for any sailing ship caught by strong south-east or south-west winds. Perhaps the most dramatic demonstration of this is the case of the seven ships lost in one night in Seaford Bay, and it is true that the diver at Seaford or eastward toward Beachy Head will rarely enter the water without coming across some evidence of a wooden wreck.

A special bonus for the wreck diver carrying out his or her own wreck research is given in this guide with the publication of the positions of the major Sussex lightships during the World War One. This will assist in the location of wrecks where the only clues are the bearing and the distance from a light vessel.

WARNING Because of the soft sea bed and silting, it is extremely dangerous to enter wrecks without some foolproof method of return to the exit. A few fin-strokes and visibility inside a silted wreck can become nil within seconds. Divers should also note that some wrecks may be fished using tangle or gill nets. These modern monofilament nets are almost invisible and can trap the unwary diver. Many wrecks in the area have been found to be draped with trawl and other nets by accident. But this does not, of course, make them any the less deadly.

Accommodation

There is plenty of accommodation of all kinds along most of the coast of Sussex ranging from grand hotels, to small hotels, to bed-and-breakfast establishments. Hotels are usually booked long in advance, and divers should be warned that even in the case of bed-and-breakfasts, spur-of-the-moment bookings in the more popular coastal resorts in high season on fine weekends are not always possible.

When this happens, the diver should try the second band of bed-and-breakfast accommodation set back from the coast in inland villages. Some of these rooms are in houses in delightful surroundings and can often provide better value than the usually higher-charging coastal houses. Parking for car and boat in these secluded places is usually easy, though divers should remember that some of the narrow lanes that service the inland villages can become traffic-choked very quickly, and should allow time for a slow trip to the dive site.

Dive Planning

Weather

The weather of the Sussex coast can change remarkably quickly, though long periods of quiet are common with winds of less than Force 4. Winds, of course, rule the diving, and the whole coastline is very exposed to strong south-easterlies and south-westerlies. Most winds in the area come from the south-west to north-west direction, though north and north-east winds are most common from February to May. These winds often provide good conditions for diving close inshore under shelter of the land.

The Meteorological Office at Bracknell, Berkshire, has details of the average frequency of gales over the Sussex sea area, and lists them as: January, 4; February, 3; March, 3; April, 2; May, 1; June, July and August, 0; September, 1; October, 2; November, 3; and December, 4. South-west to west gales are most frequent in December and January, and north to north-east gales in February and March. Wind speeds of over 80 knots have been recorded on the coast, which is Force 12 and rated as a hurricane!

At the opposite end of the scale, summer sea breezes can be as much as Force 3 in the height of summer, whereas the breeze off the land in the evenings rarely reaches 5 knots.

North-west winds bring long bright spells. One or two thunderstorms are likely each month during the summer, and diver-coxswains should look out for sudden heavy squalls during these periods. Waterspouts are seen at these times.

In general, the eastern part of the Sussex coast is drier than the west. Winds from the west are most likely and from the south-east are least likely. North-east winds are more common in spring, and gales are most likely to come from the south-west and west.

As a general rule, too, you can say that the sea is warmer than the air from October to March, and that the air is warmer than the sea from April to August. In September the two match. A wind from the south-west in the summer keeps the temperature down slightly below average, whereas a wind from the east or south boosts the temperature above average.

9

Fog over the sea can occur very suddenly, but the risk of this decreases from May and June when on average three fogs occur to an average of one only in August and September.

Weather services The Meteorological Office offers several services of use to Sussex divers. The general weather forecast for Sussex is obtained by ringing Weathercall on 0891 500402.

More important to divers is Marinecall on 0891 500456 for Brighton and the east and 0891 500457 for the west.

MetFax will give a 2-day printed forecast for the east Channel area (North Foreland to Selsey Bill) and a 24-hour forecast chart by calling 0336 400 456. A 3- to 5-day forecast and chart for Channel Waters is available on fax on 0336 400 471.

Visibility

This varies so much from place to place and time to time that only very general guidance can be given. There are some probabilities, however. These are:

1. An easterly wind will wipe out underwater visibility immediately.
2. If you are east of Beachy Head and the south-easterlies blow, you might as well pack up and go diving in Dorset – and some divers do just that!
3. Strong southerlies and some south-westerlies mean no good diving around Beachy Head (west side), Seaford, and Newhaven. The wash-back from the cliffs produces white water, which is like diving in milk.
4. A period of south-westerlies early in the spring will raise the temperature of the sea and create a plankton bloom that Eastbourne divers call the "Maybug". This destroys the visibility for some time.
5. North winds mean clear water.

Stirred-up sediment, rather than plankton, is usually the problem in Sussex waters, and the further east you go the more sediment there tends to be and the longer it takes to settle. Many of the wrecks dived out of Rye, for example, are heavily silted. Divers in the east of the zone can expect reasonable visibility for diving from the day the Sovereign Round-the-Light-Tower yacht race ends on the first Sunday in July for the next three months. After that the visibility tends to deteriorate rapidly.

On the brighter side, visibility in the whole Sussex area is generally about 4m, and after a period of north winds can be around 15m. On one or two never-to-be forgotten days it has even been in excess of 20m!

Marine life

This is prolific, and although it does not always appear where it should, it often turns up where it is least expected! Would you believe sting-rays on Bognor Reef, cod among the Mulberry units, and oysters loose among the shingle and rubble of the Mixon Hole? Divers also report seeing big lobsters going for walks over sand plains – looking like great tanks rumbling over desert dunes – but not before August.

The most common fish seen by Sussex divers must be the bib, or pouting, with wrasse and pollack coming a close joint second. To the east, it is fair to describe the plaice as very common, with big specimens coming right into really shallow water around places like Seaford with mud-bottomed chalk gullies. Soles also like this habitat.

Turbot and brill are seen by divers in inshore waters in the autumn. Red mullet are also around. Blennies and gobies are common. Angler fish are not uncommon. Dragonets are often present, as are goldsinny. Conger eels love Sussex wrecks. Thresher sharks have been seen by divers, and so have big tope. Dogfish are common in certain areas – at times the slopes of the Mixon Hole's western end are littered with them. Huge skate can be found there too.

Crabs are often buried in sand up to the top of the back shell. Spider crabs arrive in large numbers around the middle of June.

There are scallop beds, and not all are miles offshore like the ones dredged up by boats out of Newhaven. The inshore ones visited by divers have survived untrawled because of surrounding reefs. Broken trawls on these beds testify to some trawlermen's determination, but the beds have suffered badly from the huge hauls of professional fishermen-divers. Mackerel, too, are not so prolific as in past summers, and the black bream that used to make for the Bognor Rocks to spawn in vast numbers are back, but in greatly reduced quantities.

Divers who find a few oysters here and there off the coast should not be all that surprised. In the 1850s a hundred sails used to work out of Shoreham on the vast beds of oysters midway between the English and French coasts, and it was quite usual for 20,000 tons of oysters to leave Shoreham railway station every year. These offshore beds were huge – 20 miles in length by 7 or 8 miles across. In April 1874 another big new bed was discovered only 6 miles out between Shoreham and Worthing. The Shoreham boats worked this – as well as the scallops, which were an important industry too. But the oysters and the oyster industry declined in later years and by 1910 only a small quantity were occasionally brought in. Today, the diver will find the occasional oyster and many huge empty shells. One, found on the Far Mulberry Unit, measured over 6 inches across its widest part. Some live smaller oysters are found among the shingle of the Mixon Hole.

Local regulations

Most divers would not wish to dive for pleasure in any of the harbours in Sussex. But if for any reason you have to grope around in these murky waters, you must ensure that you have the local harbourmaster's permission. Diving in rivers in the area – such as the Arun, for example – requires the permission of the land-owner or their water-bailiff and the permission of the river authority as well. Some river diving is done in Sussex, mostly in search of old bottles.

The only other restrictions on divers are the same as those that apply to fishermen, and they refer to minimum fish sizes. The Sussex Sea Fisheries District by-laws do, however, have one restriction of particular importance to divers (though it is not aimed at them, but at unregistered lobster-potting). This regulation, introduced in the early 1980s, restricts each diver to two lobsters per day: "No person shall take lobsters except under a permit issued by the committee and signed by the Clerk in accordance with the conditions set out in that authority, provided that this prohibition shall only apply to persons taking more than two lobsters from the fishery on any one day. Permits will be issued on demand to the owner of any registered fishing vessel if not more than 100 pots per crew member or a maximum of 300 pots per boat are used. The allocated permit number should be displayed on all dhans or buffs used to mark pots."

At the time of going to press, the minimum sizes of fish and shellfish laid down for the Sussex Sea Fisheries District, which covers the whole of East and West Sussex and overlaps a little into Kent and Hampshire, are as given in the tables. Chief Fishery Officer is Mr Steve Holman (tel. 01323 841912), who is keen on diver-fisherman co-operation.

Skate (across width)	35cm
Bass	32cm
Mullet, grey	30cm
Turbot	30cm
Brill	30cm
Hake	30cm
Cod	30cm
Witches	28cm
Whiting	27cm
Haddock	27cm
Plaice	25cm
Megrims	25cm
Soles	24cm
Flounders	22.5cm
Dabs	15cm

Minimum sizes for fish.

Scallops (EC size)	100mm
Edible crabs (across the broadest part of the shell)	140mm
Spider crabs (length from base of rostrum spines to rear of body shell)	120mm
Lobsters (carapace length)	85mm
Oysters	63.5mm

Minimum sizes for shellfish. Landing parts of lobsters or claws from edible or spider crabs is also prohibited.

12

The Sussex Sea Fisheries Protection Vessel, the 33ft *Watchful*, is based at Newhaven. The boat is skippered by George Cole and usually has one other Sea Fisheries officer aboard. The boat is under the direction of Steve Holman who talks to her at sea on Channel 31. Having spent a considerable time under her clearing her propellers of nylon rope just before the start of a Mixon Hole dive, the author can tell you that the crew of the *Watchful* are friendly to divers, but will investigate any infringement of law or by-law reported in their three-mile-limit patrol area. The District boundaries extend eastwards of a line true south of the flagstaff on the Coastguard watchouse at Hayling Island to a compass bearing true south-east from the old lighthouse at Dungeness Point.

Divers and fishing nets

It is important that divers who use the Sussex area should be aware of the large amount of commercial inshore net fishing carried out in these waters. The major fisheries in Sussex are for sole, plaice, lobsters and crabs. There is also a fishery for herring and mackerel – though owing to unpredictable changes in the habits of these shoals in recent years, fewer and fewer boats are involved.

The main sole fishing season starts in March and runs on to mid June when the inshore movement of spider crabs and the dispersal of the soles reduces catches. However, this does not mean that it stops altogether. Netting goes on all year,

Fixed fishing nets off the Sussex coast.

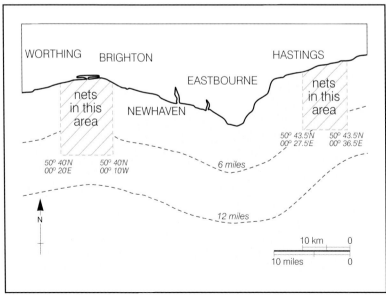

and divers should be aware that there are extensive nets in use at all times. Most of these nets are trammel nets, which have two wide-meshed outer walls and a loose interior fine-mesh wall that forms a pocket when a fish pushes through; but nets with only one wide-mesh wall and one fine-mesh net are also used.

Boats from Brighton, Newhaven, Eastbourne and Hastings are heavily involved in fishing for bottom-dwelling fish, and the main species caught are lemon and Dover sole, plaice, dabs and skate. Half the total catch of these fish in Sussex is from fixed nets.

Divers and pot fishing

The Sussex shellfish industry is mostly concentrated at the western end of the coast. All the coast is potted, but not with the same intensity as occurs on the rocky grounds off Selsey. The heavy inshore potting means that divers are bound to dive near, or surface near, pots on occasion, and will be seen by fishermen to be doing so. Even so, good behaviour on the part of divers has kept relationships between the divers and professional fishermen on an even keel and, though there have been one or two regrettable incidents over the years, there are many more cases of co-operation than of conflict. Nowhere is this more evident than in the heart of the shellfish fishery at Selsey Bill.

The majority of crab and lobster fishing in Sussex takes place on the grounds out from Selsey. Pots are usually in strings of 30 and are fished every day in summer and every other day when possible in winter. Yields of crab can reach a ton a day, with more edibles being caught than spiders. Much of this catch is exported live to France and Spain.

This means a lot of money is at stake. Yet relationships here between divers and fishermen are excellent. The main reason for this is the fine work done by Chichester BSAC, which runs a "first-aid" service for Selsey fishermen, who now know that a phone call to any one of a series of local numbers will bring them the free services of a diver within a short time.

Though members of Chichester BSAC admit that being called out four times in one evening by different Selsey boats can be a bit exhausting, they realise that to the fishermen a wire round a propeller or a lost string of pots during the height of the season can mean a serious financial set-back. Their reward is not only good relations, but also a free flow of information about the position of wrecks and underwater obstructions. And as they are usually happy to pass on this information to fellow divers, it would be a foolish Sussex diver who did anything to jeopardise this good relationship.

Contacting the Coastguard

Sussex Coastguard operations are divided into two. West Sussex (to Beachy Head) is covered by the Solent Coastguard; East Sussex (Beachy Head to Dungeness) is controlled by Dover Coastguard. The non-emergency telephone numbers (to get information on sea and weather conditions and to report intended dive boat expeditions) are 01705 552100 and 01304 210008 respectively.

Diving emergencies

In the event of any life-threatening or serious diving accident, such as a diver lost or missing, or a vase of decompression sickness or an embolism, the Coastguard must be contacted at once. For any such serious diving incident, all other Coastguard matters of lesser importance will be put on hold. This will mean that help, often by helicopter, will be on its way to you within minutes of your call.

Always call the Coastguard first. At sea, contact them direct on VHF Channel 16; on shore use your radio in the same way or dial 999 and ask for the Coastguard.

If less dramatic symptoms of decompression illness occur inland, a GP or hospital casualty department (or the Coastguard) should be contacted. Emergency transfer to the nearest available recompression chamber will be arranged for you if it is necessary. Make sure you carry the 24-hour telephone number of Portsmouth Naval Base (01705 818888), which you can pass to the doctor concerned so that specialist advice can be obtained from the Diving Medical Centre there.

Decompression illness

Decompression illness symptoms vary between those so sudden that immediate air evacuation to a chamber is vital to those that might not become apparent for some hours. Some of these less dramatic symptoms, which may well be delayed, can be more serious and produce greater disability than the excruciating pain associated with a joint bend. Tingling and numbness are included in this category.

Air embolism or severe decompression illness symptoms require prompt but careful transfer of the subject to a recompression chamber. The victim should be laid flat on their back and, if possible, should be given 100% oxygen. If at sea, contact the Coastguard for help immediately: in a small boat, any attempt at speed may bounce the victim and almost certainly worsen the symptoms rather than help the situation.

The Military Remains Act

The Military Remains Act 1986 may in the future affect the wreck diver much more than it does at present. Its main drive is to preserve the sanctity of "war graves" – the wreckage of military ships and aircraft known to contain remains of service personnel.

The wreckage of all military aircraft of any nation is automatically protected, but ships will have to be designated by the Secretary of State and will need a statutory instrument to do so. This means that ships to be named as "war graves" will have to be named and approved by Parliament in the same way that ships to be protected as historic wrecks need a statutory instrument passed through Parliament.

There seems no doubt that those who passed the Act had little idea of the number of ships that could fall under its terms, such as a merchant ship with a Navy gunner aboard – was he among the survivors? – and as a result no ships have yet been named under the Act. This does not mean that ships are not covered by the general thrust of the Act and divers should therefore treat all possible "war graves" with total respect.

However, once these ships have been named, the diver commits an offence only by tampering with, damaging, moving, removing or unearthing remains, or by entering an enclosed interior space in the wreckage. The punishment on conviction of an offence is a fine. Nothing in the Act prevents the wreck diver from visiting the site, examining the exterior or even settling on the wreckage. An offence is only committed if the diver disturbs remains or enters a proper compartment of the wreck. The punishment on conviction is a fine.

This is of course only a brief description, and serious wreck divers should study the Act itself. Your library or HMSO should be able to supply a copy.

The Merchant Shipping Acts

The Receiver of Wreck is responsible for the administration of the Merchant Shipping Act 1894 and the Merchant Shipping Act 1906, which deal with wreck and salvage. It is a legal requirement that all recovered wreck (flotsam, jetsam, derelict or lagan – whether recovered within or outside United Kingdom territorial waters) is reported to the Receiver of Wreck.

Finders who conceal items are liable to prosecution, so any object – even if it appears to have no monetary value – should be declared as soon as possible. The Receiver of Wreck can then make a decision as to the future ownership of the property.

Wreck recovered from within United Kingdom territorial waters that remains unclaimed at the end of a statutory one-year period becomes the property of the Crown, and the Receiver of Wreck is required to dispose of it. This may be through sale at auction, although in many instances the finder will be allowed to keep unclaimed items of wreck in lieu of a salvage award. This, however, is at the discretion of the Receiver of Wreck, and each case is judged on its merits.

For further information contact: The Receiver of Wreck, The Coastguard Agency, Spring Place, 105 Commercial Road, Southampton SO15 0ZD (tel. 01703 329474; fax 01703 329477).

The Protection of Wrecks Act

Divers who find a site that might be of historical, archaeological or artistic importance should leave everything as it is and report their findings, in confidence and as soon as possible, to the Department for Culture, Media and Sport (or its equivalent in Northern Ireland, Scotland or Wales). If appropriate, the wreck can then be designated under the Protection of Wrecks Act 1973, in order to control activities on the site.

Designated sites may only be dived or items recovered if a licence for that purpose has been granted; failure to comply with this is an offence and can result in a fine. All recoveries from designated sites must be reported to the Receiver of Wreck. For further information contact: The Secretariat of the Advisory Committee on Historic Wreck Sites, 3rd Floor, Department of National Heritage, 2–4 Cockspur Street, London SW1Y 5DH (tel. 0171 211 6367/8).

Chichester Harbour to Bognor Regis

This area runs from 00 56 00W to 00 39 12W and includes Chichester Harbour, Bracklesham, Selsey and Bognor Regis (for Pagham, *see* Area 2). It provides the diver with an extraordinary mix of diving possibilities. There are huge, flat, sandy areas dotted with rocky reefs. There is a sensational hole in the sea bed with a sheer wall falling to 30m. There are weird amphitheatres of Stonehenge-type rocks and boulders. There is a whirlpool, a Roman quarry, and some of the finest wreck diving in Britain.

Many of the wrecks cluster around the former position of the Owers Light Vessel (Site **46**) where U-boats in World War One took a heavy toll on merchant shipping. However, not all the wrecks in the area are the result of wartime activity. Selsey Bill is low and difficult to see from out at sea. Occasionally, vessels take the short-cut inside the Owers rocks through the Looe Channel. Not all have made it in the past. Other shipping, hoping to be totally safe from the Owers and taking the longer route south of the Owers Racon Buoy some 7 miles south-east of the tip of the Bill itself, has not always made it either.

Though just outside and to the west of the area covered in this book, the Nab Tower is included here as it is often used as a mark for locating wrecks in the Selsey area. Work was started on building this huge concrete fort (and a twin at Shoreham) by units of the Royal Engineers in 1917. The towers were intended to be the mid-Channel supports for an anti-submarine net to be strung from the surface to the floor of the Straits of Dover to stop the Flanders flotilla of U-boats getting into the Channel. There were to be six such towers in all, but the war ended before the others were completed. The Nab Tower was towed to its present position on 12 September, 1920, by two aged paddle-steamers as a replacement for the Nab lightship.

Since 1995, exploratory oil drilling has been carried out almost due south of Selsey Bill. The site of the first hole was about 1 mile south of the wreck of the *Britsum* (Site **32**). The rig is on the move, but the area of the first hole is still marked by four huge yellow buoys. You are asked not to dive inside the area so marked.

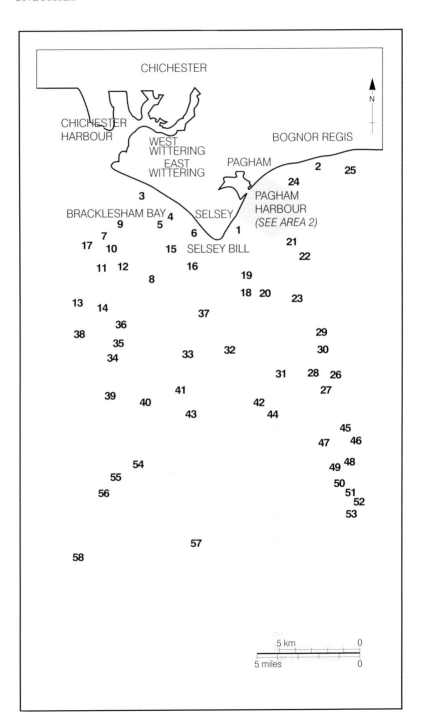

Marine life in the area can only be described as prolific, with plaice and sole, lobsters and edible crabs, spider crabs in season, skate and sting-rays, dogfish, tope, and thresher sharks. Conger eels – many very large indeed – are common, and huge shoals of pouting and pollack seem ever-present. Cuttlefish are also common.

Tidal currents are fierce at the entrance to Chichester Harbour near East Head, and very fierce around the Bill and through the Mixon Hole. They are much milder in the Bognor area, where they tend to give off circular side-streams. Offshore, tides are generally much stronger, with big overfalls in places, particularly in that spot on the Outer Owers where the depth plummets suddenly to 67m! All offshore diving –particularly on the deep offshore wrecks, on which there have been casualties – needs special care and should only be undertaken by the experienced diver and boat handler.

EAST HEAD lies at the western end of Bracklesham Bay and forms part of the entrance to Chichester Harbour. This 76-acre area of sand-dunes is bounded by a shingle bank on the outside and has a lagoon filled by the tide on the east. This land is owned by the National Trust. Divers, driven mad by endless days of rough seas, have dived East Head just inside the harbour mouth. The dive was, as expected, one of very poor visibility and a dull and uninteresting mud bottom. It is not recommended. Swimming in the entrance to Chichester Harbour is, as one would expect, forbidden – not only because of boat traffic, but also because of fierce currents in and out.

Due south of the hook-shaped East Head are EAST POLE SANDS. There are two wrecks on the sands, both deliberate sinkings for use as RAF and RNAS bombing targets. The *Armenier* is the most northerly, at 50 45 48N; 00 54 52W. This is the hulk of a 914-ton British coastal steamer of 189ft long and 31ft beam. The wreck dries about 3m. It was put in position on 29 March, 1955, and is also marked with a beacon 13m away. The hulk is badly rusted, but her frames are still sturdy and the occasional lobster can be found hiding there. The other wreck on East Pole Sands lies at their southerly edge. This is a Mulberry Harbour Phoenix Unit, sunk for the Royal Naval Air Station at Ford, near Littlehampton, for use as a temporary target on 3 November, 1959. This unit is in fairly sound condition, dries 3m, and is also marked by a beacon to the south of the wreck. The position is 50 45 23N; 00 54 42W.

Launch sites

Although the Harbour Authority at CHICHESTER stress in their leaflets that yachts should keep clear of boats flying the A-flag, it would be a pretty desperate sports diver who would dive in the huge area covered by the harbour anyway. The visibility is generally nil, the bottom soft, and what can be seen extremely dull. Much of the area dries out, and depths everywhere are shallow.

The only thing of interest to divers about the harbour must be its many launch sites. Charges at most of these are usually modest, but do remember that in

Opposite: Dive sites in Area 1, Chichester Harbour to Bognor Regis. This area is covered by Admiralty charts 2045 (Outer Approaches to the Solent) and 1652 (Selsey Bill to Beachy Head); Ordnance Survey Pathfinder map 197.

Dell Quay slipway, where you can launch at high tide.

high summer they become very crowded. Both DELL QUAY and BOSHAM are easy launching sites at high tide. There is easy launching at ITCHENOR at all states of tide and passengers can be picked up at the jetty here. There is a slipway near the lock at CHICHESTER YACHT BASIN, which can be used at high tide. LANGSTONE BRIDGE (to Hayling Island) can be used as a launch site at high tide, as can South Street in EMSWORTH. Note that Thorney Island and Pilsey Island are Ministry of Defence property and landing is only permitted below the high water mark.

Chichester Harbour is a land-locked tidal lagoon of over 4,000 acres and it is crammed with yachts of all sizes. At the entrance to this yachtsman's paradise is East Head. Moving from East Head towards Selsey there is first West Wittering, then East Wittering, then Bracklesham at the edge of the bay of the same name. Between them they offer over 2 miles of beachside development including caravan parks before the coast becomes quiet once again before Selsey. There is a launch site at EAST WITTERING. To find it, follow signs to Village Centre, then Shore Road, and finally signs to The Sea. The launching ramp by a windsurfing hut is very steep down to the shore and cannot be recommended.

BRACKLESHAM is much more suitable than East Wittering for small-boat launching, which is by tractor down a good concrete ramp. There is a charge. The ramp is very steep at the seaward end. To find it, follow the lane (B2198) through the village to its end. Here there are a car park, toilets and the ramp itself. This launch site becomes very crowded in season and is a favourite spot for water-skiers. Take great care when returning to the ramp, particularly at high tide when the surf can be, and has been, the ruin of boats whose owners thought they could do without the tractor and bring the boat up themselves. The charge is cheaper than a smashed boat!

The only approach to SELSEY is by the B2145, which leads from one of the many roundabouts on the Chichester by-pass section of the A27 trunk road. In old English, Selsey means Seal Island, and in the past Selsey was indeed an island. The sea today still nibbles at Selsey, but such attacks are nothing compared with the great inundations of centuries ago. There is little doubt that much of the area over which diving boats roam today was at one time dry land complete with towns, villages, and even royal palaces. Gold coins washed up on the west side of Selsey Bill are, so they say, evidence that one of the royal palaces under the sea had its own royal mint!

Selsey today is a fast-growing seaside village that we shall shortly have to call a town. In the summer holidays it seems to burst at the seams, despite all the extra accommodation offered by caravan parks. Most of the houses in Selsey are grouped on the eastern side of the Bill, which is a low-lying headland poking out into the Channel. Strong tides and fast currents sweep around the Bill itself. Despite the concentration of holiday-makers in Selsey during the summer, the village still has a small but thriving fishing community, with boats mostly kept in the deep channel in front of East Beach. The main fishing is for lobsters on the grounds 5 miles and more due south of the Bill, but there is some trawling too. Strings of pots are usually not longer than 30, but the catch is large. The moorings near East Beach are well sheltered from the west and south-west, and the Owers give some shelter from the south. But when a south-easterly blows there can be huge seas along East Beach. This is why if you see the trawler moorings there you will not be surprised to see the number of anchors used and the gigantic chains.

Keep a sharp eye open for keep-pots if you dive close in to the shore at East Beach. There are some around the Sluice Rocks (Site 1), and sometimes keep-pots or rafts are tied off to the supports of the staging of the Lifeboat Pier just to the west of East Beach launch site. Most fishermen in the area are friendly towards divers. This is largely due to the efforts of Chichester BSAC, who are always on stand-by to help local fishermen with fouled or lost propellers, and any other trouble a diver can help with. The fishermen now know that they have only to telephone for help and the divers turn out. Sometimes they have done so four times in one evening! However, the area around the Lifeboat Pier is still said to be "sensitive", so all divers please keep clear.

Selsey has three launch sites suitable for divers' towed boats. EAST BEACH car and boat park is free and in crush times it can be extended into an equally large field under the sea wall. From the east end of the car park a small tarmac drive leads up to a turning point for cars. Trailers are unhooked here and pulled up the slope to the top of the sea wall. Two bollards have been set into the concrete to form a chicane, but it is easy to manoeuvre a trailer around them. They are there to stop cars being driven on to the sea wall. Once on top of the wall, there is a wooden ramp over the shingle beach. The ramp is not long and there is a hard pull at low water to get afloat. There is a small café near the car park and public toilets are nearby. The inshore lifeboat and main lifeboat launch sites are to the west of the ramp. Approach East Beach by the B2145. After entering Selsey village, turn left into Church Road, which is just before the garage sign of Tony Hills Motors. East Beach is then well signposted. The car park can be full during local events.

WEST BEACH is approached by the B2145 right through the centre of Selsey village. Turn right where indicated and follow the West Beach signs, not those for

The lifeboat pier and beach at Selsey Bill.

the caravan site. The head of a first-class concrete ramp is at the foot of the Coastguard Station Tower. Parking is almost impossible, due to many double yellow lines, so trailers must be unhitched and cars taken some distance away for parking. The ramp is barred by low iron "goal-posts", but a boat and trailer can be lifted over. The ramp makes two right-angled turns to the water – but boats can be easily manoeuvred around these.

This is an excellent launch at all states of the tide. The Mixon Beacon can be clearly seen from this point for those wishing to dive the Mixon Hole (Site **18**). The "goal-post" angle-iron is locked in place with a padlock. This has been done because the ramp is not a public one and is officially only for the passage of sea-defence equipment. Prior to the entrance being locked there had been many complaints from local residents of large boats being launched and massive traffic jams. So please use this site sensibly. Though the barrier will not be unlocked, at the time of writing the local council has no objection to small boats using it.

To reach BILL HOUSE follow the directions for East Beach previously given, but bear to the right. This leads you down a road marked "private, upkeep by residents". Keep straight on over all crossings, and ahead of you just off Grafton Road you will see a very pot-holed shingle-studded road. Continue down this to the end, passing Bill House, which is the large one with a high fence and a turret on your right. This is a convalescent home, so please avoid noise. Continue to the end of the road where there is a short haul over the shingle at high tide. Look out for currents round the tip of the Bill, which is where the launch site is situated. This is not an official launch site. Use with care and consideration. Parking is limited.

Moving eastwards along the coast the next spot we reach is Pagham (see Area 2). The best road in this area is the A27, which is of good quality along most of its length from Brighton to the Hampshire border. The by-pass around Chichester gives access to the many smaller "A" and "B" roads that lead down to the coast. The A29 is the most direct route straight into Bognor, but in summer it can become very congested.

BOGNOR REGIS is the centre of miles of holiday resorts stretching from Middleton-on-Sea in the east to Pagham in the west, yet despite this is a pleasant, quiet place. The town boasts 1½ miles of sea front, much of which is occupied by a promenade. Its eastern end is dominated by Butlins Holiday Camp, but there is also plenty of family-type bed and breakfast accommodation, some excellent small hotels, and some expensive larger ones. The town has mostly managed to avoid high-rise building, and is much the same today as it was in the days when Queen Victoria called it "dear little Bognor" and King George V gave it the "Regis" in 1928 after recovering from a long illness at Aldwick.

The name Bognor comes from an old Saxon word for a rocky shore. Divers who have made the mistake of returning at full low spring tides will not recall the rocks so much as the incredibly long haul over slippery banks of clay, mud and then hard sand until the steep shingle bank is finally reached. Although there is only one public launching site at Bognor, it is a good one. From the main road, follow the signs for the sea front, then take Gloucester Road, which lies to the west of Butlins. Boats can be towed from here right up on to the promenade along to the wooden ramp that leads down to the beach. Approach from the west, continuing along the sea front until the road turns away from the sea to the left. You are then at the launching site.

There is no charge for launch or recovery, but the car and trailer must be removed afterwards to a car park. Exit and return to the ramp at sea must be made by the buoyed lane that runs from the shore out for some 300yds to the south from the mean low-water mark. The speed limit, except in the lane or more than 300yds out from the shore, is 8 knots. The 300yds of protected water is marked with buoys westward to Bognor Pier. The buoys are in position from May to September and the speed limit is strictly enforced.

Most of the coastline around Bognor, and indeed all along the coast to the west, is backed by a steep strip of shingle, which, as the tide recedes, turns into huge areas of smooth sand and slippery patches of clay. In summer these exposed areas are quickly colonised by holiday-makers as the bathing is generally safe and good. Boat divers should therefore keep a sharp eye open for swimmers a long distance offshore, especially near the partially-collapsed pier.

Shore diving sites

There are only two shore dive sites in this area that are worthy of sensible consideration – and then only when no boat is available.

1 Sluice Rocks These rocks at East Beach, Selsey, are named after the former rainfall run-off, of which some pipework still remains underwater between the second and third groyne to the west of the East Beach launching ramp. The pipework lies in the "deep" channel (4m) that runs along the face of East Beach until it comes to an end in the east at the winkle beds. Note that collection of periwinkles between 15 May and 15 September is prohibited by a Sussex Sea Fisheries District Committee Order.

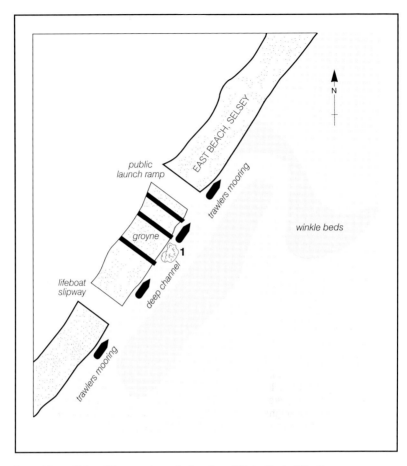

Launching at Selsey. The map shows the location of Sluice Rocks (Site 1).

Sluice Rocks are full of marine life despite their proximity to the shore, but as some keep-pots are moored by the rocks, care should be taken by all divers. The Selsey trawlers are moored in the deep channel, which is not wide and has some very shallow ground on its seaward side. At low spring tides it is sometimes necessary to push and pull inflatables across this bank into deeper water. To return to the East Beach ramp at such times it is best to approach the shore near the Lifeboat Pier and then run along the channel to the east.

2 Bognor Reef Charted as Bognor Rocks, this limestone reef curves across the face of the sea front to the west of the pier, coming in to shore at the Aldwick end close to the very high-and-dry remains of a Mulberry unit at 50 46 38N;

00 41 49W. Half Tide Rock, as its name implies, is the first to show. After that, take care when coming through the reef. Any boat that draws a few inches, such as a diving inflatable, can lose a propeller here very easily.

There are paths through the rocks, but unless you know them well it is best at full low to keep outside the rocks and come inshore, if you need to, after you have nearly reached the end of the pier. Even at near high tide the rocks should be treated with care as they are a collection of individual rocks rather than a reef wall, and some of the single rocks are very tall.

The reef can be dived from the shore if you do not mind a fair amount of wading and use of the snorkel, as the sea bed here slopes very gradually once you have reached the sand base. The rocks are heavily weeded and undercut by the tide. These holes provide plentiful hiding places for lobsters, but the area is heavily potted and lobsters are generally very small.

Visibility is often good – except after an easterly blow when it becomes nil – and there are decent-sized bass to be seen at times in search of shrimps or prawns among these inshore rocks. Large sting-rays with wing-spans of up to 2m have been seen here during hot summers resting on sand patches among the rocks.

The whole area around the pier, the rocks, and further afield off Bognor, used to be famous for black bream fishing, but this declined dramatically in the 1970s. Over the past few years, however, anglers have reported increasing numbers. The rocks are the home of many large wrasse, and there are a number of small pipefish among the broken-off weed that gathers in depressions behind the rocks.

Boat diving sites

3 Bracklesham Bay It is difficult to forget that in this area you are diving in a drowned land. Theories about the sea level in ancient times vary a great deal, but all agree that the promontory of Selsey, the Bill, was at one time much further out to sea, certainly as far as the Mixon Beacon, and probably as far as the Owers. The Isle of Wight may well have been linked by a natural causeway to the mainland and people might once have walked and worked on land now never seen by anyone but divers. Divers might well expect to find traces of human habitation ranging from prehistoric settlements to Norman buildings.

Due to the poor visibility very close in there is no shore diving. Diving in the bay is only really feasible during dead calms or after a period of northerly winds. Generally, the bottom of the bay is soft clay and that, together with the mud swept out of the entrance to Chichester Harbour, means that winds of Force 4 and above reduce visibility to nil. Even so, there are some interesting dives when the weather is kind.

4 HMS Hazardous This protected wreck site is at 50 45 10N; 00 51 47W and diving is banned within 50m of that point. Divers have been prosecuted and fined for diving on the site. HMS *Hazardous* was a fourth-rate ship of the line of 54 guns, which ran aground on 19 November, 1706 in a south-westerly gale. For some reason she was not fully salvaged and there are cannons all over the sea bed at the site today.

Some 700yds from the *Hazardous* are the keel and ribs of a wooden vessel about 85ft long. This was found by following up a report from a local fisherman of old timbers in his nets. The archaeological divers on the *Hazardous* have raised some objects such as lead musket balls, pistol shot, a copper cooking cauldron and a silver shilling of William III, dated 1697, and think this may be a small naval vessel of the late 17th century.

5 The Hounds This group of limestone rocks can provide a good dive for beginners. Lobsters and crabs can be found among the rocks, and there is enough marine life to delight any novice. The rocks can be spotted even when totally covered by the swirling surface disturbance over them. They lie at 50 44 06N; 00 50 00W.

6 LCT Discovered by Chichester BSAC divers in 1984, and close to the Hounds, this almost-intact wreck is of a tank landing-craft of World War Two. It is amazing that such a big wreck (it is 112ft long) could be concealed so close to the beach, which is only a quarter of a mile away. The craft is upside down at 50 44 06N; 00 49 30W in 7m. To find the LCT, follow the line of the Hounds until you are directly opposite the holiday camp.

A clue about the craft's sinking comes from the condition of the blades of one of the propellers. Each was four-bladed, and on one propeller one blade was bent, one chipped, and one twisted. Experts think that this shows that the craft may have run back over her own anchor. All the propellers are now missing.

7 The Old Cliff Line Running due west from the Hounds to level with East Pole Sands is a cliff-line of about 2,000 BC, though all that remains today in an average depth of 6m is a 4m-high chalk wall. This provides attractive housing for lobsters and crabs, and as a result it is heavily potted.

8 Medmery Bank Lying at 50 42 24N; 00 51 00W, this is a shingle bank with a steep fall on its south side. A favourite haunt of big skate, this bank formed part of the ancient shoreline of thousands of years ago. The original entrance to Chichester Harbour was out here too, and was a break in the shingle known to the Danes as the Hore Muth or Dirty Mouth – a clear indication of the amount of silt that poured out even then.

One of the experts on Bracklesham Bay was Alexander McKee, the man who found the *Mary Rose*. He and several colleagues carried out exploratory dives for some years to see if the Roman road that runs, straight as a die, to the Bracklesham launch site, continues underwater. Following the possible line of the road, they have made a number of discoveries and pinpointed several interesting sites for inshore dives.

9 Don's Reef This reef lies ¾ mile out on the continuation of the road line, and is named after Don Bullivant who discovered it while diving with Alex McKee. It is in 6m of water and consists of a mass of circular boulders of different sizes, some up to 2m high and 0.3m in diameter. Many are split in half, but some are intact and completely spherical. The rocks of this reef continue some way to the east.

10 Amphitheatre Lying 1 mile offshore and just to the east of the Roman road line, this is a group of standing rocks of the most extraordinary shapes in 7–10m of water. When the visibility is good, the impression given to the diver is that

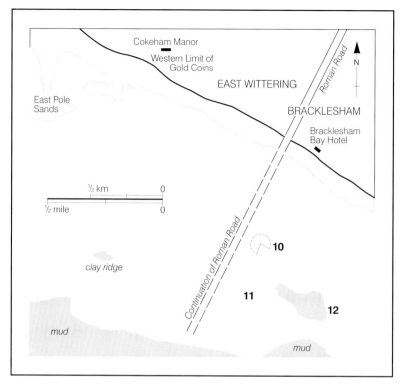

East Wittering and Bracklesham, showing the location of the Amphitheatre (Site 10), HMS A-1 (Site 11) and the Claymounts (Site 12).

you are dropping into a natural amphitheatre in which all the lines are curves: no straight lines, no right angles.

Most of the stones – discovered by Maurice Harknett – lie in pairs between 6 and 30 inches apart. They may be stones that have split. Alex McKee suggested that they formed part of a quarry known to have been submerged in Bracklesham Bay. It was a source of medieval church fonts, carved in one piece from a single stone. A large black stone in the area proved to be a fossilised palm tree and was dated with the help of Margaret Rule to 40 million years ago.

11 HMS A-1 Sitting upright on sand at 14m, the first British designed and built submarine is a designated protected wreck. Diving is banned for 100m around 50 44 31; 00 55 11. The *A-1* is not a war grave, as this is her second sinking. In the first, off the Nab Tower, 11 men died after a collision with the liner *Berwick Castle* on 18 March, 1904. The 270 ton, 100ft long submarine was raised and put back into service, before sinking again in August 1911, when unmanned and on automatic pilot as a gunnery target. She was found by a fisherman in 1989.

HMS A-1, the first submarine designed and built by the Royal Navy. She has now been designated a protected wreck.

12 Claymounts To the east of the amphitheatre are the claymounts or undersea hills. Near one hill is an eroded clay seamount with the capping rock sloping steeply to the south-east to a deep ditch before going down again to 12m. By the ditch, the hard cap has been undercut, and a "cavern" runs in some 5m underneath it. The crest of the nearby hill is only 3m under the surface.

13 Bullock Patch A good dive on a large rock area rising from a sand-and-flint sea bed with some shingle bands. Depth to top is 7m, and deeper there are many crabs and lobsters using the rocks as cover. It is known as a fishing mark for tope and skate. There is little weed, possibly due to the fast current. It must be dived at slack water. Maximum depth is 20m, though most of it is shallower.

14 Stonehenge Mark II This is the name given by diving geologist Hume Wallace to the area between Bullock Patch and the foul ground charted at 50 41 48N; 01 52 13W. As the name implies, a feature of this dive is the enormous boulders, many of which are of similar shape and size to those at Stonehenge. Could this really be the place from which the stones at Stonehenge were dragged to their present resting place?

There is an enormous amount of marine life under, around and on the boulders. At this spot and those previously noted to the north of it, diving can take place with care at almost any state of the tide. Visibility here is often 6m, which is very good for Bracklesham Bay.

15 The Streets This is a very shallow area of weed-covered rocks and shingle patches, more suitable for a snorkel than a dive.

16 The Grounds or Malt Owers Like The Streets, this area is fun to snorkel, but not really worth diving.

17 The Royal Mint It is not really fair to put this down as a diving site. In the days before the Roman conquest, somewhere to the west of Selsey between East Pole Sands and the Medmery Banks, was said to be the capital of King Commius. In that long-submerged town on today's undersea plain was said to be the royal mint. It is true that gold coins of Commius have been washed up on the beaches in the area, including some around Cakeham Manor at the west end of Bracklesham Bay, so divers should keep their eyes open!

18 Mixon Hole This is one of the top diving sites in Britain but is not for the beginner, and even very experienced divers should treat it with respect. Two divers have already lost their lives diving here. The tide is very strong, and surface marker buoys must be worn. Dive only at slack water, which is 2 hours before low water. This means that the limestone blocks around the Mixon Beacon, just to the north of the Hole, are just starting to show.

The Mixon Hole lies at 50 42 20N; 00 46 20W. Maximum depth is 28m. Average tidal speed is 2½ knots in the hole, but speeds of 9 to 10 knots have been recorded around Selsey Bill itself, which probably accounts for the continuous sea-defence work that is carried out there. There is about 45 minutes of slack water (that is, until nearly 1 hour before low water).

The Mixon Beacon is 9m high and has a metal basket on top, usually the drying-out place for cormorants after their dives. The beacon is at the extreme eastern end of the pile of limestone slabs, which are the highest point (about 1m) above the low-tide mark. A considerable area does dry out at low springs, and kelp lies on the surface. Inside the beacon, between it and Selsey Bill, there are various outcrops of rock, which dry.

The limestone slabs on which the Beacon stands are, according to historian and diver-geologist Hume Wallace, the site of a Roman fortress dating from the time when the area was all dry land and the Mixon Hole was part of a river exit to the sea. This fortress would have guarded the entrance to the former river gorge and probably had a huge catapult. If you dive into the hole some 250yds from the beacon you will find several stone balls, about 2ft in diameter, which are likely to have been fired from such a weapon.

The hole itself starts some 100m from the foot of the beacon. The beacon can easily be seen from the shore. Dive boats should aim to approach from the east and, once past, should then swing in to line up the beacon with the lifeboat station and its unmistakable ramp to the sea. A more sensational approach, from the diver's point of view, is to get into the water near the beacon and fin south. Within moments of travelling over a tangled mass of kelp and really shallow water, the bottom suddenly disappears and the diver is over the lip of the hole.

The point where the hole shelves up from the depths, as it does at both its east and west ends, is clearly marked by the troubled waters. The area over the hole is usually much smoother, though it often has large non-breaking swells. The tidal run, when diving at 2 hours before low tide, is first to the west. After complete slack it will start to run to the east. To be in the hole when the tide starts to run – it accelerates from a mere stirring at the turn to full bore within minutes – can be an alarming experience. Sheltering behind peninsulas on the wall's face is only delaying the inevitable, as sooner or later you will have to go with it. On the shingle banks leading to the eastern end divers have been seen almost "shingle-skiing" as they try to dig their fins in against the tide. However, the tidal run to the east will soon wash you up into shallow water after passing over huge mussel beds and then the pace eases dramatically. This is why surface marker buoys must always be used. Trying to follow divers' bubbles is even less practical on this dive than it is on other British dives. It is a doubly foolish diver who would leave a dive boat unattended while diving the Mixon. Launch from Selsey and leave enough time to reach the hole before diving time. Sea distance is 1¼ miles from the Bill.

The area around the Mixon is exposed to winds from all directions except northerlies. For this reason, no diving should be attempted in anything more than a Force 3 or 4. In that wind the swells can become enormous, though local fishermen who fish the area for bass and skate seem oblivious to them! These swells appear to get smaller during slack water.

Divers will find some thermoclines in the summer months, which can give the wet-suited something of a shock. Aldershot Dolphins BSAC did a survey of the hole as a special project several years ago and found that the temperatures around the 26m point varied from 8.1°C in April to 13.25°C in May, remaining stable at 14.5°C in July and August. Visibility in the hole is usually much better than the surrounding areas. It averages about 10m, but on perfect summer days has been known to reach 20m! The hole offers two completely different dives depending on whether you dive on the north face or the south bank. Though all the hole scenery is dramatic, that of the NORTH FACE is the most dramatic. Here is a sheer cliff plunging down from 5m to 20m. On a day with good visibility it looks as though only the water is holding it up – and it probably is!

At the very top are limestone slabs, which break the surface as the tide falls. It is on these slabs that the Mixon Beacon stands. From the slabs down to the start of the cliff-face at 5m is a weed-covered slope. The start of the steep face has weed hanging over it, but it is, in fact, a lip or overhang of stiff blue clay before you come to the light grey clay that makes up the bare cliff-face. This grey clay, or rather the area at its foot, is a fossil-hunter's dream as fossil shells are gently washed out of the eroding clay to fall on the soft base.

At 20m the base of the cliff slopes more gently down to the bottom of the hole at 25m. Depressions in the bed of shingle, pebbles and masses of slipper-limpets can give a maximum depth of 28m, though one diver claims to have found a shallow depression within the hole that gave him 30m. Immediately at the base of the cliff, lobsters and crabs are found among the loose lumps that have fallen from the cliff itself.

The steepest part of the north face is close to the Mixon Beacon. Further to the east it becomes very much more gentle before disappearing altogether. To the west the cliff tends to be less steep after the first 7m, but the slope is still steep enough for material to tumble down to a shelf at 10m. Sole can be found in the soft debris on the shelf. After that, the slope continues at an angle of 45° to big shingle banks at the bottom of the hole, where enormous sting-rays and skate several feet across can be found in late summer. Sticking up out of the shingle in places are enormous boulders about 4m by 2m. These are not to be confused with the catapult balls (which are about 60cm in diameter and completely spherical).

Though not as dramatic as the north face, the South Bank of the Mixon has some very steep sections falling almost sheer to the sea bed. Most of the south face, however, consists of sloping banks of rubble and shingle. There are signs of human occupation. In one spot near the east end some large oblong blocks some 2m by 4m with squared edges are perched on a shelf above a drop-off at 15m. If it is true that the Romans built a lighthouse on the south side of the river, then this may well be the remains of it.

Roofing tiles of ancient date have been found here, too, and there are unnatural circles of rocks at the top of the loose rubble bank that crowns this side of the hole. The south bank is a popular place with dogfish which, at certain times, seem to be sleeping everywhere. On the shingle are a number of live oysters, which are in no sense in a bed, but scattered at random over a huge area.

It is in this area that the real mystery of the hole is found, in the form of the "standing stones". These upright stones are on the 20m contour line of the south bank. They are pointed, and may be natural because there are strange rock shapes in the area, but they are kept upright by smaller stones packed around them, possibly by primitive people who inhabited this area thousands of years ago. The standing stones can best be located by bringing your boat in from the south on a 30° magnetic bearing to the Mixon Beacon and finding 20m on the echo-sounder on the south bank going down into the hole. You will then be slightly to the east, but a short swim holding to the 20m depth should bring you straight to the spot. You will find a stake driven in close to one of the upright stones. This was used by research divers taking measurements.

At the foot of the bank slightly to the east of this spot the author found four of these stones – lying on their sides as though they had rolled down the slope – within 10yds of each other. They were shaped like artillery shells, coming to a distinct point at one end and having a shallow depression at the "flat" end. The largest was about 4ft long and the smallest about 2ft long.

19 The Roman Quarry The stone slabs of the Mixon Mound, the walls of the Roman palace at Fishbourne and the forum in Chichester – the last two constructed about AD 70 – have all come from the same place. That place may well be a now-submerged quarry under the sea some 200m to the north-west of the Mixon Beacon in only 1m of water. Here, Hume Wallace discovered that the Mixon limestone appears to have been dug back in a series of jagged bays a few metres across. In each bay the clay bottom is littered with "quarry scrap" – small and often triangular bits of limestone quite unlike the natural slabs that have fallen from the south face of the Mixon wall. The quarry is at 50 42 40N; 00 46 15W.

20 Arno This British collier lies at 50 42 00N; 00 45 00W, having foundered here when sailing from the Tyne to Portsmouth with 1,300 tons of coal on 11 February, 1899. All but four of her crew of 17 were drowned. Built in 1871, this 1,089-ton ship was 232ft long with a beam of 30ft, but there is little of her left today. Shallow water and big seas have seen to that, and what is left is often buried under sand, though her boilers usually stand proud. The depth of the sea bed in the area varies from 5 to 10m.

21 The Park This large area of clay, sand and gravel to the south of the Far Mulberry is largely flat and uninteresting, though there are one or two depressions going down to 10m, where plaice and sole are known to gather. Despite stories that this is a vast area of drowned parkland where the stumps of old trees can be seen at low tides, it probably takes its name, as do so many offshore spots, from the land directly in front of it. In this case, the area of land was scrub or parkland that the Bishop of Chichester kept long ago for hunting.

22 Stone Boat Charted as an obstruction, this is certainly a wreck at 50 42 55N; 00 41 10W. Here, 4m proud of the sea bed at 11m, is a stack of 15ft Portland stone slabs. They are stacked as it seems they were when the barge or ship carrying them sank and rotted away from around them. This site is good for lobsters.

23 Hedgehogs This site at 50 41 58N; 00 41 06W is often (incorrectly) seized upon as the last resting place of the German submarine mine-layer *UC-16* because it is a mere 200yds from the position where HMS *Melampus* reported destroying her. Divers who get down to the spot that shows on their echo-sounder are grievously disappointed to find not a World War One German submarine, but beach landing obstructions of World War Two made from railway lines and angle-iron. They must have fallen off some of the invasion traffic in the area in 1944. They measure some 20ft by 10ft by 5ft and are some 50ft apart, and they give submarine-like echoes and outlines.

So much time and effort have gone into the search by amateur divers for the *UC-16*, without success, that the story of the loss of the *UC-16* deserves some detail. This mine-laying submarine was the first of her class of boats – *UC-16* to *UC-33*. Her keel was laid in August 1915 and she was completed in June of the following year. Of 410 tons, she had two bow torpedo tubes and one stern. In addition to this, she had six mine-laying chutes and could carry 18 mines. On her 162ft deck she had one 8.8-cm gun. Her surface range of nearly 7,000 miles at 7 knots was drastically cut to a mere 55 miles at 4 knots submerged. She could, however, manage bursts of nearly 12 knots on the surface and nearly 7 knots submerged. Her slow rate of dive – it took her a full 40 seconds to get under – almost cost the lives of her three officers and 23 men on more than one occasion and may well have been the reason she was finally lost.

But *UC-16* was a successful boat and completed many missions from her Zeebrugge base under the captaincy of Oberleutnant G. Reimarus. Just after midnight on the morning of 2 October, 1917, the *UC-16* left Zeebrugge and headed for the Straits of Dover. Her mission was to lay mines in front of Boulogne and then to move on to the "commercial war" – sinking merchant ships. On this trip *UC-16* had been briefed to attack shipping to the "West of the English Channel".

The next report we have comes from Captain C.E. Hughes White, who was commanding the Royal Navy destroyer, HMS *Melampus*. He reported that he was towing a "seaplane lighter" when the tow rope broke near Selsey Bill. While chasing the runaway lighter, *UC-16* was suddenly spotted on the surface. This was on 22 October, 1917. Captain Hughes White went flat out after the U-boat. "He was diving into the head sea and evidently did not see me, but when nearing him my safety valves lifted with a report like a pom-pom and he did a wonderful crash dive. I don't think my stem missed his conning-tower by two feet!", wrote Captain Hughes White.

According to the captain, the *UC-16* then lay silently on the bottom and for 35 minutes he searched for her, towing his explosive paravane across the area. When this apparently hooked the submarine it was detonated and then a depth charge was dropped on the position. Oil welled up, but no survivors were seen. A heavy sea was running at the time.

It seems that on the basis of this oil the destruction of *UC-16* was confirmed to the satisfaction of the Admiralty. The German High Command was not satisfied, however. They did not query the loss of the submarine – there could be no other explanation for the fact that she never returned to her Zeebrugge base – but it is clear that they never accepted that the attack of the destroyer *Melampus* was the cause of the loss of *UC-16*. The official German report into the loss says that there was clear evidence that the mines she was ordered to lay off Boulogne were laid. But then they reported: "On 26.10, the body of the Watch Officer of *UC-16* Leutnant Von Becswarzowski was washed ashore at Noordwijk in Holland." Now, as Noordwijk is some 16 miles north of Den Haag, on the coast of southern Holland, the Germans did have a point when their report continued: "This circumstance indicates that the boat touched a mine during its underwater cruise and a skirmish cannot be the origin of the loss. The closest belief is that *UC-16* either when going to sea or by returning ran into an English mine barrage, which was laid before the Flanders coast on the 22, 23 and 24 of September." They could have added that either the *Melampus* did not sink the *UC-16* at all, or the body of poor Von Becswarzowski had travelled at an incredible speed to get from Selsey Bill to Holland in four days.

That, then, is all that is known about the loss of *UC-16*. The evidence indicates that the *UC-16* is not off Selsey Bill at all, and that Oberleutnant Reimarus tricked Captain Hughes White into thinking he had been sunk, and then set off home, or that the submarine attacked by *Melampus* was another boat entirely (in which case, it too escaped for there is no record of any other U-boat missing during that period). All other losses of the time are clearly documented.

But there is in fact a submarine, probably a World War One U-boat, lying under the sea off Selsey, however unlikely it is to be *UC-16*. The "Selsey Submarine" is 8 miles out by the Nab Tower and to the south of it, but the author is unable to give a full position. The diver who found her has not finished exploring her and wishes to keep the position secret.

This submarine was found by North Sea diver Pip Maidment when clearing some snagged lobster pots for Selsey fisherman Paul Smeeton. Maidment, who comes from a long line of Selsey lifeboat men and lives there when not working in the North Sea, found the snagged pots all right, but it was what they were snagged on that took his breath away. Before him was a battered but unmistakable submarine, lying at 45° on a sandy-mud sea bed.

The submarine was badly flattened at bow and stern, but the bulkheads were intact and it was clear that she had four compartments. The single bronze periscope was intact and the hatch was open. When Pip Maidment peered in he could see unbroken gauges inside. The submarine lay in 27m of water and had twin steel propellers. Though the bulkheads were intact, she was badly damaged and heavily rusted – so much so that daylight from the hatchway could be seen when looking into the boat from one side. The torpedo tubes were clearly of steel, and had lasted better than some of the surrounding metal.

Pip Maidment is continuing to dive this submarine in the hope of finding something to establish her identity. If she is a German U-boat there are three possible candidates – all reported missing in the Channel with no survivors. She could be *U-37*, commanded by Kapitän-Leutnant E. Wilke, missing with all hands in April 1915, *UC-18,* lost in February or March 1917 when commanded by Oberleutnant W. Kiel, or *UB-36*, missing at the end of June 1917, commanded by Oberleutnant Von Kyserlinck.

24 Barn Rocks This heavily weeded area of sandstone boulders 1m high with sand-shingle pathways through them is at 50 46 12N; 00 42 24W. Depths are to 5m. The tops of some rocks dry at low spring tides. This is really a double reef with one outer band after an inner one that has many small rounded boulders in the shallows. The rocks have claimed many outboard propellers as they project farther out to sea than seems likely from the chart. This is particularly dangerous if fog clamps down suddenly and coxswains try to work their way back to Bognor from the Mulberry area by following the high shingle beach to the east. The reef is populated by pouting and the occasional lobster is seen.

This might just be a shore dive for really strong swimmers prepared to work their way along the shingle beach until they are opposite the rocks. The nearest access point to the beach through the proliferation of private estates is via Barrack Lane. To get there, head west on the sea front road out of Bognor and continue past the Ship Inn to a small roundabout. Turn left into Barrack Lane. Press on through the sprouting "Private" signs, and you will emerge at the shingle beach. This is possibly a place for an inflatable launch, but the parking difficulties are such that it would be better to launch at Bognor or Pagham. An alternative approach could be made via High Trees, a turning to the sea before the Ship Inn, leading via Dark Lane to a very small parking area with a concrete ramp to the shingle.

25 German Ju 88 At high water this crashed German twin-engined bomber lies ¾ mile offshore directly opposite Butlins Holiday Camp. Or part of it does, for there on the sand and shingle sea bed are the two massive 12-cylinder Junkers Jumo engines, and parts of the wings. One propeller has been removed by divers. Missing is the 47ft fuselage, which searches in the immediate area have failed to find. This suggests that the crash landing was an extremely heavy one with the fuselage breaking away and travelling on for some distance or disintegrating completely.

This Ju 88 may be one of those shot down during the mass attack of 63 German aircraft on Portsmouth on 12 August, 1940, when fifteen Ju 88As were detached to bomb radar installations at Ventnor on the Isle of Wight.

26 Gascony The court of enquiry into the loss of this vessel concluded that she had probably hit a mine, despite the evidence of her captain, William Melville, who said that he heard a hiss before a huge explosion from the port side just behind the bridge at 11.18pm on 6 January, 1918. The captain was right. His ship was the victim of Oberleutnant Johann Lohs – this time while he was commanding the mine-laying submarine *UC-75*. Lohs hit the *Gascony* with a torpedo while she was carrying guns, hay, and charcoal from Southampton to

The Gascogny (Site 26) struck a mine in 1918.

Calais for the British Army. She did not sink for a long time and her escort, HMS *P-12*, stood by all night. At 8am two tugs arrived and took her in tow, but she sank just before 1.45pm. Today the *Gascony* lies at 50 39 27N; 00 39 31W. She was, for many years, upside down and there appeared to be no way into her hull. Since then, the hull has cracked apart and the bow section has turned almost upright. It is now possible to swim with care inside part of the wreck where the wheels of army gun carriages are plain to see. The propeller has been salvaged. Built in 1908 in Middlesbrough, the *Gascony* of 3,133 tons, was 360ft long with a 48ft beam. The general depth is 30m and the wreck stands some 3m proud.

27 Axwell This 240ft British armed steamer of 1,422 tons was, according to Lloyds Wartime Loss Book, torpedoed "three miles west-south-west of the Owers Light Vessel", killing two men in the engine room on 13 November, 1917. The submarine responsible was *UB-56*, commanded by Oberleutnant Hans Valentiner, who had not taken kindly to being rammed by the *Axwell* an hour or so earlier!

The *Axwell* was on her way from Warkworth, Northumberland, to Rouen with a cargo of 1,850 tons of coal. At 4.45am on 13 November the second mate, who was on the bridge, spotted a dark object off his starboard bow. Closer inspection showed that the object was a submarine crossing the course of the *Axwell* from starboard to port. The mate followed the Admiralty's standing instructions and headed straight for the submarine, striking her a glancing blow along her starboard side. The U-boat then made off and was soon out of sight.

The master, William Norman Thompson, then spotted a patrol trawler and was just putting his megaphone to his mouth to tell the patrol about the submarine when a torpedo struck him in the port side amidships. The 16 survivors of the crew were picked up by the patrol vessel. At daylight the *Axwell* was found to be still afloat. Thompson and four of his crew re-boarded her and took on a towline, but at almost the first pull she lurched and sank.

Today the steamer lies at 50 38 48N; 00 40 35W and has been positively identified by the ship's bell, recovered in 1979 by Terry Barwick, Diving Officer of Newham BSAC. The *Axwell* is owned by a group of divers within that branch. She is upright in deep water (46m) with her bows to the east and is not far from the 67m hole to the east of the Elbow on the Outer Owers.

The deck of the ship is at 42m, and both the forward and aft holds are still full of coal. The forward crew area and chain locker below the foredeck can be swum through and were quite clear of debris recently. The superstructure of the bridge has collapsed, but the deck-house and bridge area can still be entered by experienced divers who know the wreck. The after-deck is taken up by the auxiliary steering gear and various winches. The propeller is iron and still in place. Her binnacle is an elegant dolphin-legged affair.

28 Menelaos This big Greek steamer was the victim of the monstrous seas that can be kicked up on the Outer Owers. In fact, she was on the west side of the Shoal of Lead at 10.40pm on 2 November, 1930, when the Selsey lifeboat, the *Canadian Pacific*, was called out. In the time it took the lifeboat, under the command of coxswain Fred Barnes (a famous Selsey figure who was coxswain of the Selsey boat from 1917 to 1956), to fight the 6 miles to the scene in a south-westerly gale, the *Menelaos* was in a desperate state. Her steering had gone, her hatches were stove in and she was drifting right into the maelstrom of the Elbow. Another ship had taken off 12 of the crew, but though there were still men left aboard, the rescuing vessel could now only stand off – she dared not go into the shallow seas around the shoal. Fred Barnes could and did. He ran the lifeboat right in alongside and took off the rest of the crew. He was only just in time. The *Menelaos* bumped across most of the Shoal of Lead, but foundered before she could get clear. So big were the seas that she started to break up almost immediately. Today she is at 50 39 24N; 00 41 06W. Derek Allchurch of Selsey, who has dived her recently, says that she is so flattened out that it is impossible to tell which part of her you are on, though her winches are still clear and prominent. The depth is often only 5m.

Pip Maidment, the North Sea diver, who is Derek Allchurch's partner when they dive Selsey waters, recently found her bell amid the wreckage. He warns that the wreck is close to the Elbow, with its fearsome tidal currents. When trying to dive the *Menelaos* in 1993, some divers instead found themselves over a broken wooden wreck of the 18th or 19th century and a number of iron cannon over 6ft long that might have been used as ballast. They were tapered but had no cascabels and no trunnions, and had a large bore of nearly 5 inches.

29 The Owers These banks and rocks are the sea-drowned continuation of today's Selsey Bill. They have always been a danger to shipping and as far back as 1788 a lightship was moored to try to stop the apparently endless succession of wrecks on them.

Oddly enough, the Inner Owers are those shore-attached sandbanks just to the east of East Beach, Selsey. The Middle Owers are out near West Head and the

Outer Owers not much further out to the east. The lightship was replaced by a "Lanby" (a large automatic navigation buoy), positioned 11 miles due south of Bognor Regis at 50 37 30N; 00 40 60W. This has now been replaced with a Racon, a radar transmission buoy.

The name Owers is a corruption of hores, the Anglo-Saxon for dirty – and signifies an area of water made dirty by the sandbanks.

30 The Shoal of the Lead There are said to be two reasons for this unusual name for a shoal of rock-capped clay, part of which can dry at very low spring tides. The first is that the name derives from the discovery by the men of Selsey of a wreck laden with lead ingots. The second is that the shoal is smothered by small mussels that give it a leaden hue. The Shoal of the Lead is at 50 39 42N; 00 40 45W, and at its southern end is the Outer Owers buoy. Between the Shoal and the buoy is a charted depth of 67m and a warning of overfalls. Neither mark is wrong. It is 67m deep here, and one diver recently described the overfalls as "huge – it was like being in a storm at sea on a calm day!"

There is a fascinating diving area just to the north of this that does not require great depth. This is the southern end of the shoal, and entry is made at the eastern tip just before slack water in about 6m. A slow descent, then a drift to the west along the edge of the bank at about 20m going slightly north following the shoal takes the diver over a mass of wreckage, mostly wood, and the many lobster pots lost or abandoned and swept by the strong tides to this particular spot.

On one particular dive in this area, Holborn BSAC member Mike Maloney reported seeing a huge and ancient anchor over 4m long. This, according to dive-boat skippers, is only one of over a dozen that have been reported by divers in various parts of the Shoal. This is surely proof that over the centuries the Shoal of the Lead has claimed more than its share of victims. Recently some members of Chichester BSAC found the wreckage of an old sailing ship to the east of the Shoal, which appeared to be carrying tin ingots.

31 The Elbow This site for scenic diving is so named because of its shape on the chart at 50 39 09N; 00 41 51W. The Elbow is formed out of the southern end of the Shoal of the Lead and provides some beautiful diving, often in water of astounding clarity. Divers have claimed over 30m visibility out here.

On the south-west side of the joint, the boring of bivalves has led to the collapse of the cap rock, and great slabs of it have broken away and fallen on to the slopes. These slopes run down from the bare rock near the surface to clean, white sand at 42m.

WARNING The tidal run here is impressive; dive only at slack. Many lobsters live under the cap-rock slabs in holes in the soft clay underneath. The south-east side of the Elbow has similar terrain. Fish life is prolific with many very large cod and big pouting.

32 Britsum This Dutch steamer was on her way to Fowey from Hull on 4 July, 1940, when a German Dornier 17 dropped out of the low clouds and bombed her. A direct hit set the *Britsum* on fire, and her captain beached her deliberately on the eastern end of the Pullar Bank in the hope that she could be towed off and

This diver has found a lobster at The Elbow (Site 31).

repaired. But a gale swept in and the 421ft *Britsum* was soon a total wreck. Permission was then given for her to be used as a bombing target by the RAF, and there is little of her now that stands more than 1m above the sea bed.

She is at 50 40 22N; 00 47 39W and belongs to two North Sea divers from Selsey, Derek Allchurch and Pip Maidment. They have done some salvage work on her and say that they do not mind people diving on her as long as they take nothing. She is very broken up over a large area in extremely shallow water in places not even 2m deep. The wreckage does, however, attract huge shoals of pouting in the area where the water is about 10m deep. Holborn diver Mike Maloney says that these shoals are the biggest he has ever seen, notwithstanding those on that well-known pouting attraction, the Far Mulberry (Site **59**)!

33 Lowmount 50 39 46N; 00 50 24W. A 2,070-ton British steamer with a 2,650-ton cargo of iron ore from Bilbao to Stockton-on-Tees, the *Lowmount* was sunk on May 7, 1917 by a mine laid by the German submarine *UC-70*. Five men were killed out of a crew of 22. Her captain, John Williams, survived and was under the impression that he had been torpedoed. The *Lowmount* was 282ft long with a beam of 38ft. She was built by S.P. Austin and Son of Sunderland in 1888 of steel, and only had one deck. After she struck the mine "four miles south-east of the Nab Tower" and sank to the bottom in 10m of water, her masts were clearly visible for a long time.

The *Lowmount* was dispersed in 1922 and visited by a hard-hat diver in September 1923. She was dispersed again in 1925 and 1951 and swept in 1965. The wreck is, as a result, very broken with only 2m showing above the sea bed.

Divers' impressions are that the sand is slowly covering her. One way of locating her is to get the Boulder and Pullar Buoys in line, then using an echo-sounder motor "down the dip and up the other side" – in other words cross the depression that lies to the north-east of her. The *Lowmount* is on the crest of the south-west side of that depression. This wreck is regularly fished by boats from Selsey.

34 Edenwood 50 40 31N; 00 54 09W. After colliding near the Nab Tower with HMS *Derbyshire* (an 11,660-ton former Bibby Line liner converted to an armed merchant cruiser), this 1,167-ton British collier let go her anchors to repair the damage. She sank shortly afterwards while still at anchor on Christmas Day, 1939. She was carrying cargo of coal and now lies in 14m on a bed of sand and shingle. The sea bed around here has foiled all attempts to sweep the wreck. It seems from divers' reports and echo-sounder traces that the *Edenwood* wreck is 138ft long and lies in a deep scour or valley 15m deep. The wreck is protected by great natural humps in the sea bed on the south-south-east and by shallows to the north-east. This means that the top of the wreck only pokes up about ½m in general sea-bed depths of 14m to 15m.

35 Robinson's Trawler At 50 40 39N; 00 53 57W, this site is only 400yds to the north-east of the wreck of the *Edenwood* (Site **34**) and is charted as an obstruction. So far, no identification by diving has been made, but the author suspects that this could well be the wreck of a trawler, possibly sunk by a mine during World War Two.

This theory is the result of a meeting and exchange of letters some 10 years ago between the author and J.R. Robinson, who was David Hillyard's engineer in Littlehampton for over 40 years. Mr Robinson described taking a high-speed motor launch out of Littlehampton during World War Two and heading for the Hamble, Southampton Water, for trials after a night of German bombing along the coast. To do this they had to get out to the swept channel and then travel along the coast. Mr Robinson wrote: "We had a fresh south-west wind, some sea which slowed us down, but soon we came up with a Bofors gun pointing to the sky, with handrails and platform awash, which I knew must be on a Mulberry unit." He continued: "The same morning when about 3 miles west of the Street and Pullar Buoys we came on to a trawler's mast sticking out of the swept channel which had only just gone down. I think mines were the cause of both wrecks." This description would put his trawler wreck almost exactly on this obstruction charted as unknown, and 13m down on a very bumpy sea bed.

36 Corbet Woodall An armed schooner-rigged steamer of 917 tons, the *Corbet Woodall* was bringing 1,250 tons of coal up-Channel, South Shields for Poole, on 30 May, 1917, when she hit a mine, laid by *UC-36*, 1½ miles east of the Nab Light Vessel. There was a huge explosion on the port side just forward of the bridge, which knocked down the master, Joseph Henry Brown. No one was killed, but she sank bow first at 50 41 32N; 00 53 21W. She lies in 12m of water on a rock bottom. Explosives were used to clear her and little now stands more than 2m high off the sea bed. She is very broken up with a good deal of her 200ft lying in pieces inside the demolition crater. The *Corbet Woodall* was built in 1908 by Austins of Sunderland.

37 The Whirlpool Hole 50 41 27N; 00 48 24W. It is this hole that deprives the Mixon Hole of its claim to be unique. For here, within 100m due east of the Boulder Buoy, is another sheer cliff with exactly the same geological formation as the Mixon. Here is the same limestone cap, then stiff blue clay and rubble-strewn slope with boulders at the bottom in 15m. Once again, the only time to dive it is 2 hours before low water.

This hole is different, though, in that it is completely circular and the tide has a clockwise whirlpool effect that will give you a circular dive around the edge of the hole. The only way to get into Whirlpool Hole is for the boat skipper to put his shot-line right into the centre of the hole and for divers to go down that. Even diving at slack water tends to produce a slightly circular dive as some vestige of current is always left to take the divers around and around. Though parts of the hole seem almost polished by the tidal whirlpool effect, there is a great deal of marine life in there, including both crabs and lobsters among the many boulders at the bottom.

38 Wilna 50 40 42N; 00 55 34W. This navy patrol yacht of 461 tons was attacked by German aircraft on 24 March, 1941, and so badly damaged that she sank shortly after being abandoned. She stood up well off the bottom until the end of the war and was dispersed with explosives on 20 September, 1945. What remains lies in a crater caused by the dispersal. The wreck extends about 1m above the crater lip. There is another small portion of wreckage 250m to the north-north-west. Depth is 13m.

39 Whale Bridge At 50 38 25N; 00 52 55W this is one of the most scenic dives of the area. It is a bridge section of the wartime Mulberry Harbour and sits upright on its pontoons in 24m at a distance of 2½ miles from the Pullar Bank Buoy.

These bridge sections rode on flotation chambers or pontoons and were designed to flex with the rise and fall of waves in rough weather. They were codenamed Whale, and were a great success when the Mulberry Harbour was established in 1944, allowing troops and vehicles of all kinds to travel along them to the shore. Each span was 80ft long and weighed 28 tons. The pontoons that carried them were 16 tons each.

Once on their water-tight pontoons, the Whales were very manoeuvrable – one tug of 1,000hp could tow 6 spans of the bridge behind it at 6 knots – weather permitting, of course. No-one knows what caused this section to lose its buoyancy; the pontoons appear intact.

Chichester BSAC, who dive this site regularly, say that it is essential to dive at slack water when visibility is usually excellent. They rate it a beautiful dive even though the Whale seems full of conger eels. There are lobster on it, too, but the congers well outnumber them. Indeed, it is an unusual dive on which less than a dozen congers are seen. They appear to enjoy the lattice-work of the bridge and are often seen swimming through it.

40 Two bulldozers, two tanks and a field gun These lie on a mud-and-gravel sea bed at 50 38 32N; 00 51 37W. There is no ship to be seen and they are jumbled together in a shallow scour in 16m. It is probable that they were being carried not as deck cargo on a ship, but on the roadway of the Whale bridge section (Site **39**), which lies only ½ mile away. As the bridge started to sink at one end, they probably slid off.

41 Wreck, name unknown 50 38 58N; 00 49 16W. This is the wreck of a World War One coaster lying east–west, with the bow to the west. She is very broken and rusted, and the highest point is the boilers, which are 5m proud of the shingle sea bed. The wreck was discovered by professional divers from Spithead in 1975 and is about 250ft long.

42 Tank Landing Craft, type unknown 50 38 12N; 00 46 19W. This vessel lies almost exactly due north–south, and there is some doubt about what kind of craft she is, as she is completely upside down and flat-bottomed. Divers think that if she is not a tank landing craft, she might have been some sort of motorised barge for use in the D-Day landings. Her hull is 4m proud of the sand-shingle sea bed in 20m of water, and she is 160ft long by 30ft by 8ft. She originally carried three small bronze propellers. The steel plate of which she is made is very thin, and holes are appearing in many places.

43 The Wallace Mountains South of the Pullar Bank in a vast area where the far-ranging Selsey fishermen pot for lobsters and an oil-rig made the first exploratory hole in Sussex inshore waters, Hume Wallace tells of mountains and gorges in the terraces, which drop down to 35m. The rock slopes are often bare, but in the valleys that run through them there is a vast amount of life. Wallace warns, however, that this is no place for small boats and stresses that he would not take even his own larger boat there except on dead calm days and at low water. There is often a very tricky big sea in the area and even on calm days it can suddenly kick up. Here, the diving time increases to 2 hours before until 2 hours after low water.

44 Dresden A small steamer of 950 tons carrying 798 tons of coke, the *Dresden* surrendered to the German submarine *UB-37* at 5pm on 23 September, 1916 after Oberleutnant Hans Valentiner had fired warning shells over her. He then sent her to the bottom by means of explosive charges after stealing her bell and chronometer. The *Dresden* was on her way from Newcastle to Rouen.

The crew were all saved, having been allowed to leave in their boats by the German boarding party. She is now at 50 37 54N; 00 43 42W. She has been identified by pottery bearing the line's insignia brought up by divers. (No, not Dresden china!)

The *Dresden* now lies in 15m of water. Although she is pretty much smashed up, her anchor chain often snags lobster pots. Divers clearing these snags and following the chain away from the anchor found nothing at first, but away from the end of the chain and to the west are her steel ribs and plates.

45 HMS Sapper This hired trawler disappeared off the Owers Light Vessel (Site **46**) on 29 December, 1917. Whether it was a mine or a submarine's torpedo no-one can say, for all her crew went with her. She is at 50 37 18N; 00 41 09W. Her wreckage is in three pieces and very broken up, so much so that there are no clues about the cause of her sinking. In 28m of water, the wreck lies east–west with the stern towards the east. The highest point is her boiler some 6m proud. Her propeller is iron. Her nameplate was recovered by divers in 1983.

46 Owers Light Vessel (1914–1918 position) This is not a wreck but is included for those trying to locate World War One wrecks when the only position given is the bearing and number of miles from the Owers Light Vessel. During World War One the vessel was at 50 37 00N; 00 41 00W, which when translated to the current Admiralty chart (1652) gives a position of 50 37 02N; 00 41 01W. This places it about ½ mile south-west of the present Owers automatic light buoy.

47 British Commerce This big steel-plated sailing ship of 1,417 tons, and nearly 250ft long with a beam of 37ft, was hit square-on by the bow of another great four-masted sailing ship, the *County of Aberdeen*, on the night of 24 April, 1883. Within moments the *British Commerce* was gone, taking with her all but two of a crew of 27, only Captain Jones and the boatswain being saved. The *County of Aberdeen*, commanded by Captain MacLean, managed to get safely into Portsmouth on the following afternoon, despite having the fore-compartment stove in and filled with water and the jib-boom shattered. The position of the collision is given as "off the Owers lightship" at 50 36 50N; 00 41 00W. The *British Commerce* is regularly dived by some small specialist groups. She is becoming well buried.

The *British Commerce* was built by Dobie and Company of Glasgow in 1874 and was outward bound from London for Melbourne with general cargo. She was owned by the British Shipbuilders Company. The *County of Aberdeen* was homeward bound from Calcutta for London and was owned by Robert Craig of Glasgow.

48 Lightfoot This wreck is now very broken and silted at 50 36 16N; 00 39 22W in 30m. The boiler, standing 4m high, is the most prominent point of this British armed steamer of 1,875 tons. She was in ballast and heading for Barry Roads when she was torpedoed on the port side in No. 3 hold on 16 March, 1918, by *UB-30*. She sank in under 2 minutes only a mile from the Owers Light Vessel (Site **46**), but all her crew managed to take to the boats and were saved. This was not her first encounter with a German submarine. On October 26 the previous year, a submarine had tried to stop her with warning shots in the North Sea, but *Lightfoot* made a rapid escape into a fog-bank.

The *Lightfoot* now lies north–south, though her 268ft hull, built in 1916, is shattered and scattered.

49 Hedwig Lunstedt 50 35 30N; 00 41 20W. This 424-ton West German ship was sunk on 28 January, 1974, after she put out a Mayday call saying that her cargo of iron bars had shifted. No more was heard of the ship, which was on voyage from Rotterdam to Cork, but four bodies of her crew of eight were recovered. She was found by Royal Navy divers and now lies on her starboard side with her bows to the north. One-third of the hull and superstructure have been forced into the clay and gravel of the sea bed at 30m. The vessel is intact as far as can be seen from the uncovered portion but the propeller has been salvaged.

50 Basil This ship, built in Belfast in 1895, was at first called *Mourne*, but after three years she was sold and renamed *Basil*. A 3,220-ton steamer, 338ft long, she had visited most ports in Europe before being requisitioned by the Navy at the outbreak of World War One. They mounted a 4.7-inch gun on her poop and she became Expeditionary Force Transport C608, carrying troops, munitions, horses, and feed, backwards and forwards from Britain to France.

On the night of 11 November, 1917, the *Basil* was doing just that, heading for Boulogne from Southampton with a cargo of ammunition when she was in collision in a fog-bank with the French steamer *Margaux* and foundered within minutes. As she sank, 13 of her crew were lost. The *Margaux*, which was going from Dunkirk to Barry, later arrived at Southampton with her bows very badly damaged.

The *Basil* is at 50 35 00N; 00 41 00W in a general depth of 35m and stands some 7m above the sea bed. The gun is still there, pointing aft. She is upright and her engine is exposed. Two decks have collapsed and some of her cargo of shells is visible. The bow section is parted from the main hull and has a 45° list to port. Her cargo is being salvaged.

51 Carbineer 50 34 59N; 00 40 52W. This 1,266-ton British cargo-steamer was carrying general cargo from London to Manchester when she was in collision with another steamer on 22 April, 1914. The *Carbineer* sank swiftly and now all 220ft of her sits upright 6m high on a sea bed at 25m. She lies north-east to south-west and is well silted. This wreck is very close to that of the *Basil*.

52 Lola This wreck is charted at 50 34 07N; 00 39 54W, but no diving reports have yet been received. A 160ft Belgian ship of 458 tons, she was on passage from Porthoustock, Cornwall, to London with a cargo of granite chippings for London's roads when she foundered in huge seas well off the Outer Owers on 20 October, 1929. She has been located by echo-sounder and is lying north-east to south-west and stands some 8m proud of the sea bed in 25m of water. Divers who have probed the Manacles in Cornwall will know exactly where the *Lola* came in to Porthoustock Beach to load her stone cargo from the chutes down from the quarry.

53 Wreck, name unknown Very close to the *Lola* at 50 33 59N; 00 39 59W, this wreck has been dived. She is some 290ft long and is very broken in 25m. Her stern is the best part. This lies on its port side with a big iron propeller still in place. The spare propeller is lying by the boiler. She is thought to be another World War One casualty.

54 Wreck, name unknown At 50 35 11N; 00 54 44W. Discovered in 1976, this coaster lies on her port side in 27m. She is very old, 200ft long and much broken amidships. The bows are badly damaged and part of the stern is broken off and tilted upright to form her highest point 8m off the sea bed. The wreck is heavily silted, but lies on a small ridge with the top of the boilers showing 2m above the bottom. Her iron propeller is clear, but broken. She lies with her bows to the north-east.

55 HMS Prince Leopold This former Belgian ship, built in 1930, was mined and damaged on 22 September, 1940 – so badly, in fact, that she was designated as an air target. However, after repairs she became an infantry landing ship under Royal Navy command. She was fitted with two 12-pounder guns and six 20mm machine-guns. On 29 July, 1944, she was torpedoed by *U-261*, commanded by Oberleutnant Hermann Struckmann, while on passage from the Isle of Wight to Normandy. The 2,938-ton ship capsized and sank.

The *Prince Leopold* now sits upright with a list to starboard at 50 34 35N; 00 55 52W, or 5.4 miles on a bearing of 171° from the Nab Tower. She is 347ft long with a beam of 46ft. The gravel sea bed is at 30m and the highest point of the wreck is the aft-mounted Bofors gun, 10m above the sea bed. There are three cases of ammunition beside the gun. Judging by the large hole in her port side, the torpedo struck her almost exactly amidships. The bow is listing to starboard more than the stern, which has a 30° list. Her superstructure is gone following sweeping.

WARNING Depth charges are still in their racks at the stern. It is possible to swim into the wreck, but only with great care as her metal is deteriorating fast and portholes are dropping out.

56 German Destroyer Just 100yds to the south of the *Prince Leopold* (Site **55**), at 50 34 35N; 00 55 52W, lies an intact German destroyer of 1900 vintage. This ship, which used to have four funnels, is remarkable for her very narrow beam. Doug Barnard, who dived her recently, says that if you come back 20ft from the bow, you can lie on the deck and put your hands over the hull on each site. Even though Mr Barnard is a big fellow, that makes her beam very narrow indeed – around the 6ft mark. The ship is about 300ft long and was obviously designed for speed with a three-bladed propeller on each of her four propeller shafts.

This narrow ship is upright and has a deck that rolls round like a Peterhead trawler. Aft there is a 75mm gun pointing dead ahead with an elevation of 30 to 40°. Behind that, at right angles to the sides of the ship, are two ready-to-use ammunition trunks with 50 live rounds in each box. Ray Lee of Littlehampton even found the rammer for this gun.

The wreck is at 37m and bears no obvious sign of damage. The fine teak decks are intact, the planking being about 2 inches wide with black pitch in between. At her after-end are masses of bundles of wire and drums as though she was being used for target towing or minesweeping.

The ship has many portholes on it, but whereas the normal porthole has eight or nine moving parts, these have 43, many of which are for a complicated ratchet locking and opening system. One scuttle raised has "N. Fehrmann and Co. Hamburg 9" engraved on it. The firm still exists and believe they may be able to identify the ship very soon.

57 The French Barque A fantastic find and a fantastic dive. After helping a Selsey fisherman who had got a string of pots tangled in the infantry landing ship *Prince Leopold* (Site **55**), divers moved over to another snagged string, and found themselves on a huge, intact sailing ship with bowsprit still erect and her four giant masts, yards still crossed, lying out to the side.

There the ship lay on a bed of white sand at 30m in 30m visibility, at 50 29 30N; 00 51 00W. Perhaps the best way to describe her is to do so in the words of the first man to see her since her sinking, Mobell diver Doug Barnard of Billingshurst: "She is the biggest sailing ship I have ever been on above or below the sea. She is four-masted and about 480ft long. She is lying on her starboard side with the foremast out over the bow. The three other masts are lying out over the starboard side. The sails are still there and the canvas of them is so tough that you cannot tear it when you pick it up.

"The hatch combings are in place around the hatches and are like curved sections of four-by-two with eight-inch square holes in it. The hatch covers, about 20ft square, are still lying there. And all around is this white, very white sand. The starboard rail is under the sand just as though a big wave had come aboard.

"The port rail is complete in eight-by-five rolled-edge mahogany and is stepped up to the stern. Big timber members are held by iron brackets on to the deck and from these there are bronze wheels – 2ft in diameter and 2½ins thick. There are eight of these on either side; they were obviously for the chains for slewing the yards.

"The wheel is in place. Even the cuddy behind the wheel is there. She has got a large counter-stern something like the *Gascony*. We went out over the bow to try to find the bell on the foremast, but we could not. The bowsprit is still there, still erect. Her holds are full of sand and she is dug well in though the stern is 8m clear of the sea bed and the bows about 6m clear.

"I have dived her three times. She is a fantastic sight – it took me the whole of one dive just to swim around her ... down one side and up the other ..."

Why the "French Barque"? No-one really seems to know. Nor will they, until her identity is confirmed by some future diving discovery.

58 UB-81 Strictly speaking, this wreck should not be in this book, as her final resting place at 50 29 22N; 00 58 12W is just 1½ miles into Hampshire waters. But as the submarine has moved around a lot – some 20 miles at least – since she sank, it may be that she will travel back into Sussex by the time this is published! *UB-81* in fact went down just 2 miles south of the Owers Light Vessel (Site **46**) on 2 December, 1917, following what is thought to have been a collision with a mine laid by her own navy. It was her maiden voyage, and 26 of her crew of 33 perished in the sinking. The seven survivors escaped through the bow torpedo tubes before the submarine was accidentally rammed by a British patrol boat during rescue operations.

How long the *UB-81* lay in the position she sank no one knows. Certainly, when the Navy had a look for her in 1961 she was gone – no Asdic contact could be obtained in the area of her sinking. When calculating positions of wrecks in World War One you must remember that distances in this area need adjustment – the Owers lightship was then stationed ½ mile to the south-west of the present automatic light-buoy.

In 1970, the *UB-81* was discovered at 50 27 00N; 00 51 00W. She was then 12 miles away from where she sank. Then, in 1974, she was discovered upright on a flat sand-and-shingle sea bed some 14 miles south-east of the Isle of Wight. The diver who found her while working for a salvage firm noted that the only real damage – and that looked slight – appeared to be to her bow.

Since then, the *UB-81* has not moved, and is unlikely to move again. She is at 00 29 22N; 00 58 12W, standing 5m high on the sea bed at 28m; when dived in 1989 she was broken in two just aft of the conning tower. The highest point is her gun, with its barrel pointing up towards the surface. The main hatch is open to reveal the heavily silted control room. To dive her, you will need to hire a boat from Littlehampton as she is some 15 miles south-west of Selsey Bill.

South Street slipway at Emsworth is one of the launch sites for Chichester Harbour.

AREA 2:

Pagham and Pagham Harbour

This area is formed by a box of imaginary lines that come to shore at 50 44 18N; 00 45 54W and 50 46 06N; 00 43 59W. The lines enclose a sea area of 6 square miles. On any Admiralty chart, this area is clearly marked by bold pecked lines to show that it contains "numerous dangers through which it is unsafe to navigate". In effect, the Admiralty is saying that though they have charted numerous obstructions under the sea off Pagham Harbour, they are pretty certain that there are a lot more they do not know about. And they are right!

It is the discoveries of divers in this area that makes the whole sea bed here so interesting. But the divers' exploration of this section of the coast has raised as many questions as it has solved. There is no doubt that anyone who dives here is diving back in time into a vast underwater museum of World War Two. The diver is also dropping down into the wreckage of an RAF bombing bonanza, with ships specially provided for bombing and strafing practice. That same diver will also be among the wreckage of units of the Mulberry Harbours, which played a crucial role during the Allied invasion of France in 1944 in supplying the troops pushing inland. The diver, too, will find evidence of air–sea rescue floats codenamed Cuckoos, concrete petrol barges, mysterious stainless-steel cylinders "stitched" with machine-gun or cannon fire, and an infantry landing craft fully equipped with oxyacetylene cutting gear. The sea bed here is covered with odd structures – and more and more are being found by divers each year.

But the award for the most enterprising diving group must go to the divers who recently hired a light aeroplane and had themselves flown over the area on a day of clear skies and flat-calm sea. During this aerial survey, the divers claim to have seen 81 separate shapes under the sea! Since then, diving with the help of their aerial photographs, they have identified even more of this sea-bed jumble.

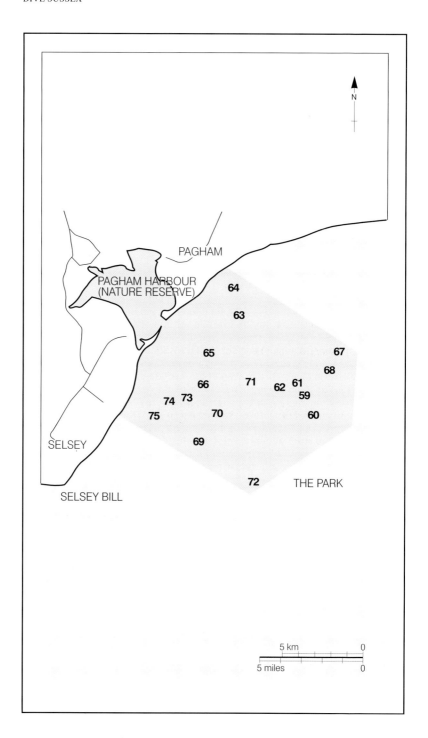

Operation Overlord

To make any sense out of diving this area, the diver needs to know about its underwater shapes and how they got there. In fact, to get the best out of it they need to know what happened here in 1943 and 1944. It is difficult to say who had the first idea of building harbours in sections in Britain, towing them to France on D-Day and putting them together there to make two harbours, each bigger than the port of Dover. Such harbours would be the only way of supplying the assault troops after they had taken the beaches and needed fuel and ammunition to fight off the inevitable counter-attack. Those troops, even if they got well off the beaches, could not afford to wait for the capture of a big port such as Cherbourg, which, in fact was the scene of weeks of hard fighting before it was in Allied hands.

The two planned prefabricated harbours had to be capable of landing 12,000 tons of cargo and 2,500 vehicles a day by D-Day plus 14, that is by the end of the first fortnight after the landings. They had to be capable too of providing berthing facilities for Liberty ships drawing up to 25ft and shelter for landing craft, which would also run a ferry service between other ships and the beaches. The American harbour, called Mulberry A, was to be set up on the east coast of the Cherbourg peninsula at St Laurent (Omaha Beach) with the aim of supplying troops who would take Cherbourg from the rear. The British Mulberry B was to be at Arromanches, further to the east near the beach codenamed Gold Beach on which the British troops would land.

Though Winston Churchill wrote a memo about do-it-yourself ports to Lord Louis Mountbatten, who had been appointed Chief of Combined Operations on 18 March, 1942, as early as 30 May, 1942, it does not mean that the whole idea of artificial harbours came from Churchill. He did without doubt give the prefabricated ports plan the codename of Mulberry, but there seems to have been some sort of similar idea current among British service chiefs soon after Dunkirk! Also, if you study Hitler's plans for Operation Sealion for the invasion of England, you will see that his engineers produced some very similar equipment to be used on British beaches by his assault troops.

The decision to go ahead with Mulberry was taken at the Quebec Summit in August 1943 and the Joint Chiefs of Allied Staff made it a British responsibility. Work on the concrete caissons, which were called Phoenix units, started in September 1943 at 26 sites, mostly in southern England.

There were six types of unit. The largest, the A1, was 210ft long, 56ft wide and 60ft in height. It displaced 6,044 tons (see Far Mulberry, Site **59**). The smallest was the D1 type – 174ft long, 27ft wide and a mere 25ft high (see Near Mulberry, Site **63**). These concrete boats – for that is what they were – had upswept or "swim ends" at both bow and stern, like lighters for easy towing. Ninety-eight of them were built in basins dug out of the banks of the Thames. Once the concrete lower portion had set, this keel section was floated out and built up while moored alongside a quay. Other smaller units were built on the foreshore

Opposite: Dive sites in Area 2, Pagham and Pagham Harbour. This area is covered by Admiralty charts 2045 (Outer Approaches to the Solent) and 1652 (Selsey Bill to Beachy Head); Ordnance Survey Pathfinder map 197.

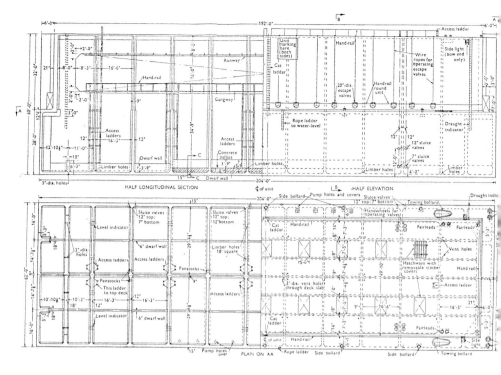

*An Admiralty plan of the Phoenix A1 type, the largest of the Mulberry units.
The unit at Site 59 is of this type.*

near Southampton. More units were constructed inside London's East India and Surrey Docks and in an Admiralty floating dock at Portsmouth.

The Phoenix units were made of concrete strengthened with steel reinforcing rods. The outer walls were 15 inches thick and were divided into compartments by internal walls of 9 inches. The A1 had 22 such compartments and the D1 under 20. Some of the internal walls on all types were linked by foot square holes to allow the Mulberry units to sink on an even keel when the harbour was put together on the French coast. There were valves in the outer side walls to allow sinking (and raising with pumps). With all valves open, a big unit could be sunk to a depth of 40ft in 20 minutes.

At the busiest building time, 20,000 men were at work day and night building the Mulberry units. In fact, 213 were built, of which 147 were used after D-Day to build two harbours, each with 3 miles of concrete walls. The surplus unit were used for repairs and extensions to the harbours until the end of 1944.

Some idea of the effort put into the building programme can be gained from the materials that were used – 542,000 cubic yards of concrete, 49,170 tons of mild steel bar for reinforcing, and hundreds of thousands of tons of rubble from the Luftwaffe's bombing of London and their blitzes on other cities. Together with the floating piers and pierheads, the Mulberry units cost £30 million.

It is odd to discover that though construction of the units was well planned and well executed, no one seems to have thought of what to do with them until

50

they were to be used in France. It seems to have been generally accepted that they would be moored in some harbour. It came as a shock to the planners of Operation Overlord that every likely harbour was already jammed with invasion shipping and there was no space for these massive concrete blocks. The only solution was to sink them to the sea bed. This needed a flat sandy sea bed without rocky outcrops and, not too deep. Nor could the chosen places be too far from the French coast. Eventually, 80 units were lowered to the sea bed between Selsey Bill and Bognor Regis in Sussex and most of the rest sunk in the shallows near Littlestone, Kent.

These parks also met one final condition – the water must not be deep enough to flood the crew's quarters. Each Phoenix unit had crew, part Navy, and part Royal Engineers or American Seabees. These men were to cope with the towing and sinking of the unit and were put aboard immediately the unit was completed. They were accommodated at each end of the units, which were the only parts with roofs, though on the bigger ones a Bofors anti-aircraft gun was mounted amidships on its own light steel platform, which allowed 12 tons of ammunition to be stowed around it.

The guns were a wise precaution, for by the time the units had been sunk in place, their lack of depth made them stick up from the surface like concrete blocks of flats. It was hardly a sight that could be concealed from the prying cameras of German reconnaissance aircraft. The official British cover story was that they were intended for the protection of harbours against air attack, especially by flying bombs. Officially, they were described also as "Anti-Bomb Defence Units".

It was a story that would not have been believed by anyone in the German High Command. In fact, "Lord Haw-Haw", the traitor William Joyce, specially dedicated one of his broadcasts beamed at Britain to "Those USN Seabees and soldiers on the concrete caissons off Selsey Bill" and then went on to say: "We know exactly what you intend to do with those concrete caissons; you intend to sink them off our coast in the assault. Well, we're going to help you boys. We'll save you the trouble. When you come to get underway, we're going to sink them for you!"

But the Phoenix units were not the only amazing sights on the Pagham waterfront. Attached to huge concrete-block anchors (Site **64**) or to the units themselves were other vital parts of the Mulberry Harbours, the floating pierheads, piers and roadways codenamed Whale (Site**s 39, 70, 104**). More concrete pontoons, called "Beetles", which were to hold up the roadways to the shore, were moored in the area and were to allow tanks and trucks as well as other supplies to travel over them.

In addition to the Mulberry Harbours, there was to be an outer wall of blockships, old ships filled with rubble or cement. These ships were called "Gooseberries" and those that can still be dived today off Arromanches are *Elswick Park, Lynghaug, Sirehel, Aglos Spyridon, Ingman, Winna, Modlin, Parklaan, Flowergate, Vinlake, Innerton, Njegos, Georgios, Saltersgate* and *Alynbank.*

Inside those concrete and steel walls was the harbour. Jetties were headed by the Whale pierheads, floating up and down on guide rails between massive legs. They were some 300ft long and coasters could berth alongside them. Landing ships carrying tanks and trucks had a rather more dramatic way of unloading by means of a buffer pontoon. The landing ships would ram the buffer forcing it down in the water, ride up over it, open the bow doors and let the vehicles out onto the floating roadway from pierhead to shore supported on the small Beetle pontoons. These roadways were nearly ¾ mile long and 10 miles were used in all.

But this was all in the future when on 20 May, 1944 the first Phoenix, the one that divers today call the Far Mulberry, was raised in a test operation and then allowed to settle back to the sea bed. Though the salvage men cheered as she came up, the test was really a disaster. It had taken too long – 3 days – to get her up and at that rate only a few of the 80 parked around Pagham would be ready to be towed to France on the day after D-Day.

The same day, the Admiralty Salvage Department were told of their role in Operation Overlord, the part of the plan called "Neptune". To their horror, they found that it envisaged nine Phoenix units being raised each day and sent to France from D-Day onwards. They were given only a few days to complete the operation and all they had were two small Dutch tugs with pumps aboard. They could not even raise the one they had used for a test – she had broken her back when she settled down again, but this time across the hole she had previously made for herself in the sea bed.

The whole operation was a mess. One of the salvage men described Selsey East Bay in these despairing terms: "There were dozens of these monstrosities sitting on the bottom and moored to them were other fantastic pieces of equipment floating on small pontoons. The whole area of the bay for 3 miles offshore was cluttered with concrete and steel equipment resembling nothing I had ever seen before, ashore or afloat". The detailed plan was a mess too. The units meant to be sent to France first were the closest inshore and there was little chance of towing them through the others moored further out. So the raising plan had to be rewritten. The salvage men despaired and told their superiors that Mulberry would be a disaster before it even started.

The Admiralty suddenly got the message and swung its full weight behind the lifting operation. The naval chiefs knew that if Mulberry failed, the British and American troops ashore would quickly run out of ammunition and the first big counter-attack would fling them back into the sea. There could never be another Dunkirk miracle – thousands of men would die on the same beaches they had stormed across only days before.

Suddenly the salvage crews had only to ask and it was given. The biggest salvage operation of all time began. All other work was halted in salvage depots in Falmouth, Portland, Southampton, Dover, Harwich, Hartlepool, Leith, Aberdeen, Scapa Flow, Glasgow and Liverpool and skilled men were switched to Littlehampton with their pumps, air compressors, welding and cutting tools and diving gear. Launches were requisitioned, tugs were taken over. Trucks jammed the roads to Selsey. The Admiralty commandeered the small Littlehampton shipbuilding yards and the harbour. Ammunition barges loaded for D-Day were moved up-river to make way for the salvage craft.

Divers were lowered into the water inside the Phoenix units to block holes in the central walls that were making the units unstable when they finally floated. Pumping went on day and night. But only four units were floating by 3 June, when Captain J.B. Polland, Deputy Director of the Admiralty Salvage Department, who was in charge of the operation, was told that D-Day was to be 5 June. He had no shortage of equipment. What was needed was men. The diving crews were exhausted and the salvage teams were literally staggering from lack of sleep.

So a call for volunteers went out to all the yacht and motor-boat clubs along the south coast for anyone who could handle a boat. The next day the men were there, crewing all the launches and small boats and releasing the naval salvage experts to get on with the big lift.

That extra manpower made it possible for Polland now to report that he could meet the nine unit a day requirement for D-Day, D-Day plus one and D-Day plus two. But he could forecast no further ahead. Then came the welcome news – at least to Polland and his men – that D-Day was to be delayed for one day owing to the bad weather. It gave them the time they needed.

Each day the drill was the same. Eighteen salvage ships would close in on nine more sunken Phoenix units. One ship would moor on each side of a unit. Pumps would be landed on the gangway slab and connected to stand-pipes. Then the flooding valves down at the base of the unit would be closed and after 4 or 5 hours of pumping, the Phoenix would arise. Then two small tugs, still pumping, would tow the unit out to sea where it was handed over to the "Despatcher", the title of Commander Kitcat of the Royal Navy, who had his headquarters in the paddle-steamer *Queen of Thanet*, anchored to seaward of the furthest "parked" unit.

When the big sea-going tugs took over, the pumping still went on while salvage crews clambered inside the "egg-box" compartments, plugging leaks and installing small portable bilge pumps to make sure there would be no danger of a capsize. Then from the *Queen of Thanet* came a transit crew of ratings to take the unit to France, coming back on the towing tug to collect another one after handing the

Mulberry units in action at Arromanches in Normandy.

53

unit over to the "Planter" – another Navy commander whose job was to sink each Phoenix in its correct position in the shallows off the designated French beach. In the case of the Mulberry at Arromanches this meant sinking the first units in a line inside the notorious Calvados Reef, which wreck divers will be interested to know has a gully called the Fosse d'Espagne (The Grave of Spain) and may well be the site of a Spanish Armada wreck.

Back and forth went the tugs. Some towed the Whale units for the piers and some towed roadways, six sections at a time. The first units and the Gooseberry blockships were in place between D-Day plus one and D-Day plus four, before the British and American troops were very far inland. Soon the Mulberries were carrying out their purpose. By D-Day plus 12, the flow of ammunition and stores peaked at 24,412 tons, well above target. Tank landing ships were able to discharge 60 vehicles in 30 minutes. However, on D-Day plus 13, violent storms wrecked the harbours and the American one was abandoned. The British Mulberry, however, was repaired with new units being brought across the Channel to fill the gaps.

The parking area between Selsey and Bognor still looked like a scrapyard. In 1945, the great bulk of the Phoenix A, which had broken its back, still towered up from the sea opposite Pagham Harbour (Site **59**) and another smaller concrete unit was stranded closer to shore (Site **63**). There was debris all around – dark shapes underwater indicated concrete Beetles, holed with part of a Whale roadway on their backs, concrete petrol barges (Site **60**), a Whale buffer pontoon, Whale hinges, towing cables, even an infantry landing craft, laden with welding gear.

That scene changed dramatically when the RAF, practising for low-level support of the troops in France, hit the Phoenix unit with rockets from Typhoon fighter-bombers. Soon all that was left of the Phoenix was underwater and she only broke the water at low springs.

The RAF had not finished. "The Park", as the area was now marked on naval charts, was too useful as a bombing and strafing range to give up. So they continued to blast everything that showed above water and even towed some 30ft Cuckoos into the area to act as extra targets (Site **62**). Finally, the war in Europe was over and only then was The Park left in peace.

But today the interest of the area is not totally concerned with wreckage. Although the sea bed is generally of flat sand, this does not mean that the sea life is any less prolific than elsewhere. Plaice and sole are common; big turbot and brill have been seen around the Mulberry units, as have massive pouting and large shoals of pollack. Bass come in to hide and hunt in the weed on and around these concrete "wrecks', and mullet are often seen too. One such place hides what must be the largest conger in Sussex inshore waters – over 13ft long. Estimates of his weight from looking at his barrel-sized body all start well above 100lbs! He does not seem to mind divers, but then he is much bigger than most of them!

PAGHAM HARBOUR is not a harbour any more, and certainly not a diving area. But it is a nature reserve of great importance, with some 1,000 acres of mud flats. There is no road around the outer edge of the reserve, and coming from Selsey the road stops at Church Norton. On the other side, the road stops at Pagham.

To get from one side of the "harbour" to the other using proper roads you would have to drive on the B2145 from Selsey to Hunston and North Mundham and come back down to the coast at Aldwick using the B2166. There is a footpath all around the reserve. The shingle banks on either side of the sea entrance used to seal the entrance to the saltings. Anyone who wants to bathe or paddle in the harbour entrance (heaven forbid!) should look out for very strong currents both in and out at spring tides.

Pagham Harbour is a comparatively new name, being first recorded in the 18th century. Before that it was called Selsey Harbour or Sidlesham Harbour.

Launch sites

PAGHAM BEACH is the nearest launch site to the Mulberries. To find it, follow signs "To Sea" before you go down Beach Road to East Front Road, which runs behind the shingle bank of the beach.

There is access to the sea beside Pagham Yacht Club and opposite the Beach Amusement Arcade. Stone bollards block the way, but they are not high enough to prevent an easy lift over them. From the top of this alley there is a long haul (200m) across shingle to the sea – and that is at high tide! The nearest car park is Pagham Beach Car Park at the top of Beach Road, which charges for car and trailer separately. There are other pay car parks nearby.

NOTE The Pagham Yacht Club lays a runway for its yachts and boats over the shingle, and when it is not in use there would seem to be little harm in using this to ease the haul over the shingle. But please do not do so without asking permission first from the clubhouse.

Shore diving sites

For all practical purposes there are none in this area. A strong swimmer might be able to turn the Near Mulberry (Site **63**) unit into a shore dive at low spring tides, but there seems little point.

The Mooring Blocks (Site **64**) can be dived from the shore, but they are difficult to locate and are a waste of air.

Boat diving sites

The joy of this area for the boat diver is that there is plenty to see and to explore, and the water is shallow enough to give plenty of time underwater. The visibility, except after easterlies, is often quite good.

It is, of course, the Mulberries and the huge fish population around them that attract divers in their scores to this area. It is a particular favourite of underwater photographers, and more and more novices are lucky enough to make their first sea-dive here.

59 The Far Mulberry The largest of all the Mulberry artificial harbours units built for the D-Day landings in World War Two, this is the one most divers simply call "The Mulberry". It is only when they want to distinguish one Mulberry unit from another that she becomes "The Far Mulberry". This is the Mulberry unit at 50 44 38N; 00 42 19W, which lies on the sea bed 2 miles offshore in only 9m of water and is of the A1 type, the largest of them all. She measured 204ft in length, was 56ft wide, 60ft high, and had a draught of 20ft. Her displacement was 6,044 tons.

A Phoenix unit being manoeuvred by two tugs off Bognor in 1944.

The Far Mulberry is, without doubt, one of the best dives along the whole Sussex coast for those who want to see fish. Clouds of big pouting and pollack hang around her, probably because she is a large object on a mainly featureless sea bed of mud and sand. Bass hunt around the concrete wreckage of this floating egg-box with its steel reinforcing rods. The top of her is heavily weeded, and the broken internal walls and hull provide thousands of hiding places for shellfish and conger eels.

The Far Mulberry is now an important diving site, and it is not unusual to see over a dozen diving boats moored about her. She can be dived in all states of the tide provided the divers shelter on the "right" side of this great concrete structure, which is now snuggled well down into the sea bed yet can still reach up to the surface on low spring tides.

Though it seems almost certain that this unit was left behind because she broke her back, there is another reference in the records to a Phoenix unit at Selsey that did not make it across the Channel. "A small tug rammed and sank a unit just as it was being taken over for the cross-Channel tow," says the report.

Despite being used as a bombing target by the RAF in 1945, the Far Mulberry can still be a threat to larger boats. Several large motor boats are said to have lost propellers on her at extreme low water.

The layout of the wreck is as follows. The northern end or stern is the best preserved part of the unit. Whether this is, in fact, the bow or the stern is difficult to tell because Phoenix units used the same "Noah's Ark" shape at both ends; but presumably if she was about to be towed to France the bow would have been to the south.

The "stern" is a gloomy place. Here a few real rocks litter the sea bed, but all the rest is shingle right into the angle where it meets the concrete surface of the unit, which is covered with thousands of white and orange dead men's fingers. The white polyps of the anemones give a ghostly glow to the stern as it shelves out above you. Under the angle there are usually some starfish hunched over a meal of mussels that have fallen from above.

To the east of the stern is a sharp clear-cut corner, which marks the beginning of the eastern side or wall. The unit on this side is better preserved for the first 15m than anywhere else. Here the wall towers up sheer to the top where there are a pair of towing bollards. Down at the sea bed two vent pipes open and offer dark holes through which at times invisible currents stream. These were the sluice valve outlets used to flood the Mulberry unit when in position.

The sea bed on the eastern side changes character as you swim seaward, the bare shingle giving way to large patches of kelp and pod-weed. After 15m the wall finishes and turns into a tangle of debris from collapsed compartments with mild-steel rods poking this way and that from each hummock of weed-covered wreckage.

At the southern end or bow, the true shape of the hull is almost impossible to follow. Much of the concrete wall has completely collapsed, but the sand does cover huge sections of it, judging by the heavy weed growth, which must mean that the holdfasts of the weed are gripping something pretty solid. It is at this end of the Mulberry that the larger schools of pollack are found. The bib or pouting are inclined to congregate much more at the northern end.

Nothing like so well preserved as the first part of the eastern wall, the western wall section allows access (careful of the tangle of rods) to some of the broken compartments. The low wall along which you will find yourself swimming is, in fact, part of the top of the unit, complete with large flat towing bollard and two smaller bollards for mooring, which has tumbled down on its side.

It is here, in the gap between the wall and the Mulberry proper, that the biggest pouting gather. It was from the scour under the wall that a 10lb lobster was taken in the early days of exploration of the Mulberry. There are a huge number of congers in the wreckage as any night dive there will tell you. In the autumn, big brill and turbot can be found sheltering close to the unit.

Do not overlook normal diving safety. One incident here showed the danger of burrowing too deeply into the wreckage. A diver probing in did not notice that his harness had somehow threaded on to one of the steel rods, and when he tried to surface he found that the rod was still quite strong enough to hold him down. His diving buddy unthreaded him, but the incident shows how careful divers must be when near any sort of wreckage.

In the 1980s the Marine Conservation Society carried out a survey of the Far Mulberry (or Outer Mulberry as they call it) and in the spring of 1995, the Nautical Archaeology Society started another, and now intend to use the Phoenix as a training site for archaeology qualifications. Their survey is planned to extend in time to cover the whole bay and is part of the West Sussex Sites and Monument Record being compiled by the Royal Commission for Historic Monuments of England.

60 The Concrete Petrol Barge This wreck lies at 50 44 56N; 00 42 00W, 200yds south of the Far Mulberry (Site **59**). Parts of this concrete boat are covered in weed, particularly at the northern end. A tangle of cables and other debris lies close by. The barge is tilted on one side and has three hatchways, none of which will admit the average diver's shoulders and were for inspection purposes only. At one end, the barge appears to have been blown apart, and reinforcing rods poke out of the shattered concrete. It would appear that this barge was a victim of RAF bombing practices. The petrol barge stands 3m high above the sea bed, and the remaining section is some 25ft long. Two hundred of these petrol barges were built for the invasion of France, and they normally carried some 200 tons of petrol each. The concrete proved highly resistant to aviation spirit in particular. Other concrete wreckage in the area could be part of this barge.

61 Infantry Landing Craft At 50 44 42N; 00 42 15W and sitting upright on the sand is this intact LCM Mark I. The craft is only 100yds away (on a compass bearing of 325° true) from the Far Mulberry (Site **59**). She is 100ft long by 10ft beam. The winch is in place on the stern, and the Chrysler 6-cylinder petrol engines are visible. Some of the stern superstructure has broken off and now lies on the sand to one side. The landing ramp at the bow is in position and the hinges are clear. The brass propellers are missing.

It is possible that this craft was being used for salvage work when she sank. The first divers on her found oxyacetylene cutting equipment (tubes, flame cutter, bottles and gauges) on board, and it is suspected that she was being used in an attempt to raise the wreck of the nearby Cuckoo refuge vessel for World War Two pilots (Site **62**).

The latest date on items found in the landing craft is 6 March, 1943.

62 The Cuckoo At 50 44 37N; 00 42 24W, this wreck is only 150yds from the Far Mulberry (Site **59**) in line with the lifeboat slipway at East Beach, Selsey. In fact, it is so close that the Far Mulberry, the Infantry Landing Craft (Site **61**) and the Cuckoo can all be visited on one dive.

For a long time the identity of this strange-looking boat of steel was not known. Chichester BSAC used to call her "The Work Boat" and Billingshurst Branch used to know her as "The Old Lifeboat", owing to the rounded shape of the top of her hull. But she is, in fact, a British air–sea rescue float – one of those vessels codenamed Cuckoo, 21 of which were moored at various points just off the English coast. It is interesting to note that the Germans had the same idea, except that their versions were codenamed Lobster Pots and were moored along the coast of occupied France.

The thinking behind each version was the same. When an aeroplane was returning from a mission and was damaged so that it could not land or reach an airfield, it was better that it should put down on water. The crew would then either inflate their dinghy and paddle to the float or swim to it. So the cuckoos were moored along the Sussex coast – and other coastlines – to offer a refuge to ditched pilots and their crews. The RAF rescue floats all had boat-shaped hulls 30ft long, which were painted bright red and orange.

Each Cuckoo was fitted with grids and bars extending below the surface to give foot-and hand-holds. The stern of the float was cut away at an angle so that a ladder hung over it could be climbed easily. The sides of the float were raised to give some protection to a man lying on the deck too exhausted to get into the cabin straight away. Inside the cabin, the ditched airmen would find a radio to get in touch with the shore, food (preserved meat and vegetables, biscuits, tea,

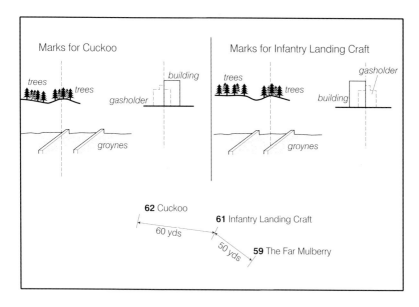

Transit marks for the Cuckoo (Site 62) and the Infantry Landing Craft (Site 61). Just to the south is The Far Mulberry (Site 59).

cocoa, sugar, brandy or rum) and drinking water. There was a paraffin stove on which to cook, several complete changes of clothing, sleeping bags, towels, washing gear, cigarettes, matches, books, games and playing cards. There was room for at least six men. Bunks were also provided. It sounds as though the crews were expected to be in the float for a long time, but in fact the food and supplies were more to reduce the shock of their crash-landing than to prepare them for a long stay.

Some 20 Cuckoos were made and each was numbered. The fast RAF air–sea rescue launches visited each one as often as possible – as, so they say, did the German E-boats who not only liked the supplies, but were always ready to take the British survivors of a ditched crew back to prison camps in Germany. It is also said that British MTBs performed similar operations on the German air-rescue floats moored off the French coast.

The early British rescue floats had the Red Cross symbol painted boldly on them, but later this was painted out as it was felt that saving airmen so that they could fly and bomb again was not really a Red Cross matter and would probably lessen the symbol's effectiveness on real hospital ships. There is no record of whether the Cuckoo on the sea bed near the Mulberry was ever involved in saving lives. There are clear signs of an attempt to lift her at some stage.

Two divers at a time can get inside the cabin, and though the sand level is creeping up the sides it is possible to sit inside and look out through the portholes – a view blocked at times by a conger or two looking out as well! There is some rusting of the deck plating. Some of the laddering on the port side has collapsed,

A British air–sea rescue float photographed off the Sussex coast in 1943.
These floats were codenamed "Cuckoos".

and when first found by divers none of the rescue equipment remained on board.

A careful search in the files at the Public Records Office provides a great deal of information about these air–sea rescue floats. But what it fails to explain how it was that in 1943 British forces seemed to be in possession of a number of German floats, which were added to the ones already stationed around our coasts. Could it be that the British would have gone so far as to steal such craft? It hardly seems likely that all the German floats drifted across the Channel of their own accord! One such German float is dived off Peacehaven (Site **206**).

The floats were inspected daily by aeroplane and as often as possible by air–sea rescue launches. There were two off the Owers and another off Brighton and other places along the Sussex coast. Some were specifically positioned for bombers returning to Tangmere Airfield near Chichester.

63 The Near Mulberry So called because it is very near the shore at Pagham, this Mulberry unit lies just ½ mile out to sea, and dries 2m at low tide. The beacon welded onto it is bent over at a steep angle by the waves, but shows above the water at all times except during extraordinarily high spring tides. The unit lies at 50 45 36N; 00 43 36W.

This little D1 unit, the smallest of all the Mulberry units, makes an excellent dive for novices in a maximum of 9m of water. Plumose anemones decorate the walls inside the "cathedral", where, on sunny days, light streams down through the girders at the north-east end. Lobster are sometimes seen under the overhang created by the tidal scour. Mullet feed on the bootlace weed around the outer edges of the concrete walls, which have been breached in places to form caves.

Underwater photographers will find the fine silt that covers the lower parts of the unit after each storm a nuisance. Another drawback is the fact that this wreck can become overcrowded on sunny summer Sundays, with strings of divers weaving in and out.

64 Mooring Blocks These mooring blocks, or concrete "anchors" over 2m high, with huge eyelets for the mooring cables set into their tops, lie in less than 3m of water at 50 45 48N; 00 44 00W. Some are square, others cone-shaped. They were used to hold the big Mulberry units in place once they had been raised. You will find a lot of these moorings in this area, for there were 80 big Mulberries parked here in 1944.

65 Low Concrete Structures Lying at 50 45 00N; 00 44 00W are these low, concrete, open-topped structures, the purpose of which is unknown. They only stand 1m high, and there are two of them set one behind the other almost directly in line with the entrance to Pagham Harbour.

66 Crumbly Mulberry 50 44 30N; 00 44 13W. This is a D-unit of the same size as the Near Mulberry (Site **63**), but is in a much worse condition. It looks as though it has been blown to bits and stands only about 8ft high at its highest point. Rods poking up from the crumbling remains come very close to the surface and could be a real danger to an inflatable at low water. The distance to the Barge (Site **75**) is about 900yds.

67 Mulberry Top (1) This small section of wreckage lies not far from the Bognor Sewer Outlet Buoy at 50 45 08N; 00 41 30W, and appears to be part of the top of the Far Mulberry (Site **59**) ripped off by the sea or by the 1945 bombing. It consists mainly of a tangle of piping, with no sign of the Bofors gun, which would have been there with a large quantity of ammunition. These were probably salvaged when the unit sank.

68 Mulberry Top (2) A smaller section of wreckage lies at 50 44 54N; 00 41 36W. It is dominated by a huge towing cleat, and has a pile of small stones and debris around it.

69 The Beetles These two small concrete chambers some 20ft by 10ft and only 50yds apart are possibly the remains of two Beetles – the flotation chambers used to carry the bridges and roadways of the Mulberry Harbours. Today they are the home of big wrasse and congers. The one to the west stands a mere 1m high; the other is 2m tall. They are at 50 44 09N; 00 43 54W.

70 Whale Float Lying at 50 44 12N; 00 43 48W, this float appears to have been ripped off some other piece of equipment such as one of the Whale bridge sections (Site **39**). It is sitting upright on a flat sea bed in 6m, and is home to a big conger. Such chambers or pontoons were, of course, meant to be water-tight and were air-tested for leaks before launching. This one is concrete, 30ft by 15ft, and looks just like a complete concrete boat.

71 Three Concrete Puzzles At 50 44 52N; 00 43 18W are three more concrete structures, but no diver who has seen them can come up with a good suggestion as to their original purpose. They look like concrete boats that have gone wrong. They are crumbling now and may have been bombed to their present unrecognisable shapes.

72 Intact Mulberry Lying at 50 43 37N; 00 43 14W, this wreckage looks much bigger than the Near Mulberry (Site **63**), so is probably that of a C1 unit. She is intact except for a big hole in one side, which probably sank her. The Mulberry is in 6m of water and is home to at least three big congers, which are not worried by divers poking their heads through the hole to look at them.

73 Stainless Steel Mystery One of the strangest objects on a sea bed that has more than its fair share of odd obstructions lies at 50 44 19N; 00 44 32W. At first sight this would appear to be another kind of beetle or flotation chamber, but inside the crust of rusting mild steel is a lining of extremely tough stainless steel. Adding to the mystery is a line of holes across the top from what appear to be either cannon or machine-gun fire. Although some of these holes penetrate both skins, others have merely dented the surface. It is difficult to guess what the 35ft tank was originally used for – perhaps it was water, or something more dangerous such as battery acid.

74 Big Aeroplane Engine with Propeller Just to add to the mysteries on the sea bed in this area, at 50 44 15N; 00 44 48W, you will find a big radial aeroplane engine with the propeller still attached. Whether this is just one part of an aeroplane crash of which the other pieces have not yet been found it is impossible to say.

75 The Barge Though known locally as "the Barge" this is, in fact, another piece of the Mulberry Harbour. It is one of the 50ft buffer pontoons designed to enable tanks to unload directly on to the Mulberry roadways. The pontoon is made of mild steel with heavier plate chequered on the top in a lattice-work construction. There are conger in it and the occasional lobster. At low spring tides the unit can be seen from the surface as it lies in only 5m of water.

Because of the growth on it the Barge makes an interesting inshore dive. Even though it is necessary to have a boat to reach it comfortably, the wreck is not far off the edge of the winkle beds that dry out to the east of the East Beach launching ramp. If you swim out to it, you will pass over scaffolding lying on the sea bed. The Barge, which lies at a shingle bar, may well have caused the bar to form, and some divers suspect that much more of the pontoon lies under the shingle. One area appears to have been ripped open. It is at 50 44 03N; 00 44 54W. To the south of the Barge lies an extensive system of pipework that seems to go nowhere in particular.

AREA 3:

Littlehampton

This area runs from 00 39 12W to 00 28 00W, and includes Felpham, Middleton-on-Sea, Climping, Littlehampton, Rustington and East Preston. LITTLEHAMPTON, with its big dive boats, dominates the area and welcomes divers. It is this – plus, of course, the offshore wrecks and all the boating facilities and easy launching for inflatables and other small boats – that brings divers here from a very wide area. It is no surprise to find that a report on the future of tourism in the town recommended providing even more facilities for divers.

Of course, wrecks do attract divers, and the Littlehampton dive boats specialise in wreck diving. As a result, some 50 diving clubs book a year or more in advance to make sure they get their favourite Littlehampton dive boat for the much-valued neap tide weekend dates. Nearly all the boat skippers are divers themselves, and their boats sport the latest in location equipment. Some have proton magnetometers. All are good sea boats because a large number of their wreck dives are beyond sensible inflatable range. The *Moldavia*, for example, is over 24 miles due south of Littlehampton.

But not all the diving out of Littlehampton is for wrecks. Within easy range are reefs that support a varied and plentiful marine life. There are many lobsters and crabs, and even a small scallop bed. Plaice and sole are present on the sand flats, and brill and turbot are often seen by divers.

FELPHAM occupies a low area of land forming the ancient marine plain that reached right back to the Downs. Today the sea is held back by stout marine works including a wall. Protecting this low-lying land has dramatically changed the scenery as far as the coast further along to the east at Middleton and Elmer where five huge blocks of stone, each 150m long, have been dropped into the sea about 75m out from the beach. These 10-ton blocks each stand about 5m proud and have created miniature islands off the coast. They not only protect the beach from erosion, but make it easy for rod fishermen to cast farther out!

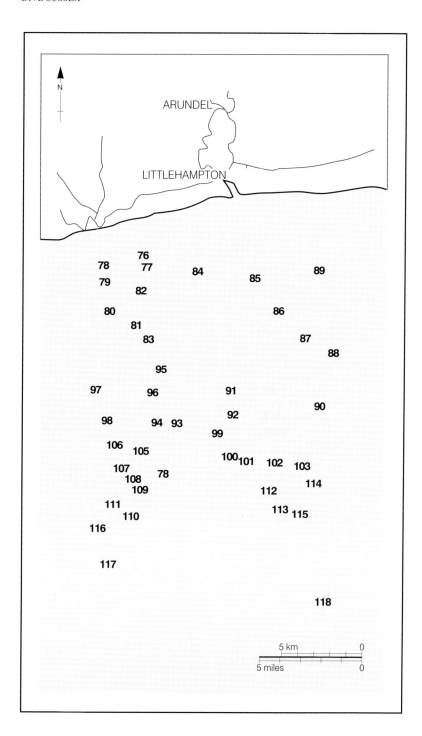

Launch sites

To launch at Felpham, pass the George Inn after taking the signposted turning off the A259 at the traffic lights and carry on towards the sea. Turn down Sea Road. The first turning on the left is Canning Road, at the end of which is a very low barrier (low enough to lift a boat over when padlocked) leading to an excellent gently-sloping ramp running parallel to the sea down to shingle, then sand. It can be used at all states of the tide. No parking is available at the ramp, so remove trailers and cars back to the main road or car parks. Do not leave cars blocking houses or other boats.

Alternatively, take the third turning on the left down Sea Road. This is Outram Road, at the end of which is another launching ramp similar to the one in Canning Road. A notice says that the ramp is for sea defence works, but it provides an excellent launch for inflatables and small boats. It is used also by the Yacht Club. There is no chance of parking in the road as this blocks access to both the houses and the Yacht Club. There is no parking either further down Sea Road where a group of holiday homes made out of railway carriages are sited behind the high sea wall.

To reach CLIMPING from Bognor, take the signposted turning off the A259 shortly before the road crosses the new bridge over the River Arun at Littlehampton. The road to Climping runs past the Black Horse Inn on the left, and the Bailiffscourt Hotel on the right. It continues for ½ mile before ending in a car park scarcely large enough to cope with the many summer visitors. Boat launching is possible over the shingle beach between groynes. The shingle leads down to sand, which has some large weeded boulders dotted here and there. Plaice have been found here by snorkellers, who should keep an eye open, especially after storms, for the remains of the medieval church and houses of ancient Atherington, which is said to lie under the sea here.

At least seven large dive-boats for hire are based at LITTLEHAMPTON. There are easy launching facilities for inflatables and other towed boats. Air is handy too, and the diving is well organised. Approach the town either by the A259 from Worthing or Bognor, or by the A284 from Arundel. Note that a one-way system and pedestrian precincts are in operation.

FISHERMAN'S QUAY is on the east bank of the River Arun, and is the public launching site. This wide area has recently been the site of sea defence works following flooding in the town, and the steep, concrete launch ramp provides perfect access up to plus or minus 1 hour of low water. The launching ramp ends in mud, and this can cause some problems for the unwary at low water. Fisherman's Quay can be reached via the one-way system by bearing left at the first roundabout in Littlehampton and working along to the east and south of the pedestrian precinct. Another slightly longer, but simpler, route is by following the signs for Bognor on the A259 and continuing as though going out of the town. After passing the railway station in Terminus Road, there is a sign on the left saying "Rope Walk 2mls". Immediately after this sign turn left just before the

Opposite: Dive sites in Area 3, Littlehampton. This area is covered by Admiralty charts 1652 (Selsey Bill to Beachy Head) and 1991 (Littlehampton Harbour); Ordnance Survey Pathfinder map 197.

The public launching site at Fisherman's Quay on the east bank of the River Arun.

Arun View Inn at the east end of the retractable footbridge, into River Road. Continue down River Road, past the Littlehampton Museum, which has a good deal of local wreck material, to the pay-and-display car park at the back of Fisherman's Quay. Launching from the quay is free, but boat owners are expected to pay harbour dues.

LITTLEHAMPTON MARINA is on the west bank of the river, and is reached from Littlehampton by heading for Bognor on the A259 and crossing the Arun road bridge before taking the first turning on the left. A left turn at the end of this road where it confronts the western end of the retractable footbridge leads along through the boat-parks to the marina office. Next door to the manager's office is the compressor room with a huge bank of storage bottles.

Launching is down a wide concrete ramp. There are two charges here. If a group of divers wish to park their cars and trailers in the marina and carry their boats down the launching ramp the charge per boat is reduced. If, however, the divers want to have their boat launched from its trailer for them, then highly-skilled tractor drivers can manoeuvre the most awkward trailer down to the water without mishap. This entails a higher fee for launching and recovery. You cannot launch your own boat on its trailer yourself. No cars are allowed on the slipway.

Close by are petrol pumps to fill tanks while boats are afloat. On return, the fact that you have paid to use the marina ramp entitles you to use all the toilet facilities including hot showers. The marina uses Channel 37 for marine radio calls. At the marina is a floating bar-restaurant and there is a camping and caravan site close to the bigger boat mooring pontoons where the diving boats are kept.

The Ship and Anchor Marina is up river at Ford, 3½ miles by water to the sea. It is built around a pub built in 1624 and has a caravan and camping site, moorings, a boat-park and crane and shops, including a chandler. At least one of the big diving boats is berthed here. Launching at the slipway is by tractor only.

The charge is reduced if you are staying at the camping site, but there is no objection to divers launching their inflatables free over the river bank at the marina.

At LITTLEHAMPTON HARBOUR (Admiralty chart 1991) the harbourmaster's office (tel. 01903 721215/6) is on the port side as you go down the River Arun to the sea and almost opposite the Arun Yacht Club with its crowded moorings, many of which dry out at low tide.

There are certain basic rules and regulations in force in the harbour. The first of these is the speed limit of 6½ knots in the river (it goes without saying that there is no water-skiing anywhere). Secondly, boats going up and down river have priority over those crossing the river – with the exception of the pedestrian ferry, which runs across from near the harbourmaster's office and has priority at all times. Thirdly, boats and ships moving against the tide must give way to those moving with the tide.

Large merchant ships do use the harbour, so when the pilot boat is flying a white-and-red flag or showing a white light over a red by night, all boats must keep clear as this means that a large ship is about to enter or leave the harbour. A signal of one long blast followed by two short blasts is also warning of a ship's approach.

International regulations for the prevention of collision at sea are strictly adhered to in the harbour. Rule 14 – boats meeting end on to alter course to starboard – and Rule 9 – in a narrow channel keep to the starboard side of the mid-channel – are particularly important here.

The harbourmaster warns that the bar at the entrance to the harbour extends for 650yds to seaward from the refuge at the end of West Pier, and is not a true sand bar in that it does not shift. "You see", he says, "the beach runs from Selsey right past here and on towards Beachy Head. The River Arun has cut a furrow in

The entrance to Littlehampton Harbour.

67

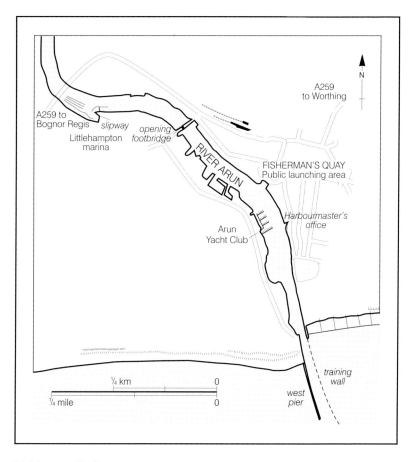

Littlehampton Harbour.

it here. Think of it as a hurdle; you have to get over the beach to get in and out."
He warns, too, that although the Admiralty charts show the bar as drying, it never
does so because of the river water running out over it.

There is always about 6 inches of water on the bar, even at low-water spring
tides, and this can trap the unwary who do not study the tide boards showing
the depth of water. The divisions on the boards are in feet. At spring tides,
anyone drawing 3ft should keep away from the bar for 2 hours each side of low
water. A north or easterly wind at low-water neap tides can blow the water away
and leave only inches over the bar.

To the east of the harbour entrance, the Dickerworks, or Training Wall, guides
the river out. Skippers should know that this becomes covered at half tide. Its
course is marked by seven beacons.

TIDAL STREAMS

Tidal streams between the piers and in the river are extremely strong – up to 7 knots – as you will realise if you see dinghy sailors clinging desperately to the piers and trying to pull themselves along.

Shore diving sites

There are none in this area.

Boat diving sites

76 Middleton Ledge The Ledge is basically a chalk outcrop, which makes this inshore area in front of Middleton practically an underwater desert.

77 The Dog Rocks Lying at 50 46 24N; 00 37 12W, the Dog Rocks are the shallowest part of Middleton Ledge and are a small boulder patch of heavily-weeded sandstone. Less than 1m of water covers them at low spring tides. Archaeologist Hume Wallace says the presence of sandstone at the Dog Rocks makes him suspect that this is ancient building material.

78 Bognor Spit At 50 46 12N; 00 39 00W, this rocky area is really a continuation of Bognor Reef. Once again, there are rocks here that come too close to the surface for the boatman's comfort. This area to the east of the pier provides interesting diving, with large rock clumps shooting straight up from a sand-and-shingle sea bed at 14m.

The gloomy holes under the rocks look like splendid places in which to find lobsters, but the holes go back in and up too far to provide easy pickings. Be aware, too, that these holes are also home to many congers; 40lb specimens have been taken by anglers at night.

Further to the east, the rocks give way to a low rubble of rock and stones with short weeds sticking up like bristles. It looks and is barren, though divers have seen the occasional skate here.

79 Luff Bucknell This is directly south of Bognor Spit (Site **78**) and is another rocky area in 10m of water with rocks rising to within 3m of the surface. Divers will find plenty of life here among the rocks, which seem to appeal to dogfish, congers and pouting. Many underwater visitors have also reported being escorted by large inquisitive garfish – curling their long bodies into great question marks, they peer intently into face-masks and seem totally unafraid of the air bubbles spurting from the strange creatures they are examining! The area is a black bream angling mark.

80 Boulder Reef At 50 45 30N; 00 38 54W, this strangely-built reef rises to within 2m of the surface. On the outside of the reef the rocks rise from the 15m sea bed to about 9m. This base has boulders piled on it. Some divers think that the top layer of boulders is the result of bigger boulders splitting up. The area is the haunt of bass, but there is little other life.

81 The Waldrons An unusual sea bed with massive sandstone boulders in great quantity. Some are as big as 3m in diameter, and are round except for the undercutting of their bases where lobster and crab now hide. Some caves are big enough to swim into. Other misshapen rocks in the area are also circular, but flatter, rather like ancient millstones. There is some growth on the top of the boulders, which are in 25m of water, resting on a shingle bed. The Waldrons are at 50 45 00N; 00 38 00W. Many wrasse inhabit the area.

82 Shelley Rocks 50 46 00N; 00 37 24W. This area is not so much a rocky reef as a great shingle bar. There are pebbles and cobbles, patches of sand and gravel and some boulders. The distinctive red markings of the Shelley Buoy is to the south of the shallowest part, which can be less than 1m deep at low water. The anchor chain of the buoy has swept a great circle clear of any living thing. This area is not really worth diving.

83 Scallop Grounds 50 44 31N; 00 37 00W. This inshore bed is not extensive, and much collecting in recent years has left the sea bed with more depressions, where the big scallops used to be, than live scallops. The bed exists in a dip with a mud, rubble and clay floor. The dip is protected from trawls on all sides by rock outcrops. Some local fishermen obviously found this out the hard way as there are some broken trawls and boards by the rocks at the eastern end. There is a large amount of silt here, and when they sense the approach of a diver the scallops often give their position away by shutting of their shells and puffing a cloud of silt into the water above them. Depth is 16m.

84 Winter Knoll 50 46 12N; 00 34 00W. An outcrop of chalk in a predominantly sandy area, this site seems to be one end of low chalk cliffs that appear now and then at other sites such as the Worthing Lump or the Loo Gate at Brighton. The odd thing about this little cliff is not that its top is roundly corrugated, but that it seems to face east in places and in towards the shore in others. The occasional turbot has been seen around the Knoll in late autumn.

85 The Mud Hole Lying at 50 45 36N; 00 31 42W, this site is exactly 1¼ miles due east of the Winter Buoy. Not so much a hole, but more of a mud-filled depression in the sea bed, it is the lying-up place of sole, dabs, plaice, and sometimes turbot. The marks are the funfair at Littlehampton in line with the east side of Arundel Hill and the Winter Buoy in line with Selsey Bill.

86 Meteor 50 44 25N; 00 30 30W. Until quite recently this aeroplane was intact, but some recent salvage has deprived her of one engine and part of a wing. The tail is gone, and shingle is starting to fill her cockpit. Depth is 10m.

The Armstrong Whitworth Meteor NF.11 came from 29 Squadron based at Tangmere, near Chichester, and bore the tail number of WD 603 when she ran out of fuel and crashed into the sea on 20 October, 1953. The pilot, Flying Officer J. Sneddon, ditched the aeroplane perfectly and he and his navigator, Pilot Officer Sweetman, who was later reprimanded for an error in navigation, were winched from the sea by helicopter and taken to Ford Naval Air Station near Littlehampton.

Do not be misled by divers' tales into thinking that there is a Westland Wyvern in the sea near the Meteor's position. Although it is true that two Wyverns collided in this area on 17 September, 1957, both went down on land. One was in a field opposite Littlehampton Cemetery. The other, which was at first thought to be in the sea, was later discovered in a field north of the main Brighton to Portsmouth railway line, and only 400yds from the other Wyvern. Both pilots ejected safely and landed unhurt.

87 The Mussel Beds These cover a wide area around 50 44 00N; 00 30 00W. They lie to the south of the Meteor site (Site **86**) and are the haunt of very large plaice.

88 Kingmere Rocks 50 43 36N; 00 28 00W. This used to be a famous fishing ground for the black bream that arrived in late April and early May and stayed until the end of June, but the numbers of these strong fish declined dramatically in the 1970s and 1980s. However, anglers now report catches that suggest bream shoals are returning in good numbers.

The diver will know the Kingmere as a collection of rocks with sand and shingle patches between them. The bases of these big black rocks are heavily undercut by the strong tidal stream in the area – so much so, in fact, that some of the rocks have what amount to caves inside them. In these caves, on a tide run, the diver will find large bass sheltering.

There are lobsters here, too, but the amount of under-cutting makes many of the holes under the rocks where the lobsters hide very difficult to get at. Crabs in the area tend to be small. Divers have reported finding large numbers of big plaice on the shingle ground between the Kingmere and the shore.

To locate the Kingmere Rocks, which are 5½ miles south-south-east of the mouth of Littlehampton Harbour, keep the Convalescent Home (a very conspicuous building) near Rustington in line with the east side of Arundel Hill until Bognor Water Tower is on the bluff of trees at Felpham.

89 Frode This Norwegian coaster of 697 tons was originally owned by a Dutch company. When built in October 1917 – 180ft long with a beam of 28ft – she was called *Hollandia I*. She was seized on 25 April, 1918 in the Skagerrak by *U-19* and taken to Germany.

She was returned to her Dutch owners in 1919. In 1924 she was sold to the Norwegian firm of A/S Garm, and was re-named *Frode*. Later she was sold again to another Norwegian company, Rederi A/S Steinmann. On 15 January, 1941, she was beached at Oban after a fire caused severe damage, but was re-floated in August.

The *Frode* was wrecked on 13 April, 1943 after leaving Newhaven in ballast for Mumbles, near Swansea. She was heading for Littlehampton in the "swept" channel when she hit a German parachute mine and sank with the loss of seven of her 17 crew. Another two men died in hospital later.

The *Frode* now lies scattered at 50 46 06N; 00 28 54W in only 6m of water, which makes her a good second dive. You should have no difficulty finding her, as a large dan buoy is usually fixed by local fishermen to the largest piece of wreckage, the boiler. She is very badly smashed up, with even the boiler broken open, but items do still come to light from the sea bed of sand and gravel. Do not be tempted to drift dive to the east of this site. The further east you go the more barren (shingle and weed) the sea bed becomes.

90 The Ore Wreck lies at 50 40 45N; 00 28 47W, and is heavily dived. No-one knows her correct name; all we know is that she was a coaster laden with iron ore. A lump of the cargo, which lies in great mounds where her holds should be, has been analysed to prove that it really is iron ore.

The wreck lies in 15m of water with her bow section practically all gone. There is an iron propeller lying off the starboard side of the vessel. This is the spare; the other one is where it should be at the stern on the propeller shaft, which has a bronze bush that is very firmly attached. The three-bladed iron propeller has the old hatchet, square-tipped shape. The boilers and engines are still there, with the engines standing about 4m proud. In the winter this wreck is a good site to see big cod and pollack.

91 Metal Bars That is exactly what this obstruction is – just a heap of rusting metal bars. Once again, they are probably a left-over from the Mulberry operation. The position is 50 41 48N; 00 33 10W.

92 Glenlee A victim of *UB-57*, the *Glenlee* was sent to the bottom by one torpedo on 9 August, 1918. The torpedo struck her in the starboard side between holds Nos. 3 and 4. She was 4 miles east by north from the Owers Light Vessel (Site **46**) and sank stern first in 15 minutes. One of her 68-man crew, a gunner for one of the three guns with which she was armed, was drowned when she sank. Captained by George Lumsden, the 4,915-ton 400ft steamer was carrying 2,100 tons of steel billets for the Government from Dunkirk to Portland.

Swept and salvaged, the *Glenlee* is well broken up and lies in 20m of water. Three boilers stand 5m proud, but the rest of the ship is largely flattened, with a number of her plates lying on the bottom. Well silted, she lies with her bow to the north-east at 50 40 28N; 00 33 52W.

93 Shirala At 50 40 55N; 00 35 10W, this 5,306-ton liner lies in 24m of water. In this case "liner", the word used when she was ordered from A. and J. Inglis and was launched in 1901, did not mean a cruise liner, but simply a ship belonging to a shipping company that would carry passengers as well as cargo on scheduled routes. The shipping company in this case was the British India Steam Navigation Company, and the *Shirala* made her last voyage from London on 29 June, 1918. She was bound for India, and some of her cargo seemed at first sight rather strange. On board were large quantities of African elephant tusks being routed through London to carving experts in India.

Packed into the four holds were also cases of wine, crates of Dundee marmalade in stone jars, and spares for lorries and Model-T-type cars including tyres, axles and radiators. There were telescopes, binoculars and ammunition for the Indian army – shells packed in metal crates, thousands of detonating caps and some large bombs for aircraft use. In addition to her crew of 100 she carried over 200 passengers, many of whom were Indians bound for Bombay.

On 2 July, 1918, as the *Shirala* zigzagged down the Channel in her dazzle paint, she was being watched and followed. The eyes behind the periscope lens were those of Oberleutnant Lohs, captain of the German submarine *UB-57* – which was later to sink the *Glenlee* (Site **92**). Lohs had made the area around the Owers Light Vessel his own killing ground, and when the *Shirala* was about 4 miles north-east of the lightship he added to his score by loosing off a torpedo

The Shirala (Site 93) was sunk by the German submarine UB-57 in July 1918.

from a bow tube. This struck the *Shirala* on the port side amidships at 5.12pm on a hazy and perfectly windless day.

There is some confusion in the reports of what happened next. Captain E. G. Murray Dickinson is quite clear in his report that a few seconds later there was a second explosion that carried away the main steam pipe and the wireless aerials and put the engines out of action. However, Lohs' report does not mention a second torpedo, and the second explosion may have been caused by water rushing into the stoke-hold. Eight men were killed.

Despite the fact that her engine room and stoke-hold were full of water, *Shirala* floated for some time, and the survivors had time to watch her go down. Lohs' torpedo must have broken her back because the ship was sinking amidships with her still-buoyant bow and stern supporting the deadweight in the centre and she literally folded in the middle until her forefoot at one end and her propeller at the other came right up out of the sea. That is how she went down.

During 1978, Metal Recoveries (Newhaven) Ltd used explosives to get into the holds and were reported to have salvaged £150,000-worth of elephant tusks as well as a great number of brass shell cases. They still own the cargo, and while they have no objection to divers taking a souvenir such as a wine bottle or marmalade jar, they object strongly to the removal of any brass.

The *Shirala* is a popular dive over 5 miles out of Littlehampton. She lies almost north to south with her bows to the south. Her holds are now open, and the highest point of the stern is about 8m off the sandy sea bed. Divers are warned that the bombs in her cargo – some are said to be 200-pounders – are scattered around the wreck. On a recent dive six were sighted on deck amid the debris. Among the cargo, too, can be seen the butts and stocks of many rifles, the metal parts of which have completely rusted away leaving just the wood. A diver recently found the big brass letter "S" of the ship's name.

94 The Bottle Wreck This vessel rises 3m off the sea bed in a depth of 22m at 50 40 53N; 00 36 28W. She is more of a mound than a ship really, but is the remains of a sailing barge of about 70ft with one mast set well forward.

The basic cargo was a triangular stack of large cast-iron pipes, 8 inches in diameter and about 20ft long, each pipe having a bulbous section at one end. This makes it possible that these were Victorian gas pipes. (Each seems now to contain at least one conger!) But it is the rest of her cargo – some 500 bottles of porter – that is fascinating and gives the ship her diving name. All the bottles are tightly corked, and when the corks are drawn there is still a strong beery smell about the undrinkable contents. The bottles appear to come from the 1825 period.

Other clues to the identity of this vessel include a quantity of cut-throat razors, some inscribed with the word "Liberty", and a picture of George Washington. There is some pottery, too, each piece with a slight flaw. These "seconds" bear a design last used in 1840. The Bottle Wreck also carried a lot of cheap knives, forks and spoons and glass salt-cellars. On board too were large barrels of beer (54-gallon hogsheads), one of which had the words Barclay Perkins Pale Ale burnt into the wood. Archaeologist Ed Cumming of Chelmsford BSAC is researching into the wreck's history. One of the intact bottles of porter recovered from this wreck can be seen behind the bar of the Britannia Inn in Littlehampton.

95 HMS Pine This vessel now lies at 50 43 05N; 00 37 10W, but the torpedo from an E-boat that finally sank her hit her some 40 miles away. The *Pine*, a well-armed Admiralty Tree class trawler of 530 tons, was escorting a small convoy some 10 miles to the south-east of Beachy Head when, in the dark of the early morning of 31 January, 1944, they were located by a pack of E-boats out of Cherbourg. These German E-boats were from either the 5th or 9th Flotilla based at Cherbourg, and the *Pine* could not have chosen a worse group of adversaries. The 18 boats of the two flotillas often worked together and were the largest and newest of all the E-boats operating at that time. They were 95-tonners, 106ft long, and each had three diesel engines, giving these slim killers a top speed of 46 knots. In addition to their torpedoes they carried quick-firing cannon.

Guided to the main target area by a form of radar, they then broke up their flotilla of nine boats into groups of three and spread themselves over a 10-mile area to pinpoint their targets. *Pine*, built in 1940, was no match for them with her very much slower speed. She carried a 12-pounder, two 0.5-inch calibre anti-aircraft guns, and two twin Lewis machine guns. But it is doubtful whether she got the chance to use any of them.

The attack started at exactly 2.45am, and the *Pine* was one of the first vessels hit. Ten men of the 35 aboard died in that attack, and she soon listed heavily from the torpedo hit. The steamers *Emerald* and *Caleb Sprague* sank on the spot at 50 38 15N; 00 25 29W. The 806-ton *Emerald*, laden with coal, did not get off more than one shot, and her crew of 12 and three naval gunners were all lost. The *Caleb Sprague*, of 1,813 tons and full of 2,305 tons of steel and timber, went down so swiftly that she took all 25 on board with her (Sites **329** and **330**).

As soon as the confusion had died down and it became clear that there was a chance of saving the *Pine*, all casualties and crew were taken off and she was

HMS Bay, sister ship to the armed trawler Pine (Site 95).

towed towards Portsmouth. Why she was not taken into Newhaven we shall never know, but the long tow towards the Isle of Wight started long before dawn. They tried hard for hour after hour, but in the end she was too badly damaged to make it, and, at exactly 1.25pm on a bearing of 90.5° from Selsey Bill 6 miles away, she sank.

Today, the wreckage of her 164ft hull and superstructure is scattered over a wide area and she is very broken up in less than 10m. She is a good "rummage", and in calm conditions makes a pleasant second dive.

96 Unidentified obstruction Though it certainly lies at 50 42 31N; 00 37 42W, no one has yet, to the author's knowledge, identified this one. It is likely to be another bit of Mulberry, as the main concentration of that invasion wreckage is not far away to the north-east. At the last echo-sounding it stood up only about 1m off the sea bed in 14m, so is extremely difficult to find.

97 Wreck, name unknown 50 41 18N; 00 38 39W. Close to the East Borough Head Buoy, this is said to be a ship of not more than 100ft, standing up nearly 3m from the 18m sea bed. Those who have dived the spot have, however, found only a rock pinnacle.

98 Zaanstroom This Dutch coaster of 900 tons, built in Amsterdam in 1895, lies at 50 39 07N; 00 36 54W. She foundered on 21 December, 1911, 2½ miles east-north-east of the Owers Light Vessel (Site **46**), when water began leaking into her cargo of china clay on the way home from Fowey to Amsterdam. All the crew were saved.

The 215ft *Zaanstroom* has recently deteriorated rapidly. When first dived by Newham BSAC in 1975 she was a whole ship, but she apparently now resembles a barge, lying on the bottom with all her superstructure collapsed into her holds. The bows are now the most prominent part of the ship with the anchors still in place, but the winches have collapsed into the forward hold. The boiler stands proud as the bridge has collapsed around it. The valves and gauges of the engine room can be clearly seen. Aft is the spare propeller, which has collapsed into the after hold along with some winches and the auxiliary steering gear. She lies in 30m of water.

It is interesting to note that a predecessor of the same name – this time a barque on the Amsterdam to Batavia run – went ashore on Church Rocks, Shoreham, on 13 November, 1870, but was later re-floated.

99 HMS Northcoates 50 39 41N; 00 35 19W. This Royal Navy trawler was built in 1918, and launched the following year at a cost of £21,000 under the name *George Corten*. Sold off in 1921 as part of the slimming-down of naval forces, she became a fishing trawler under the name of *Zencon*. In 1939, she took the name HMS *Northcoates* after being requisitioned for mine-sweeping in World War Two. She sank on 2 December, 1944, owing to "stress of weather" while under tow.

Today, all 277 tons of HMS *Northcoates* sit upright in 26m with just a slight list to starboard. Her stern is to the north, and she is sanded up to her gunwhales. There is 12-pounder gun (dated "1939" on the breech) on her foredeck, and a box of shells nearby were made by the "Enfield Cartridge Company" and dated 1942. A derrick on the bow has a tangle of sweep wire around it. Twin 0.5-inch machine guns are mounted on the port side towards the stern. For years she was known to divers simply as "the Armed Trawler", but divers from Ruislip and Northwood BSAC found details on the ship that enabled her to be named.

Shells from HMS Northcoates (Site 99).

100 Ship Shape Charted as an obstruction caused by a pile of stone blocks, this is in fact nothing of the sort, rather a big mound of hard blue clay, 50ft long, in the perfect shape of an upside-down boat. This "ship" shape looks as though someone has made a huge jelly mould of a ship, filled it with clay, and slapped it down on the sea bed. It is obviously a very old wreck, which either carried a load of clay as cargo, or filled up with silt which then set. The timber of her hull rotted away long ago, but there can be no doubt that this was once a ship. It is even possible to tell her bow from her stern by the shape. The "vessel" stands 4m high at 50 39 20N; 00 32 25W.

101 Eden This is a Norwegian ship at 50 39 03N; 00 32 12W in 22m on a rippled sand sea bed. She was spotted by *UC-70* on 30 April, 1917, "ten miles south of Worthing Pier", while carrying a cargo of 1,800 tons of coal from South Shields to Rouen. The *UC-70* fired a torpedo at her, but missed. The *Eden* ran for the shore, but when the U-boat surfaced the crew abandoned ship. Another torpedo sank her.

Of 1,304 tons, she was built in 1879 by W. Gray and Company, for her owner, H.S. Horgen of Norway. Just over 245ft long with a 34ft beam, she is now very broken up with her highest point only 2m off the sea bed.

102 Tank landing craft 50 38 46N; 00 30 51W. Lying in 20m, this LCT stands 7m high and is 220ft long. She is rarely dived.

103 Jenny This 53ft MFV caught fire and was abandoned by her crew on 14 September, 1979, and later sank while anchored to the sea bed by her trawl. Her position is given as 50 37 24N; 00 29 54W. A recent dive could find no trace of her. Divers instead found themselves amid a "forest" of rock pinnacles in 35m of water. A magnetometer search of the area has shown that the wreck as such does not exist, small pieces of her being spread far and wide.

104 Whale Bridge These two sections of Whale bridging were to be part of the Mulberry Harbours during the Normandy invasion. They obviously did not get there, but are still mounted on the pontoons (called "Beetles") and have twisted at right angles to one another. They lie at 50 37 29N; 00 34 06W.

105 War Helmet 50 37 23N; 00 36 30W. This was one of the "Liberty" ships of World War One, a mass-produced, British-standard ship built to combat the vast losses caused by German U-boats. The 8,184-ton *War Helmet* was built in 1917 in Japan, and was sunk on 19 April, 1918, when travelling in ballast from London to Barry.

She was yet another victim of German U-boat ace Oberleutnant Lohs, this time when he was commanding the mine-laying submarine *UC-75*. The *War Helmet* carried a crew of 86 of whom 66 were Chinese. They all behaved with commendable calm after their ship was hit in the port side aft and as a result all the crew were saved.

The *War Helmet* now lies in 27m with her stern to the south-east and her bow to the north-west. She is 445ft long, and is well-flattened amidships. Her three boilers are clear and the engine room easy to locate. The bow is complete, but the stern is well broken.

The 445ft Liberty ship War Helmet, built in Japan in 1917 (Site 105).

106 Huntsholm This armed merchantman was empty when torpedoed in her port side amidships by *UB-40* on 11 June, 1917, 4 miles east-by-south from the Owers Light Vessel (Site **46**). She was on her way from Dieppe to Southampton. All the crew were saved. Up until then the *Huntsholm* had borne a charmed life. That same year in the Channel on 24 April a torpedo had hissed past her stern, and less than a month later, on 17 May, another torpedo had just missed her. Ironically, the *Huntsholm* was a war prize – the former German ship, *Telde*, a single-decker of 291ft and 2,073 tons.

    Her position is given as 50 37 26N; 00 37 30W, but divers say that all they have found there is the side of a wooden ship, though the very broken wreck of the *Huntsholm* lies nearby.

107 Wreck, name unknown 50 35 09N; 00 38 50W. This ship in 25m of water stands 5m proud of the sea bed. She has been called many names – *Vernon, Marlborough, Algiers, Kennett* – but so far no firm identification has been made.

108 Afon Dulais A British steamer, despite the name, of 988 tons and 208ft, with a beam of 33ft, the *Afon Dulais* was sunk by a mine while carrying coal from Seaham to Poole on 20 June, 1942, and now lies at 50 35 05N; 00 38 26W. In 26m of water she stands 3m proud. She is broken in two and much silted. The sea bed is of sand.

109 Algiers 50 34 34N; 00 38 09W. A British steamship of 2,361 tons and 300ft, the *Algiers* was torpedoed by *UC-65* on 26 February, 1917, 3 miles south of the Owers Light Vessel (Site **46**). Eight of the crew died in the attack, which sent the *Algiers* to the bottom in 36m. There is some doubt that the wreck at this position is the *Algiers* as salvage divers found over 100 tons of 18-pounder shells, dated 1916 and 1917, but the *Algiers* is listed as being used for coal and being in ballast at the time from Calais to Barry Roads.

The wreck lies upright to the south-east of an area of sand waves and stands 10m high with her bow to the east and stern to the west. She is very broken.

110 HMS Ganilly A well-armed naval trawler launched on 22 May, 1943, and one of the Isles class, the *Ganilly* was completed in September of the same year. She sank after hitting a mine on 5 July, 1944, and a sight of the wreckage makes it clear that she was either sweeping and pulled a mine on to herself, or fouled a mine cable with her propeller to the same effect.

The *Ganilly* was a ship of 545 tons and 164ft, with a beam of 28ft. She was capable of 12 knots, and carried a 12-pounder gun on her bow as well as three single 20mm anti-aircraft guns. Her crew numbered 40. She now lies at 50 34 01N; 00 37 48W, and care must be taken when diving her, not only because of the depth of 37m, but also because she lies on a slope that runs down steeply to the 48m mark. There have been several cases of bends while diving this wreck, which is often just called "The 37" by Littlehampton dive-boat skippers.

The bow, the gun and the ammunition on her decking are all intact. However, as you move towards the stern the effect of the mine becomes obvious and she gets more and more crumpled until there is a mad tangle of wreckage at her stern.

111 HMS Vernon II This wreck has been reported as having been found about 1,000yds north-north-west of HMS *Ganilly* (Site **110**). The author has, however, been unable to contact the diver who found her. It would be impossible for him to mistake her for anything else. She was a Royal Navy vessel originally named HMS *Marlborough*. She weighed 6,300 tons, and sank after capsizing off Brighton while on tow to the breakers on 29 November, 1924. Just over 245ft long, she was built in 1855 and designed to carry 131 guns. This was later reduced to 121, including one 110-pounder, 16 8-inch guns, six 70-pounders, 10 40-pounders, and 88 32-pounders. For all that, her active career was soon over, and she was turned into a training ship in 1878 and renamed *Vernon II* in March 1904.

112 Alert This small steamship of 289 tons is at 50 35 00N; 00 32 00W, though this position should be regarded as approximate, as it is the result of a distance and bearing from the position of the Owers Light Vessel (Site **46**) during World War One. The *Alert* was on the way from Le Havre to Littlehampton and was captured by the *UB-39* on 28 November, 1916, on the same day and by the same submarine as were the *Alison* (Site **179**), and the *Ramsgarth* (Site **159**). The submarine's boarding party put bombs in her hold and the engine room. The *Alert* is in 45m of water.

113 Atlas A Norwegian steamer of 989 tons, requisitioned by the British Government, the 217ft *Atlas* was torpedoed by *UB-56* on 13 November, 1917, when on voyage from Amble, Northumberland, to Rouen with a cargo of 1,300 tons of coal. The crew was saved. Today, the *Atlas* stands upright on the sea bed in 41m. It is easy to see where the torpedo struck – there is a large hole in the starboard side amidships. She lies east–west with her bows to the east. Her decks and some of her superstructure are still intact, though there is some more wreckage on the sea bed on her starboard side. She stands 8m proud at 50 34 35N; 00 32 52W.

114 Vesuvio 50 35 33N; 00 30 28W. Sunk on 6 April, 1916, this 1,391-ton British steamer was carrying 1,100 tons of general cargo from Sicily to London when she struck a mine laid by *UB-29* 6 miles east of the Owers Light Vessel (Site **46**). Of her crew of 21, seven men died, including the ship's master, when the mine exploded on her port side. The boiler burst at the same time and a mass of boiling water carried away the bridge. She now lies close to the south of a big rocky reef, and rises some 5m high in 42m of water. The reef appears slightly higher than the ship, which lies on her port side and is broken and silted. She lies east–west, with her bows to the east. The latest diving information is that she is broken in three places on a gravel sea bed, and that her propeller has been salvaged.

115 Candia An armed British merchant steamer of 6,482 tons carrying 8,000 tons of general cargo, including lead and zinc, the *Candia* was torpedoed by *UC-65* eight miles south of the Owers Light Vessel (Site **46**) on 27 July, 1917, while on her way back to London from Sydney. One crew member was killed. Built in 1896 as a twin-screw vessel 450ft long, it was the measurement of the overlapping arcs of those twin screws, that in 1952 enabled salvage divers to identify her. Those same divers salvaged 1,025 tons of lead and 1,000 tons of zinc from her forward holds. Today she is still reasonably intact in an area of great sand dunes in 45m at 50 34 18N; 00 30 41W. She stands 18m proud, and lies north–south.

The Candia (Site 115) was torpedoed by UC-65 eight miles south of the Owers Light Vessel, while on her way back to London from Sydney in 1917.

116 Duke of Buccleugh Inside the *Moldavia* (Site **118**), but still many miles due south of Littlehampton at 50 29 32N; 01 26 02W and only reached by the bigger dive boats, lies this 380ft long iron steamer of 3,099 tons. She was found by chance when a group of veteran divers, including several Littlehampton dive-boat skippers, came across her while magnetometering for another lost wreck in the area in 1990. When they dived they found her upright and almost intact with her masts lying across her. A china plate with the words "Ducal Lines" printed around a crown motif gave them the first clue to her identity.

The *Duke of Buccleugh* sank with all hands after a collision with the *Vandalia*, a 210ft wooden sailing ship, during the night of 7 March, 1889. From the damage to the steamer – a huge split in the starboard side close to the bridge and about 180ft back from its bow – it would seem that the captain of the *Vandalia* lied about the collision when he told the court of enquiry that the steamer rammed him head on. The wreck is on a shingle sea bed at 58m from which she is 8m proud. In her holds are 600 tons of hand-painted Belgian porcelain and china and glassware of all kinds, much of it broken and all intended for the hotel trade in India. The rest of her cargo comprised 2,533 tons of iron rails and machinery also destined for Madras. Visibility on the wreck is usually

Above: A decorated porthole cover from the Duke of Buccleugh (Site 116). Below: The steamer Duke of Buccleugh was discovered in 1990, a century after she sank off Bognor.

good, although because of her depth light levels are low. The *Vandalia,* with massive damage to her bows, was beached in the shallows off Brighton and soon broke up.

Divers should take care when diving the *Duke of Buccleugh* because of her depth. One diver has been bent on her already. Intriguingly, some professional salvage was carried out on her in 1992 using a sea bed chamber. As a result stories were passed quickly around Sussex diving circles that the professionals had raised something worth over £1 million!

117 Highland Corrie 50 32 30N; 00 38 20W. This 7,583-ton armed merchantman was nearly lost in the first year of World War One when she hit a mine in a field laid by *UC-1* 3 miles east-north-east of North Foreland on 14 August, 1915. However, she managed to stay afloat and get into Tilbury. She survived until 16 May, 1917, when she was torpedoed by *UB-40* 4 miles south of the Owers Light Vessel (Site **46**). Five of her crew were killed, and her cargo of 3,500 tons of chilled meat, which she was bringing from La Plata (in Argentina) to London, went down with her. She now lies on her port side in 40m of water and is owned by diver John Salsbury.

118 HMS Moldavia A long way out at 50 23 08N; 00 28 43W lies the giant wreck of the *Moldavia,* a 9,505-ton liner that became an armed merchant cruiser in World War One. She went down on 23 May, 1918, the victim of a single U-boat torpedo. Fifty-seven Americans died, 56 of them in the explosion and one during a leg amputation operation on board a rescue ship. These were the only casualties

The armed merchantman Highland Corrie (Site 117) was sunk in May 1917.

82

inflicted on the Americans during the whole trooping operation in which over 1 million US troops were carried in British ships. The U-boat responsible was Oberleutnant Lohs' *UB-57*.

The *Moldavia* and her sister ship the *Mongolia* were the first of the famous P&O "M" series of passenger liners. The *Moldavia* was 521ft long with a beam of 58ft, and was built at Greenock by Caird and Co. She was a huge ship, and if there was any criticism of her design it was that there were so many portholes (over 1,000) that, according to the builder, her sides seemed "unduly perforated".

The *Moldavia* cost £336,178 when she was launched in 1903. On 11 December, 1903, she made her first scheduled sailing – London, Colombo, Melbourne, Sydney – and proved that her 12,000hp engines could push her along at a top speed of 18.5 knots with the help of her twin 18ft-diameter propellers.

Now she lies on her port side at about 45m, with the depth to her highest point 28m. The wreck is just over 24 miles due south of Littlehampton, and the ideal dive time is slack water at neap tides. Most diving takes place on the stern, which is the nearest place to the surface. Visibility is often so good that when sitting on the stern the diver can see almost one-third of the massive ship. She was fitted with eight 6-inch guns, and the two near the stern point straight up. Others have fallen into the wreckage amidships where the torpedo struck.

Forward, the ship appears more damaged and collapsed, though the actual bow appears untouched. Near the stern, which drops vertically downwards to the sand and shingle sea bed, much decking is still in place. The twin propellers have been salvaged, as have the condensers. As the wreck is so far out, the Littlehampton dive boats only go when conditions are likely to be ideal – and then only in pairs. The voyage takes about 3 hours, so careful planning is needed in order to be on site and ready to dive at low-water slack.

WARNING This is a very deep dive on a very big ship. Take great care – divers have died on this wreck.

The liner Moldavia (Site 118) is a very deep dive, 24 miles south of Littlehampton.

Above: The entrance to the marina at Shoreham, showing (in the centre) the slipway at Shoreham Yacht Club.

Below: RIB returning to Shoreham Marina.

AREA 4:

Ferring to Hove

This area runs from 00 28 00W to 00 10 00W, and includes Ferring, Goring-by-Sea, Worthing, Lancing, Shoreham-by-Sea, Portslade-by-Sea and Hove. It features many offshore wrecks, and some particularly interesting chalk walls and rocky reefs. Dive boats out of Shoreham are centrally placed, but hard boats from both sides (Littlehampton and Brighton) also roam well into this territory.

Divers must be warned that this area is heavily netted, with both gill and trammel nets being used. Some nets are encountered very close to the shore. An indication of the amount of netting is shown by the fact that the area bounded by 00 20 00W and 50 40 00N along to 00 10 00W and 50 40 00N was at one time a no-go area for all trawlers, and fixed nets were in operation all the year round. Unfortunately, as far as the netters were concerned, the agreement with the trawlers, though put into operation with the support of the Ministry of Fisheries, was simply a gentlemen's agreement and had no teeth. Nevertheless, a great deal of netting is still used in the area, and divers should keep a sharp look-out at all times. Most of the fishing by nets is for lemon and Dover sole, plaice, dabs and skate. Divers who visit the area regularly say that the very number of nets means that you rarely see many flatfish close inshore.

The movement of beach material is now to the east. In fact, the covering and uncovering of sites in the area is, to a large degree, dependent on this movement, which is at its greatest during storms, so that diving after a storm when the visibility has improved may well present the diver with a totally different sea bed.

There are a number of places where it is possible to launch an inflatable over the shingle beaches that are typical of this area; but it is best to use the launch sites provided whenever possible. There is usually a ramp down from the sea wall, and car parks are not usually far away.

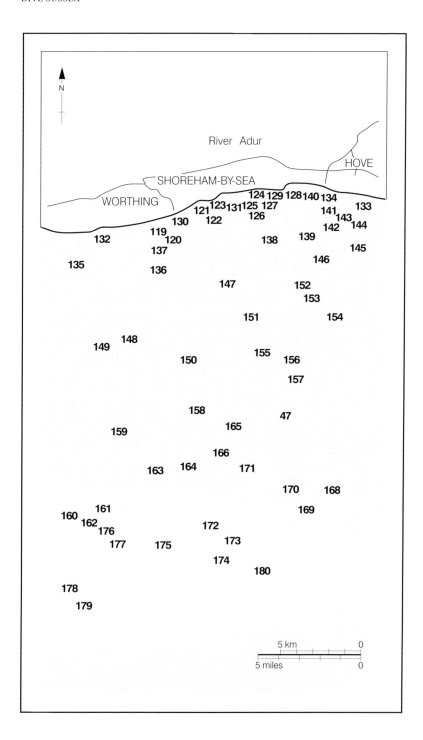

Launch sites

There are two first-class public launch sites at GORING. Both are awash for about 3 hours either side of high water. Both have car parks beside them, but the usual warning must apply – in season, be early.

Coming from the east, from Worthing, follow the Marine Parade along the sea front heading west until you turn away from the sea at a roundabout. Drive up George V Avenue, turn first left and left again back to the road along the sea front. Just before Worthing Yacht Club, turn left down Sea Place with the yacht club dinghy park on your right. This leads to a car park and toilets to the left of the foot of the "barricaded" ramp. The Ordnance Survey reference for this ramp is TQ 124 019. Both the ramps at Goring have barriers over the approaches that will not allow any combination of boat and trailer over 4ft 6 inches high to pass under them.

At SEA PLACE, there is a steep pull up to the top of the shingle bank then along in front of the dinghy park to the top of the stout wooden beams of the ramp that runs over the shingle to the sand. This ramp has a gradient of 1 in 7.

The ramp at ALINORA car park lies a few hundred yards further to the west. It is clearly signposted (the Sea Place one is not) off Marine Crescent. This ramp has the same barrier and a decent curving roadway from the car park to the top of the shingle bank. From there, the stout wooden beams go down over the shingle to flat sand. The gradient here is 1 in 10. There is a hand winch. The Ordnance Survey map reference is TQ 120 018.

Travelling further along the coast, all of which is built up, sometimes quite dreadfully so, we come to SHOREHAM-BY-SEA, a town that has a great deal to offer divers, with a number of excellent dive boats. Shoreham Harbour consists of a western arm – the mouth of the Adur River – and an eastern arm leading through lock gates to the Southwick Canal. Shoreham is a very busy commercial port, and the chimney of its power station provides a landmark that is extremely difficult to mistake from the sea. The chimney is marked by red lights at night, and is about 1 mile east-north-east of the harbour entrance, which lies between two huge concrete breakwaters.

Inflatable coxswains and dive-boat skippers should note that the sea area just off the entrance of Shoreham Harbour can be very rough indeed in onshore winds. Outside the entrance, the west-going stream starts about 2 hours before high water, and the east-going one 6 hours later. There are strong eddies in the entrance itself. Ships leaving the harbour have priority.

NOTE All diving in the commercial harbour and the harbour entrance is forbidden and all divers must observe this ban.

To reach the ROPETACKLE launch site, take the Shoreham road from Brighton, and at the Norfolk Bridge roundabout turn down "Ropetackle". Here, a public ramp gives easy access to the river. There is parking nearby. Use this site at high water plus or minus 3 hours.

Opposite: Dive sites in Area 4, Ferring to Hove. This area is covered by Admiralty charts 1652 (Selsey Bill to Beachy Head) and 2044 (Shoreham Harbour and Approaches); Ordnance Survey Pathfinder map 198.

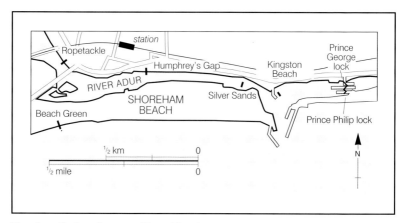

Shoreham Harbour has several launching sites.

There is also a launch site at SILVER SANDS. At Norfolk Bridge roundabout continue along the road and across the bridge. Take the turning marked "Shoreham Beach" at the next roundabout. Take the first left and follow Riverside Road and Harbour Way back towards Shoreham. At the end there are railings and a raised wall and parking overlooking the river. This is Silver Sands, which gives an easy launch at any state of tide.

BEACH GREEN is a public area near West Beach at the end of Beach Green Road. Launching is over a shingle beach.

KINGSTON BEACH can be used at high water plus or minus 3 hours. It is an easy launch down a gently sloping shingle beach to the east of Lifeboat House and Shoreham Rowing Club. The marker for finding the site is the lighthouse on Kingston Road, which is part of the A259. Trailers can be left immediately in front of the lighthouse, but cars must be taken away and parked either on the opposite side of the coast road or in the car park 500yds away in the Portslade direction. Take great care not to obstruct access to the lifeboat house. There is a small toilet block on site.

Shore diving sites

Good shore sites are not plentiful in this area, and those that are worth diving are really much better tackled by boat anyway. The movement of the sea bed in this area makes the location of wrecks that were driven ashore very uncertain, but several examples of this sort of wreck have been included here to add interest to the dives of the shore-bound.

119 Junkers Ju 88 This German twin-engined bomber was shot down in March 1943 and crashed into the sea off George V Avenue, Worthing. The site of the crash was 200yds offshore from the Marine Gardens Bowling Club.

120 Capelia of Hamburg This 1,000-ton barque was wrecked onshore on 11 November, 1891. The wreck site is described as "off Heene Terrace". She was in ballast.

121 Lancing Beach This used to be a simple shore site where divers in shallow water were bound to see plaice, but divers say that in recent years fish numbers have declined in strict tempo with the increase in offshore netting. Beware of boat traffic here in the summer.

122 Ophir This big schooner was wrecked on the beach opposite the Three Horseshoes, Lancing, on 6 December, 1896. Her cargo was salt!

123 Kong Karl of Horten This is another schooner wrecked onshore between "Lancing Toll Bar and the Coastguard Station" on 23 July, 1895. So violent was the wind at her wrecking that she was spun completely round and ended up with her stern to the beach.

124 Church Rocks 50 49 24N; 00 16 27W. This is only a shore dive for the fit. The rocks start 300yds offshore, stand 2 to 3m high, contain tunnels, and are home to bass, congers and some lobsters. The rocks are well weeded, and some of them dry at low spring tides. They are easily silted by strong blows. They lie directly off the little Church of the Good Shepherd, on West Beach. There is an easy approach to the water over the shingle beach, though parking is restricted close to the site. Depths are shallow. It is a good site for second boat dives.

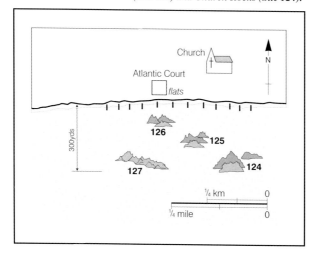

Shoreham Beach, showing the location of Atlantic Court Rocks (Site 126), Dave Barnard Rocks (Site 127), Supermarket Rocks (Site 125) and Church Rocks (Site 124).

125 Supermarket Rocks Lying just to the west of Church Rocks (Site **124**), this site is so named because of the vast number of lobsters that used to inhabit the area. The terrain is very similar to Church Rocks, but with more debris.

126 Atlantic Court Rocks Lying still further to the west, this site takes its name from the Atlantic Court block of flats, which stands almost on the beach in front of them. These rocks are smaller than Church Rocks (Site **126**), standing only 2m high. To the east between them and Supermarket Rocks (Site **125**) is a big ledge of rock that runs some way out almost from the beach itself. This ledge is the home of several congers.

127 Dave Barnard Rocks So called after a local spearfisherman who found this a happy hunting ground, these rocks are so honeycombed with holes that some of them seem almost hollow. They are home for lobsters and congers.

Some idea of the amount of wreckage lying near the shore in this area comes when you look at the huge number of losses recorded. Several of these occurred on the day of the Great Storm: 2 June, 1860. Some of its victims are described below.

128 Pike This barque carrying a cargo of coal from Hartlepool struck the shore 100yds to the east of the entrance to Shoreham Harbour and became a total wreck.

129 Mary Ann This brig became a total loss after coming ashore on the west side of the harbour entrance.

130 Lord Nelson Once a large lugger, the *Lord Nelson* is now a total wreck just east of Worthing.

131 Plough This Whitby vessel laden with stone for Arundel was wrecked near Shoreham.

132 Marys This large coal brig from Portsmouth was wrecked west of Worthing.

133 Transit The *Transit* was a brig from Shoreham, wrecked on the shore to the east of the Chain Pier at Brighton.

134 The Inner Jenny Ground 50 49 18N; 00 12 30W. The Inner Jennies is an area of small rocks almost directly in front of Portslade gas-works. There is a shallow hump in the middle. Depth in general is 6m. Plaice and dogfish are often seen. Hollows at the foot of these rocks are traditional spawning areas for black bream, but a mine discovered and exploded in 1984 right in the middle of a spawning season killed hundreds of these fish, and anglers say they have not returned in anything like their former numbers.

Boat diving sites

135 Kingston Rocks This is rocky ground, but it is very shallow and heavily weeded and the area is not really worth diving.

136 Indiana 50 47 03N; 00 22 12W. This homeward-bound British steamer of 2,266 tons was laden with oranges and lemons from Sicily when she ran into thick fog close to dawn on 1 March, 1901. She collided near the Owers Light Vessel (Site **46**) with the German cross-Atlantic steamer *Washington* on her way to New York. The *Indiana* was struck slightly aft of midships and seemed to be sinking. The crew of 23 was taken off by a tug assisting the *Washington*, which before the collision had been having engine trouble.

But the *Indiana* was not quite ready to go. In fact, after several hours she was still afloat, and a tug took her in tow. However, she soon began listing heavily, and then, finally – and literally – ground to a halt 1 mile south of Worthing Pier in about 10m of water. A storm soon put paid to her, and her cargo of oranges and lemons was washed ashore on beaches all along the coast.

Today, despite the shallowness of the wreck and the fact that she has been dispersed with explosives, this is a good dive. There is a great deal of movement of the sea bed here, and recently the *Indiana*, or parts of her, started to emerge from the sea bed. Her magnificent brass steam-whistle was then recovered by Eric Smith and is on display at the Marlipins Museum at Shoreham. A condenser plate was found in 1983, and a 400lb brass pump the following year. A bathroom in the old ship was also exposed at one point. It contained part of a marble bath, brass taps, lead pipes, a china washbasin, and brass door hinges.

Slack water is 2 hours before both high and low. The wreck is potted heavily.

137 Slate Boat Lying at 50 47 48N; 00 21 24W and slightly to the east of the pier at Worthing, this is possibly the remains of an old barge, but there is nothing to be seen now but her slate cargo. To find this dive, align the conspicuous chapel of Lancing College with the beacon at the landward end of the old sewage pipe at Worthing. The slate lies in 3m among weed.

Transit marks for the Indiana (Site 136).

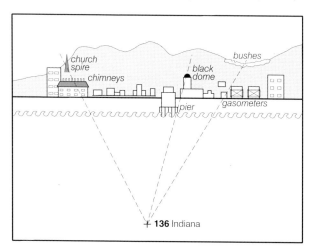

91

138 Miown This small British steamer of 379 tons was carrying a cargo of cement from London to Bristol on 13 February, 1914, when she struck a low reef and sank 1½ miles from Shoreham Harbour during a south-easterly gale. She is now at 50 48 19N; 00 15 23W in 10m.

The shallow water in this area has played a part in the destruction of the *Miown* in the years since her sinking. But by far the worst damage was done when she was blown apart to give a clear freeway to Shoreham Harbour. Though she was originally 135ft long with a beam of 23ft, she is now more of an oblong lying south-west to north-east, with her boiler in the south-west corner. She is often buoyed for divers by divers.

It would be a mistake to say that there is nothing left of interest on the wreck. Local divers say that she is emerging more and more from the sea bed. There are lots of iron plates lying on the sand, and in the mid-section some of her ribs stick up. The cement cargo is now stone (she is often called "the Cement Boat" by locals), and is scattered around as rocks.

The *Miown* makes a good night dive. If you get right down on the sand you can shine your torch nearly a dozen feet into the wreck in places and light up a lot of lobsters at home there. But there is not the slightest chance of getting at them! This is just as well because the wreck and the area 500yds around it has been declared a voluntary marine reserve by a number of Sussex diving clubs, who have appealed to all divers to refrain from taking any life from the site.

Transit marks for the Miown (Site 138), off Shoreham.

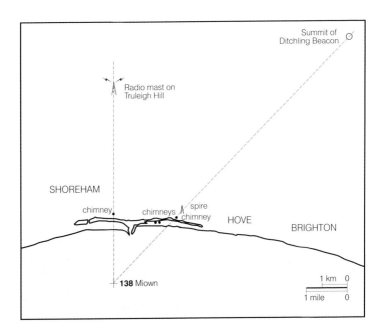

139 Man o' War Anchor Wreck The anchor is at 50 48 30N; 00 12 54W, but the wreck may be further in towards the shore near the Shoreham Dredger (Site **142**). Though there is no local record of a large warship being wrecked here, the ship must have been big because a diver can stand inside one of the flukes of the anchor. Other signs of a sunken ship are the cannon, cannonballs and musket shot, all of which have been found in what seems to be a direct line towards the shore from the anchor. If you line up on the old harbour entrance (roughly where the end of the Aldrington Basin is), and go straight offshore, this is the line on which the wreckage lies. Local divers say that this is an indication that either the ship was making for the old harbour and missed it, or that all heavy objects were being dumped overboard to lighten a ship in trouble.

140 Flying Fortress Although it is difficult to imagine that two four-engined bombers came to grief in almost exactly the same area (*see* Site **152**), Eric Smith of Shoreham has found the remains of yet another big aeroplane straight off Shoreham power station's cooling-water pipe. He believes his discovery is the engine from a Flying Fortress. There is some documented proof for this. During World War Two a badly-damaged Fortress homeward bound from a daylight raid over Germany did break up in the sky over Shoreham. One engine landed on shore, one somewhere inside the Jennies (which would be Eric Smith's), and one on the sea bed out by the *Miown* (Site **138**). What happened to the fourth engine no one knows.

141 The Outer Jenny Ground This is deceptive because it is generally thought of as just a low reef of rocks, but parts of it have caves into which a diver can swim. The Jenny Ground is really two reefs of rock – the Inner Jennies (Site **134**) and the Outer Jennies – which run along the coast. There is evidence on the outer reef of a large wreck hundreds of years old. This may be the wreck the anchor of which lies at Site **139.**

One diver has shown the author a massive heavy bronze pulley wheel, some 7 inches in diameter from the Outer Jennies. Another recovered a big sounding-lead. In Mike Davies's Shoreham Watersports you can see part of a three-legged bronze cauldron, which could be Roman or from the late 1500s, also discovered on the Jenny Ground.

The Outer Jenny Ground offers depths of up to 9m, and must be dived by boat. Some of the bigger diving boats use this as a second dive area. The sea bed is a mixture of large rocks and boulders, with patches of sand in between. There are some big ledges, and undercutting has, in places, formed caves big enough for divers to turn round in. Lobsters, crabs, and flatfish are often seen in this area.

142 The Shoreham Dredger This vessel lies on the Jenny Ground. Its remains are scattered far and wide, though two large wheels and seven or eight buckets are still to be seen. The boiler is sometimes clear too. As the main wreckage is only ¾ mile offshore in shallow water, this is often used as a first sea dive for beginners. The area is the haunt of big pollack, bass, congers and lobsters.

143 Roman Villa (possibly) This site at 50 49 07N; 00 11 24W was found by a spearfisherman ½ mile out to sea from the end of Wish Road, Hove, in 5m of

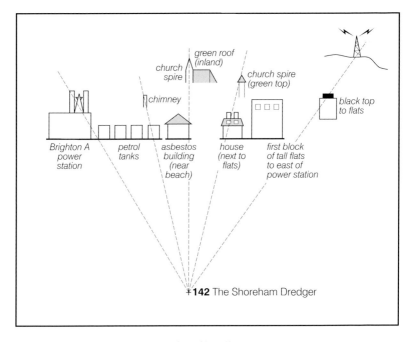

Transit marks for The Shoreham Dredger (Site 142).

water. He found rows and rows of tiles and took one to the curator of a local museum, who identified it as Roman. Further exploration of the site was cut short when a sand movement covered it up again.

144 John Roberts This sailing ship laden with slates was caught in the terrific storm of 11 November, 1891, and was driven ashore "east of the gasworks" at Portslade-by-Sea. The crew, a man, his son, and a youth, died in the wreck. A grave in Aldrington churchyard records the occasion of the wreck, along with the deaths of "William Williams of Carnavon, aged 45, his son William, aged 14, and John Griffith Thomas of Llanwnda aged 17".

145 Rock Lump Though marked on some Admiralty charts as wreckage with the "position approximate" sign, this is in fact a lump of rock rising 3m from a flat sea bed in 7m. The position is 50 47 58N; 00 10 37W.

146 Billy Boy Or is it the *Billy Bee*? Or the *Billy B*? Certainly the local name for this wooden wreck is the *Billy Boy* (though the author has found a chart of 1850 that marks it as "the Bee Wreck'). Anyway, she and her cargo of stone are at 50 47 23N; 00 13 13W. The ship is believed to have capsized and sunk in about 1826 when the Middle Pier of Shoreham Harbour was being built out from the North Bank. This was done to keep the two ebb currents apart and so get them to

You can launch at Kingston Beach either side of high water.

deposit their silt out at sea. Certainly, the Middle Pier, which shelters the launch site at Kingston Beach, had to be built without the *Billy Boy's* granite blocks, which now stand 2½m high on a 10m shingle sea bed and lie north–south as though the ship was heading in at the time of her loss.

The *Billy Boy* has another claim to fame. The wreck is the haunt of massive congers, and it was here that Eric Smith of Shoreham made the 66lb catch that became the British conger spearfishing record. This has not, however, frightened off other big congers – oddly, these do not conceal themselves among the blocks but lie lengthways in the open in the gaps between the piles of stones. This gives divers a good opportunity to observe them, and on one recent dive nine were seen lying out in this way.

There are some wooden planks still trapped under the square stone blocks, and in good visibility the outline of the ship can be seen clearly. Out to one side is a big anchor, and a winch can be seen too.

147 Mike's Mushroom

Shoreham diver Mike Davies was 4 miles out at sea directly opposite Lancing chapel clearing a trawl for a local fisherman. The trawl was hooked around a mushroom-shaped rock. As he cleared the trawl Mike Davies realised that he was under a huge stone mushroom about 12ft high and 15ft across at the widest part of the cap. The top was circular, as were the stem and base. He thought it an odd shape even for Sussex rocks, which do tend to have strange outlines. He then got a real shock for the "rock" was made of masonry, with, around its base, huge flagstones some 6ft by 5ft.

Mike Davies offers no explanations for the identity of this strange object, except to say that it is clearly man-made. On surfacing, he found that a heavy mist

95

had clamped down, which means that the position of 50 45 00N; 00 19 00W is very approximate.

His discovery is included here as it is a prime example of the objects found by divers in Sussex that seem to fit in with the many tales and legends of buildings, even towns, under the sea off the coast. There is no doubt that much of the Sussex sea bed over which diving is carried out today was once dry land.

148 Betts Reef Lying just to the east of Worthing Lumps (Site **149**), this reef at 50 43 34N; 00 24 39W is a meandering chalk wall sometimes as much as 5m high. At the eastern end it merges into rough ground of chalk and weed. At the western end gullies run through the wall, ending in a sandy bed. Some 200yds long, the wall varies in height along its length and is sometimes less than 1m proud. The wall with its overhangs, and the debris around it, is the home of many lobsters, and is heavily potted. It is believed that this reef is named by local fishermen after a well-known diving doctor, who used to tell friends about this lobster superstore, calling it El Dorado!

149 Worthing Lumps 50 44 00N; 00 25 00W. These are part of the face of the chalk wall, which emerges in places from the sea bed on this part of the coast. Here, there are only big lumps of chalk, but the wall can reach 6m high in places. It disappears under the sand and then re-emerges and is usually easy to locate because of the number of lobster pots along it. There are also many crabs in the area.

A drift dive to the west following the edge of the Worthing Lumps will take the diver out over sand and then on to a rock reef. In about 15m, this is another good area for shellfish. Take care, however, for in this reef is a sea mine – though broken, it still sprouts horns!

150 Wreck, name unknown At 50 43 09N; 00 19 27W, and almost completely buried in the soft sea bed off Shoreham. All that is known is that the wreck is some 180ft long, with a beam of 28ft, and lies in 19m of water.

151 Wreck, name unknown At 50 45 03N; 00 16 54W, this vessel is some 90ft long with a beam of around 12ft. She lies – perhaps wallows would be a better word – so deep in the 13m sea bed that she is at times almost completely buried. After a storm from the south-east some of the sea bed is scoured away, and more than the usual few iron plates on top of the sand show. But the snag is that the south-easterlies ruin the visibility, and when the visibility clears the wreck is buried again!

152 Stirling Bomber Found by Brighton and Worthing BSAC in 1970, this bomber was upside down with her wheels down at 50 46 21N; 00 14 00W. The divers found her when recovering a trawl that had caught on the wreckage. Though all the engines were there, one wing appeared to be missing. She stood 2m off the sea bed, but is now widely scattered. The RAF Stirling, a Mark III of 75 Squadron, was returning from a raid on Frankfurt. The crew were picked up by a Walrus amphibian rescue aeroplane after they ditched.

153 Wooden trawler Only yards from the remains of the bomber and to the south lies the wreckage of a small wooden trawler about 40ft long.

154 The Steam Trawler 50 44 45N; 00 11 18W. This one is much dived and it is fair to describe her as a "fun wreck". She stands upright with just a slight list to starboard, is covered in mussels, has her propeller and rudder intact, and is in 17m of water. She is 98ft long and has a beam of 31ft. Most of her superstructure is gone, but if you want to show a novice a ship-like ship under the sea, this is the one. Even her hatches are in position. She stands 5m proud, and the joy of her is that she has not sunk into the sand at all, but sits there on her keel with a 3m scour under her bow on the port side.

WARNING Some nets have been reported on this wreck.

155 Pentyrch The wreck of this 3,382-ton British steamer laden with coal lies on the sea bed at 50 43 22N; 00 15 43W. The *Pentyrch* was sunk by a submarine on 18 April, 1918, "five miles west-north-west of the Brighton Light Vessel" (Site **222**). One of the crew was killed in the explosion. We know that the torpedo came from *UB-40*, which survived the undersea war only to be blown up on 2 October, 1918, by the Germans themselves when they evacuated their Flanders Flotilla base in Bruges.

Locally known as "the Six-miler" (referring to its distance from Shoreham), the *Pentyrch* is very broken up amidships. Her big boilers are, however, still prominent, with the stern and bow sections standing 7m proud in 19m. Although the *Pentyrch* has been picked clean by the multitude of divers who have visited her over the years, she makes a good dive for novices as she still looks ship-like.

156 Maaslust A dive at 50 43 12N; 00 14 28W in 1983 identified this small wreck as the 40-ton *Maaslust* by her bell. The diver who found the bell described her as a steel, barge-shaped vessel standing about 2m off the sea bed. Later dives by other divers showed that she was sinking in, and now only about 1m of her shows above the silt. In fact, so far in is this 40ft vessel that echo-sounders become useless in any sort of sea. The depth is 20m.

The *Maaslust* went down following a howling south-west gale in July 1956. She was a Dutch-built ship called a boeier, and was designed with apple-shaped bows and stern, a rounded bottom, and big leeboards, for sailing in the very shallow waters of Holland's canals and inland seas. Later examples of these craft were built of steel and were much sought after as pleasure vessels when fitted with modern engines. When the *Maaslust* sank three men, one woman and two children were saved by the Selsey lifeboat.

157 City of London This vessel lies at 50 42 18N; 00 14 17W, but there is some confusion over this one. The Navy think she might be the *Ikeda*, a 6,311-ton, 410ft steamer torpedoed on 21 March, 1918, by the German submarine *UB-40* while sailing in ballast from London to Galveston, Texas. The Shoreham lifeboatmen used to call her the *City of Waterford*, but that wreck lies further to the east. Somehow, though, the local name for her became the *City of London*, but no-one can find a ship of that name lost in these parts.

If the wreck is the *Ikeda*, then she reported being 7 miles west of the Brighton Light Vessel (Site **222**) at the time of the submarine attack. If that is right, she must have drifted eastwards a bit before sinking, because now the wreck is only 3 miles west of the light vessel's position in 1918.

The Navy have located a big wreck here conforming to the measurements of the *Ikeda*, but a diving report in 1982 from a salvage firm says that they found only the upside-down section of a small wreck, probably one of less than 1,000 tons. It therefore seems likely that there are, in fact, two wrecks here.

Whichever ship it is, the wreck most commonly dived in this position lies upside down in a dip in the sea bed (which takes the depth to 23m). This is a very silty area, but you can swim along the keel and get in part of the stern and around the boilers. There are still some portholes left.

NOTE Just to confuse the issue still further, there was a small coaster of 351 tons, built by Schlesinger Davis of Newcastle in 1891, called the *City of London*. There is evidence of her being owned up to 1925 by the Brussels Steamship Company of 28 Billiter Street, London EC3, but then suddenly she is not listed any more. Could she be the small wreck the salvage divers found? If so, it only goes to show that local names are often right.

158 Steam drifter, name unknown 50 40 39N; 00 19 44W. This wreck is lying on her starboard side some 7m proud of the sandy sea bed at 23m. Apart from her missing superstructure she is intact even if the plates are rusted through in places. With great care divers can go inside the wreck through the forward holes right down to the keel. In this way there is a route through from bow to engine room. Do not go any further. There is a way through to the stern, but it needs a thin diver and a lot of wriggling to exit underneath the engine. It is not recommended.

The rest of the wreck makes a good dive, with some very pretty areas. One diver compared the sunlight striking down through the hold as like being in a cathedral. There are lobsters and congers aboard. Some portholes were recovered recently, but only the opening section of the glass was brass-rimmed.

The funnel, 4 to 5ft wide, disappears into the sand at a sharp angle. There was a brass pipe of 2 to 3 inches in diameter leading from the engine room along the funnel, but that has been taken now. The steam whistle, however, is probably still there under 10ft of sand. Eight years ago the wreck was upright, but she has now rolled over.

159 Ramsgarth In the early days of World War One, the German U-boats often captured merchant vessels, then sank them with explosives. This was done to save torpedoes, though a pretence was often made of inspecting the ship's papers; the British use of Q-ships and the arming of merchant ships made this a less frequent occurrence in the later years of the war.

The *Ramsgarth*, a small British merchantman of 1,553 tons, was not armed when she was captured by *UB-39* on 28 November, 1916, and boarded 11 miles east-by-south of the Owers Light Vessel (Site **46**) when on her way from Cardiff to the Tyne in ballast. The German charges blew holes in her bottom and she went swiftly to the sea bed. The crew in their boats were all saved.

The *Ramsgarth* now lies on her starboard side on the sea bed in 22m of water at 50 40 01N; 00 23 33W. Her bow is still upright and is the highest point of the wreck, standing 5m proud. The stern is also intact, but the mid-section has collapsed. The boiler is clear and the engine can be seen. A beam trawl has hit her amidships, so beware of netting.

Visibility in this area is often good and can be over 15m. A very big, almost frightening, angler fish regards the wreck as home. A good spot, though, for lobsters, which are often seen out in the open around the wreck.

The *Ramsgarth* was identified by her bell, which has been recovered by divers.

160 Jaffa A blue pennant in a white circle and the words "Wilson Line" were positive clues to the identity of this wreck at 50 38 33N; 00 27 01W. The insignia was found on an intact dinner plate recovered by a diver in June 1977, and the find confirmed local belief that this was the 1,383-ton British steamship *Jaffa*, which was torpedoed by the German U-boat *UB-30* in the early hours of 2 February, 1918.

The *Jaffa* was going from Boulogne to Southampton in ballast when she was hit in the port side amidships. She sank quickly, taking 10 men down with her. The survivors in the port lifeboat were questioned by the U-boat's commander when he surfaced nearby. The interrogator was Oberleutnant R. Stier, who was not to survive long himself, for he and all his crew were killed on 13 August that same year, when *UB-30* was rammed and then depth-charged by an Royal Navy trawler off Whitby.

Today the *Jaffa* lies on her port side in a general depth of 22m. Her four boilers stand proud by 6m. There is a heavy scour along the keel, which is broken in places. The 260ft wreck lies north-east to south-west close to a 3m-high shelf of shingle and rock with her bows to the south-west. She was armed with a 4.7-inch gun, shellcases for which, dated 1916, have been recovered though there is no sign of the gun, which is probably buried in the silt.

NOTE The Wilson Line plate is identical to several recovered from the wreck of the liner *Mohegan*, a famous wreck-dive on the Manacles in Cornwall.

161 Ariel When the mist cleared as suddenly as it had come on the evening of 10 June, 1892, it was easy to tell where the wreck of the 2,200-ton steamer *Ariel* of Hull lay – her two masts stuck up 10ft above the water.

The 300ft ship had been carrying a cargo of wheat from Varna, the Bulgarian Black Sea port, to Hamburg, via the Bosporus, the Dardanelles, along the length of the Mediterranean, then out by the Straits of Gibraltar and up into the Channel. It seems a long way round for a cargo for Hamburg – and a harsh fact that having come all that way the *Ariel* should collide in the mist with the steamer *Lancashire* 5 miles east of the Owers Light Vessel (Site **46**). The *Lancashire* was on her way from London to Liverpool.

The wreck of the *Ariel* lies at 50 38 54N; 00 24 48W in 28m and has been identified by dinner plates and her bell, which was lifted in 1981. Her bow section lies in deeper water to the south-east, and leans heavily over to port. The bow itself is intact, but the decking has collapsed and the ribs stick out. She is broken up about 30ft back from the bow, though the stern section is upright on the keel. To the west is a large scour.

A swim up over the rounded stern will show the rudder wheel exposed to full view. Forward of that is the boiler and engine room. There is no brass left on the wreck.

162 Wreck, name unknown 50 38 36N; 00 25 30W. This is a wreck that we know was carrying steel plate and coils of wire. We know, too, that she is broken in two. The stern lies on its port side and is very smashed. The propeller, which presumably was of bronze, has been removed. It is clear, too, from the stern that she had chain steering gear. The bow leans away from the stern at more than 90°, and is buried in silt. Depth is 25m.

163 Ny-Eeasteyr A British MFV despite the Dutch name, this German-built 61-ton boat sank on 8 December, 1980, on the way from Great Yarmouth to Ramsey, Isle of Man. She lies at 50 39 28N; 00 21 42W, with her stern badly damaged in 26m on a mud sea bed.

WARNING Look out for nets draped over this wreck.

164 Wreck, name unknown 50 39 35N; 00 20 26W. There seems little chance that this old wreck will ever be identified. She seems to be about 145ft long on a sandy sea bed into which she is now well sunk at 29m.

165 Unidentified obstruction 50 40 08N; 00 17 19W. This small obstruction stands 2m off a sea bed of sand, shells, and stones, at a depth of 27m. More diving information is needed.

166 Lulonga This small British steamer of 821 tons was one of the early victims in World War Two of the German E-boats in the Channel. She was torpedoed on 26 July, 1940, 10 miles south of Shoreham, and now lies at 50 39 49N; 00 17 03W. Those who have dived her say that it is hardly worth it as she is almost completely covered by sand and going under fast. Depth is 28m.

167 Ingo The crew of this 49ft British steel MFV, which sank on 13 December, 1980, were rescued from their life-raft off Brighton; but the vessel itself drifted awash before sinking at 50 40 58N; 00 14 28W. The wreck was located by Peter Van Der Boon of Shoreham in 1983. He says she is 5m high on a 26m sea bed, and that her superstructure at the stern is hanging over the starboard side. She is already silted up, which prevents entry. The propeller is of iron.

WARNING This is a small wreck lying in trawling grounds which is consequently covered in nets.

168 Wreck, name unknown 50 38 35N; 00 11 20W, she stands upright and 10m proud of the sea bed at 46m with her bows to the south-west. Her superstructure is still there amidships, and she has two holds, which were carrying coal, either side of it. This wreck is called the "North-easter" by some dive-boat skippers. A fine ship's decanter and glasses have been raised.

169 Pagenturm Sometimes called "the Other *Moldavia*" because of her size, this is not a liner, but a big merchantman of 5,000 tons. The *Pagenturm* lies at 50 38 01N; 00 12 56W on her starboard side, and it is still 24m from the tip of her bow to the 44m sea bed, and even deeper on the east side where there is a 10m scour. She is easily located by the large area of "boiling" water on the surface over her.

    The *Pagenturm* had an exciting life. She was originally a German ship, but was unfortunate enough to be caught in British India at the outbreak of World

War One. Having been taken as a prize, she was requisitioned by the Admiralty and armed with three 4.7-inch guns – one on the poop, and one on each of the port and starboard quarters. She was then put to work for the British war effort carrying Government stores, and on 16 May, 1917, she was on her way from London to Barry when the U-boat *UB-40* caught her "16 miles west from Beachy Head". Four men died when the torpedo ripped into her starboard side, and within minutes she was gone.

The *Pagenturm* now lies north–south with her bows to the north. Her decks are almost vertical, but despite this much of her superstructure and the three guns are still in place. How long she will stay in her present condition it is difficult to say, but quite recently a crack has appeared running right across her amidships. Many nets and fishing lines are draped over her as she is a popular fishing mark, especially for conger, which abound.

Some of the first people to dive this one were a group from London BSAC. When they did so in 1975 the wreck was already suspected of being the *Moldavia*, but the London divers were able to inform everyone, including the Admiralty, that she was a large cargo vessel and not a liner like the *Moldavia*. Once again, it was a dinner plate marked with a crest, found in 1982, which confirmed that this was indeed the *Pagenturm*.

170 HMS Minion This is the name of this World War One destroyer, which is lying on the sea bed at 50 38 37N; 00 13 53W. This is a deep dive with a minimum depth of 43m, from which this old warship stands 8m proud on an even keel.

Three holes in the deck were thought to be where the funnels had collapsed, but dive-boat skipper Tim Bennetto says that the holes are each circled by rails, probably for gun turrets. These three gun turrets led him to identify the wreck as HMS *Minion*, an M-class destroyer launched in September 1915. The *Minion* was one of six Admiralty M-class boats built by Thornycroft – the others were the *Michael, Milbrook, Munster, Nepean* and *Nereus*. They were all 1,025 tons, and 276ft long with a 26ft beam. They were armed with three 4-inch guns, one 2-pounder pom-pom and four 21-inch torpedo tubes in pairs. Each had three boilers and 25,000hp engines, driving three screws, which gave them a maximum speed of 34 knots.

The *Minion* survived the war and was sold for breaking up in Germany in 1921. It is believed that the old ship had been stripped of her guns and was under tow to the breaker's yard when she foundered. She lies north-east to south-west and her bridge has collapsed on to her foredeck.

Despite the depth, she is dived frequently. Positive identification was made when a diver raised her maker's nameplate. It reads: "JOHN I. THORNYCROFT & Co. Ltd / No775 / SOUTHAMPTON / 1915 / ENGINEERS & SHIPBUILDERS".

171 Obstruction, type unknown This lies at 50 39 14N; 00 17 31W in 30m. It could be a buried World War One wreck, but is charted as an obstruction. Diving information is needed.

172 Quail This vessel is a very old iron steamer-sailer lying in 42m at 50 38 02N; 00 18 26W. She was built in 1870 by Palmers in their Jarrow yard for the Cork Steamship Company, whose fleet all bore the names of birds. Among her sister ships were the *Grebe,* the *Buzzard,* the *Auk,* the *Cygnet* and the *Hoopoe.* The *Quail* was 224ft long with a beam of 28ft and 924 tons gross.

On 24 August, 1886, with Richard Reynolds in command, the *Quail* left Antwerp for Glasgow with a general cargo that included glassware, wool and potted foods. On the Friday she was in dense fog off the Sussex coast sounding her whistle and barely moving. Suddenly she was struck on the starboard bow by the *San Martin,* a French steamer bound from Bilbao for Dunkirk, which made such a big hole in the *Quail* that she started to sink at once. Most of the crew jumped across to the *San Martin* as she drew away, leaving captain, chief officer, carpenter, cook and stewardess on board the sinking ship. They managed to launch one of the lifeboats, but the stewardess refused to jump in and went down with the ship 11 minutes after the collision.

Today the *Quail* is upright with her bow broken off and lying with its port side to the west and her large counter-stern lying to the east. There is no sign of her masts, and her superstructure is gone too. Her two-cylinder 120hp engine can be seen clearly. The hub of a massive ship's wheel is on the counter-stern. Her bell has been raised. There are many wooden deadeyes around her, and one diver recently found a sounding lead. The potted food of her cargo is mainly in jars, some with their lead seals embossed "Liebig's Extract of Meat". Do not bother taking any home; the contents stink! There is a lot of broken glass near the bow. This is the remains of Victorian light ale glasses (pub rummers), wine glasses and water jugs. If you are lucky enough to find a whole one, take care how you bring it up as any rapid change in temperature will cause it to crack.

The area around this wreck is known as The Holes after the shape of the sea bed, which has great holes in it, yawning open like bomb craters.

173 Wreck, name unknown Either there are two wrecks at 50 37 43N; 00 19 35W, or this one has broken in half and moved apart. First dives established this wreck as a 260ft freighter lying in a north-west to south-east position, 10m high in 30m of water. Then someone spotted depth-charges, still armed, close by. Next came the report of more wreckage not far away from the original find. This wreckage, in an area of sand waves, was much longer than the original, at 370ft. One thing is certain, both pieces of wreckage are old and heavily broken up.

174 Porthkerry The steamer *Porthkerry* (1,920 tons, 280ft long) was unarmed when she was torpedoed by *UB-40* on 20 May, 1917. Her captain and six crew were killed outright. Built in 1911 for the Porthcawl Steamship Company, at the time of her loss she was carrying 2,600 tons of coal. Today, at 50 37 35N; 00 18 58W, she provides a dramatic scene. The wreck lies in a deep hole, or valley, with the bow jutting 10m upwards and almost vertical. The ship is lying east–west, is broken in at least two places, and is in 42m of water. Her bows are to the east. There is a 3m scour on the north side and a great sand wave nearly 20m high is poised above her. A mast lies across the wreck near the broken mid-section. Her large steam engine can be seen. She has been identified by her bell.

Close by this wreck, divers should find the 3,216-ton *Tycho*, which was sunk seven minutes earlier by the same submarine. The reason for the sinking of the *Porthkerry* was that she stopped to pick up survivors from the *Tycho*. Fifteen men and the master of the *Tycho* died in the double sinking.

175 Stanwold 50 38 00N; 00 20 02W. This British collier of 1,020 tons was nearly sunk in dock when she became one of the first casualties of the German daylight bombing offensive on British ports in World War Two. It happened on 15 September, 1940, the most vital day, according to Winston Churchill, of the Battle of Britain, and the day on which the Luftwaffe made its greatest concentrated effort in the attacks on south-east England and London. On that day, 56 German aircraft were shot down by the RAF.

On 26 February, 1941, the patched-up *Stanwold* was in a convoy going from Southend to Cowes when she was seen to have a list to port. Later that evening her captain reported that she was steering badly. In the dawn of 27 February she was seen listing to starboard. Nothing more was heard of her and her crew of 22 men, but the bodies of some of them were washed ashore much later in Pevensey Bay.

The *Stanwold* is a good wreck to dive, even though she is lying on her port side and is three-quarters upside down. The hull is still intact apart from one section near the stern, which has collapsed. She stands 10m proud on a 36m sea bed of rippled sand. It is possible – with care – to dive inside her. Her bows are to the south-west and are the highest point. There are piles of coal on the sea bed beside her. The iron propeller is still in place, and there are still a number of portholes almost falling out of her rusting hull.

176 Wreck, name unknown 50 37 37N; 00 26 25W. Divers have found this to be the wreck of a small Admiralty drifter or trawler about 190ft long and lying in 25m of water. She is broken in two, lies north–south, is much silted, and at best is 3m proud of the sandy sea bed. Many years ago divers recovered a box of 13lb howitzer shells from her, dated 1914. The wreck is so close to that of the *Cairndhu* (Site **177**) that the two ships may share the same howitzer ammunition! Local divers have not yet found enough to identify her firmly, but two names are popular choices. These are the *Klondyke*, 155 tons, sunk on 4 June, 1916, after a collision near the Owers Light Vessel (Site **46**), and the *Evadne* of 189 tons, sunk on 27 February, 1917, by a mine off the lightship.

177 Cairndhu 50 37 27N; 00 26 14W. This armed British merchantman of 4,019 tons was torpedoed by *UB-40* on 15 April, 1917, while on a trip from the Tyne to Gibraltar with a cargo of 6,250 tons of coal. She was hit on her port side amidships and sank swiftly, although not all aboard had time to get into the lifeboats. It was nearly midnight when a U-boat surfaced, ramming the port lifeboat and tossing out all those in her. Eleven men were lost. The other lifeboat reached shore safely.

In January 1918 the masts of the *Cairndhu* could still be seen above water so she was dispersed and swept. Now she lies east–west with the bow to the west, and is largely broken up, though her engine and boilers stand some 6m proud of the gravelly sea floor. A howitzer gun and ammunition dated 1916 lies 30ft from the stern, which is broken off and listing to starboard. Another gun, a long-barrelled 4.7-inch, is still bolted to the stern. The identity of the *Cairndhu* was confirmed by the boss on the ship's wheel found in 1980 by Newham BSAC. The boss was unusual in that it carried not only the date and the builder's name, but also the name of the ship.

178 Molesey The one and only victim of *UB-81* (Site **58**), the *Molesey* was a 3,218-ton armed merchantman, which was torpedoed amidships by Oberleutnant Reinhold Saltzwedel on 1 December, 1917, as she made her way up the Channel on passage from Sfax in Tunisia to Hull with a cargo of 4,867 tons of phosphate. The hit failed to sink her, however, and the U-boat surfaced and planted the explosive charges that finished the job. *UB-81* was herself sunk the next day. The *Molesey* is today at 50 35 23N; 00 27 24W. She is badly rusted in 45m of water. Divers say that she is almost completely upside down, and that her hull has rusted right through in places. She stands 6m proud on the side of a sea bed ridge. Her iron propeller is still in place.

179 Alison A little British steamer lying at 50 34 48N; 00 26 34W. Just 286 tons and 121ft long, the *Alison* was captured by *UB-39* on 28 November, 1916, and was sunk by explosive charges planted by the German sailors in the boarding party in the same way as the *Alert* and the *Ramsgarth* (Sites **112** and **159**). The *Alison* was on the way back to Littlehampton from Le Havre at the time. She now lies in 54m on a ridged sea bed and stands 8m proud.

180 Glenarm Head 50 36 58N; 00 16 29W is the position of this 3,908-ton British armed steamer sunk on 4 January, 1918, by Oberleutnant Stier in *UB-30*. The *Glenarm Head* was torpedoed "5 miles south-west-by-south from the Brighton Light Vessel" (Site **222**). The master and another member of the crew were killed. This is a very deep dive – the steamer stands 10m proud in 52m of water and is consequently mostly intact.

AREA 5:

Brighton to Burrow Head

This area runs from 00 10 00W to 00 02 00E, and includes Brighton, Rottingdean, Saltdean and Peacehaven.

If you wanted three words to sum up this area, they would be wrecks, walls and chalk. The shore diving and the close inshore diving is dominated by the chalk cliffs both above and, to the east, under the water. The deeper diving offers an astounding variety of wrecks, ranging from German air–sea rescue floats, to aircraft, to "submarined" merchantmen of all shapes and sizes, to great sailing ships.

Then there are the walls. Basically, the inshore sea bed off Brighton is of sand, but two bands of rock run across this sand from east to west. It is these chalk bands that provide some of the best diving in the area. The chalk is often in the form of a wall some 3 to 4m high, and these are easily reached by inflatables, giving local divers some pleasant evening dives in the summer. A good tip for locating this north-facing wall wherever it outcrops from the sand is to drag your boat's grapnel from north to south.

The fact that the wall is north-facing means that it is a rock fault and not an ancient cliff line. Some divers believe that this fault runs along the coast for some considerable distance to the west, and they are certain that it connects Loo Gate with Ship Rock (*see* Sites **185** and **186**). The debris at the foot of the wall provides excellent ground for crabs and lobsters, and big plaice can sometimes be seen sheltering from the incoming tide.

Launch sites

Brighton is good RIB country, and there are a number of suitable launch sites. But on many of the swimming beaches, boats may not to be launched or come close inshore. The best launch sites are described below.

King Alfred Swimming Pool, HOVE, is a beach launch, but nearby parking is easy. Launch is possible at any time.

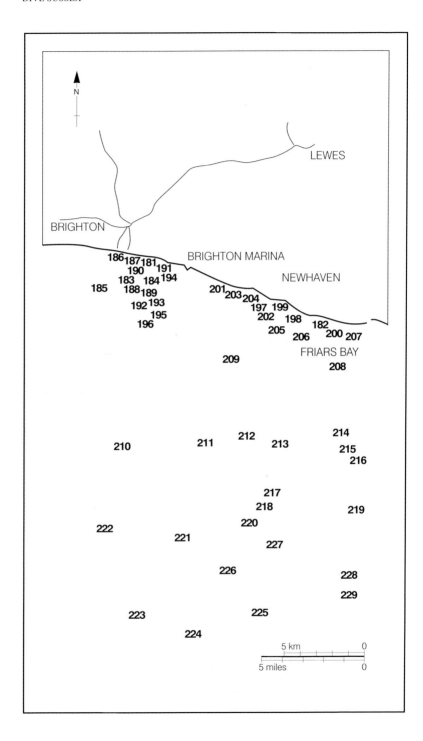

The concrete ramp to the beach near King Alfred Swimming Pool, Hove.

At BLACK ROCK boats can be launched over shingle beach at the end of the electric railway that runs along from Palace Pier from high water plus or minus 4 hours. At complete low water it is too rocky. There is a car park here.

FISHERMAN'S HARD is another launch over the beach at any time of the tide. It is right in front of Brighton BSAC clubhouse under the Kings Road Arches. Parking is prohibited on the hard area at all times, so remove car and trailer swiftly.

If anything makes BRIGHTON MARINA unique, it is its size. The two breakwaters, made up of 110 caissons and each as tall as a four-storey house, enclose 126 acres with berths for 2,000 boats. The marina is divided into two harbours. The outer harbour is tidal, but at low spring tides it can still take boats drawing up to 2.5m. The inner harbour is non-tidal owing to the lock system. The speed limit in the marina is 5 knots.

At the main cross roads at ROTTINGDEAN you will find a sign "To Sea". Turn down this and you will come to a large slipway. Parking is on the opposite side of the main road. Launch at high water plus or minus 4 hours. The White Horse pub is at the crossroads.

To launch at PEACEHAVEN, park at the seaward end of Steyning Avenue, which is a turning off South Coast Road, the main road out of Newhaven to Brighton. Parking for about 15 cars is on hard, if rutted, ground before and alongside the mammoth roadway cut down through the chalk cliffs to the coastal defence promenade. The gate at the top of this broad avenue down to the sea is padlocked

Opposite: Dive sites in Area 5, Brighton to Burrow Head. This area is covered by Admiralty charts 1652 (Selsey Bill to Beachy Head) and 1991 (Brighton Marina); Ordnance Survey Pathfinder map 198.

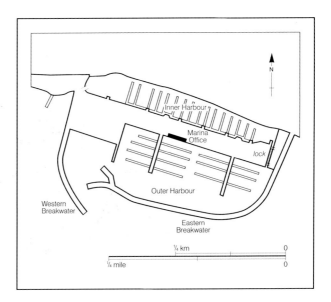

Brighton Marina.

as the roadway is part of the coastal defence works, and is not intended for public use. Notices at the top of the run-down state quite clearly that no responsibility will be taken for any mishap that might occur to people using it.

Having said this, however, this roadway represents one of the best launching sites along the Sussex coast. The wide road winds down through the sheer cliffs to a huge concrete promenade from which it is possible to launch in normal weather conditions at high water plus or minus 4 hours. Obviously, you will have to lift your boat and trailer over the barrier at the top, but this should prove no difficulty.

Those with a navigational turn of mind will be delighted to find that the Peacehaven launch site at Steyning Avenue is only a few yards from the spot where the prime meridian crosses the coast. At the seaward end of Horsham Avenue, a few streets west of Steyning Avenue, a memorial with a shabby green globe on top, the King George V Memorial, marks the spot.

Shore diving sites

181 Cod Rocks These are close to the shore by Black Rock, and divers should be careful not to infringe on the historic wreck site here. Cod Rocks is only one of a group of little reefs slightly to the west of the Black Cat site (*see* Site **194**). Water depth is about 6m, which makes this area ideal for novices. The rocks support a great deal of marine life including lobsters and crabs, but this tends to deteriorate as you move west. Returning to the shore at low water is awkward because of the exposed rocks. Remember that there are swimming-only areas between Black Rock and the Palace Pier.

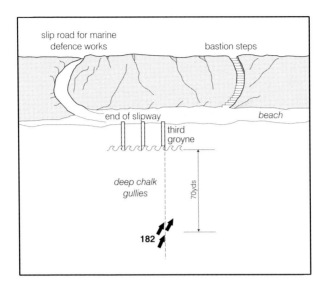

How to locate the cannon site at Peacehaven (Site 182).

182 Peacehaven Cannon This site lies just off the Bastion Steps at Peacehaven and calls for great determination – and strength – on the part of the shore diver, who must carry his or her gear down to the sea from the cliffs above. The slip-road (*see* Launch sites – Peacehaven) does at least enable the determined shore diver to walk down with the gear without tackling all those steps! From the end of the slip-road, go to the third sea-break to the east. The cannon lie some 50yds away directly out to sea in one of the deep chalk gullies running out from the coast. These gullies vary in depth according to the amount of sand in them. Some of them are 10m deep with the sand depth varying from 1 to 3m.

Sometimes, six cannon are well exposed, and several 8ft wooden spars can also be seen quite clearly. However, the sand moves and when it is very high in the gullies only two cannon will be seen.

Take care that sea conditions are calm, otherwise the return to shore can be extremely difficult.

Boat diving sites

183 Pier Reef Two hundred yards south of the Palace Pier is a reef in 10m of water – a favourite haunt of flatfish. The problem here, however, is that the reef tends to get heavily silted after more than a couple of windy days. Winds from every direction except north seem to affect the visibility and the amount of silting on the rocks.

184 Cannon Site, Brighton In 1963 antique dealer Dave Berry was spearfishing off Black Rock when he spotted a cannon in 6m of water. The cannon was later raised with the help of a trawler and turned out to be a bronze minion of nearly 8ft in length, which weighed 15cwt, and bore an indecipherable coat-of-arms. Barely readable, too, were the letters "AE" or "AG", which might indicate Dutch origin. The minion is now in the Tower of London armouries. The cannon was locally known as "Berry's Banger" and is dated at around 1550. Later Dave Berry found another cannon on the site, this time of cast iron and very corroded.

The artefacts may well be from the same vessel as those at the protected site at Black Rock, but there seems to be no record of the wrecking of a big ship – one big enough to carry the minion and other cannon – during the relevant period of history.

185 Loo Gate The Loo Gate wall is 2 miles out at a depth of 14 to 18m. The top of the wall is a sand desert. The marks are St Paul's Church over the end of West Pier and square on to the front of the Sackville Hotel. The rocks run from this point for at least a mile in either direction and possibly all the way to Ship Rock. Divers will not need telling that a wall like this in the middle of a surrounding area of sand means a good dive with plentiful marine life. In this case, nothing could be more true. Strangely enough, the site's name is totally accurate – there is a 2m-wide "gate" or gap in the wall just to the east of the mark.

186 Ship Rock or South-west Rock These are possibly two names for a single site, or two sites lying side by side. There are big mussel beds here on which plaice love to feed. These are large and extend over an area about of 20 square metres. The wall here is 2 to 3m high, and once again the top of the wall is sand and is easily missed. Once in the shelter of the wall, however, you can cope with most tidal conditions. It runs east–west, but the area of "scrub" – a local diving name for rubble, small rocks, and other debris – leading up to the wall is only 10m wide and is not easy to find. Average depth is 12m.

Parts of the wall turn into slabs of rock like a collapsed pack of cards. This is a really good dive with plenty of life. The marks are St John's Church over two trees at the top of Adelaide Crescent and the television tower over the end of Palace Pier.

187 Montpelier Road The sea bed here is small stones, small rocks, debris and a good-sized bed of large mussels. As a result, it is a very good spot for plaice. Depth is 10m. The marks are St Paul's Church over the end of West Pier and looking straight along Montpelier Road, which stands out as the very straight road it is.

188 The Spires This is a rock wall 1m high in 15m of water running east to west and, like the other outcrops in the area, its face is to the north. The top of the wall is sandy. At the foot is "scrub" debris of low rocks, stone chunks, and rough ground. Brighton divers suspect that this is part of the main wall and that it joins up after zig-zagging across the sea bed. Sussex Diving Club has been carrying out a survey to establish the wall's exact pattern. The marks are St Michael's Church on the left-hand corner of the Metropole Hotel and St Mark's Church over the second house (from the west) in Chichester Terrace, whose tall regency houses are easily spotted at sea just to the west of the marina.

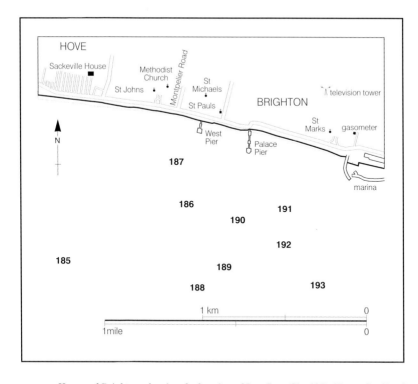

Hove and Brighton, showing the location of Loo Gate (Site 185), Montpelier Road (Site 187), Ship Rock or South-west Rock (Site 186), The Spires (Site 188), Cole's Hole (Site 189), Rock Tow (Site 190), the Inner Manors (Site 191), the Outer Manors (Site 192) and Measor's Rock (Site 193).

189 Cole's Hole A mixture of low rocks and debris together with beds of very large mussels, this area not only attracts plaice, but is obviously a paradise for starfish, which have been seen to be three deep in places. Depth is 10m. The marks are Holland Road Methodist Church over a large square conspicuous block of flats in Brunswick Square and St Mark's Church over the third house (from the west) in Chichester Terrace.

190 Rock Tow Often called "the Anchor Lump", this part of the wall is 3m high in places. The anchoring lump in question consists of 5 to 6m-high slabs in 16m of water and was the place where they used to anchor warships as the only decent piece of holding ground in the area. The blocks of rock are big – up to 10m by 15m – and are piled this way and that so that it is possible for the diver to find "caves". This area is not, however, as rich in marine life as the section of the wall further to the west. The site tends to silt up easily, so the variation in the height of the lump off the sea bed can vary by as much as 3m.

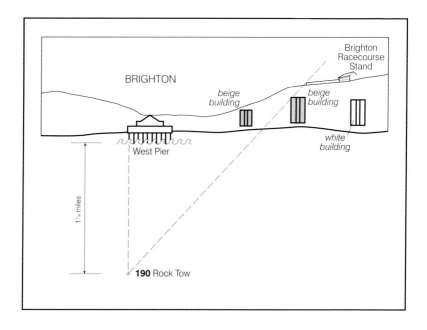

Transit marks for Rock Tow (Site 190).

The site is quite close to one of the yacht-racing turn marks, and is named after the trawlermen's "tows" in the area, which usually ended up full of rocks. It is an especially good area for lobsters. The marks are St Mark's Church over the first house (from the west) in Chichester Terrace and the Norfolk Hotel on the end of West Pier.

191 Inner Manors This rock, shingle, and mussels site has the low rocks and shallow depressions that flatfish love. It is quick and easy dive in 12m of water after an inflatable launch from Black Rock. The marks are St Mark's Church over the seventh house (from the west) in Chichester Terrace and the National Car Park at the top of North Road over the Amusement Arcade on Palace Pier.

192 Outer Manors This is similar to the previous site, but the rocks are much bigger with table-sized slabs. There are the same shingle and mussel beds, but these are deeper, at 18m. Flatfish can be seen here too. The marks are St Mark's Church over the 10th house (from the west) in Chichester Terrace and the east corner of Brunswick Square over the end of West Pier.

193 Measor's Rock The sea bed here is a collection of 1m-high boulders, which seem very attractive to lobsters, crabs, and – at certain times in the season – large spider crabs. The marks are St Michael's Church over St Paul's and the gasometer on the corner of the marina's western arm.

Brighton Marina.

194 Brighton Marina Protected Wreck Site That is its official name, but it is known to most divers as the "Black Cat" site after the Black Cat Special Branch BSAC of Basildon, the members of which found the first cannon here in 1974. The site is now designated as being of historical and archaeological importance under the Protection of Wrecks Act, and diving and salvage operations other than those carried out by the Black Cat divers under the leadership of Stan Merralls, who is the licensee of the site, are prohibited. The archaeologist in charge is Adrian Barak of the *Mary Rose* operation.

The protected area inside which you must not dive is bordered by the following Ordnance Survey National Grid co-ordinates: 533 370E by 103 025N; 533 370E by 102 875N; 533 170E by 102 875N; and 533 170E by 103 025N.

The known area of the site at present lies between No. 6 to No. 17 of the west wall caissons of Brighton Marina, and extends some 200m to the west. Depths in the area are from 5 to 10m, and the sea bed is flat chalk with shallow gullies filled with fine sand.

From this site have come several cannon and a rare bronze hackbut, a type of swivel-gun from the 15th century. The cannon seem to date from around the 15th century, too, and a stone cannonball on the site would seem to be of Spanish, or possibly French, origin. Breech chambers from other guns have been found, and there is clear evidence of more metal objects lying under the sand. To date, the ship's identity has not been established.

113

195 Working Barge 50 48 03N; 00 06 12W. This one lies almost straight out from the marina, so beware of boat traffic. To find her, line up the end of Palace Pier on St Ann's Church, and the west tower of the marina on the central white column in the striped block onshore behind the marina. The barge is well preserved and has one winch on top and another on the sea bed beside her. She is usually circled by large shoals of pouting.

196 Infantry landing craft This small infantry landing craft is at 50 47 26N; 00 07 00W. She lies the right way up on a 17m sea bed and stands 4m proud. Both her bronze propellers have been removed.

The area immediately in front of the great chalk cliffs running along from ROTTINGDEAN towards NEWHAVEN is a pretty standard sea bed of fingers of chalk running out to sea. These form gullies filled with sand and silt deposits. Such places are favoured by flatfish. Some also contain wreckage from the many ships that have perished under those cliffs. In addition to the *Diana*, the *Dragon* and the *Brazen* (Sites **204**, **207** and **243**), the following wrecks might be worth looking for.

197 True Christine This wreck lies near Portobello Gap. Cargo being carried included sugar, coffee, tobacco and cotton. Two crew drowned when the ship was wrecked on 16 March, 1780.

198 Nuestra Señora de Begona This was a Spanish ship carrying chestnuts and walnuts. Her captain and three crew drowned when she was wrecked between Telscombe and Newhaven on 27 November, 1786. There were four survivors.

Transit marks for the Working Barge (Site 195).

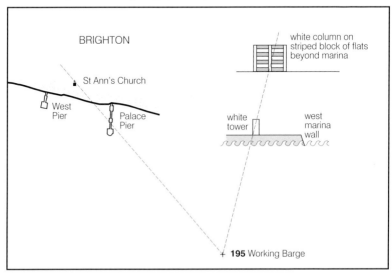

199 George The *George* was a brigantine from Sunderland that ran ashore between Rottingdean and Newhaven while being chased by four French privateer luggers on 5 February, 1808.

200 Minerva The *Minerva* ran ashore in thick fog about 2 miles west of Newhaven in 1832. Her cargo was salt.

201 Sir Charles Keith This schooner, bound for Dartmouth from Leith, was wrecked on 13 November, 1840, to the west of Rottingdean. A report states: "All hands saved by Captain Manby's apparatus".

202 Captain Long The *Captain Long* foundered off Saltdean in 1890 and was said to have sunk "opposite Cranleigh Avenue". The vessel was carrying marble.

203 Lufra Lying off Rottingdean, this Swedish ship, whose nameboard used to be in the billiard room of the White Horse pub, sank in 1895.

204 Diana This 14-gun brig of 140 tons was driven ashore during south-westerly gales on 30 May, 1803. Details of the wreck are sparse, but the place is given as the Saltdean Gap. *Lloyd's List* of Tuesday, 31 May, 1803, gives the captain's name as Pirera and says that the *Diana* was on the way "from Porta Port to Hambro". Hambro is presumably Hamburg, but the nearest names to Porta Port today are St Peter Port, Guernsey, and Port-au-Port in Newfoundland. To confuse matters further, *Lloyd's List* gives the wreck site as "near East Dean".

Transit marks for the Diana (Site 204).

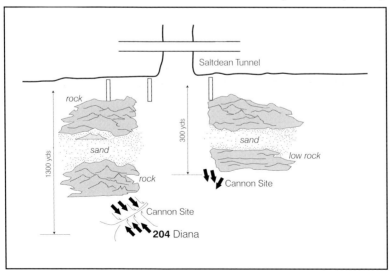

The cannon thought to belong to the *Diana* lie among the ribs and massive keel of a big ship on the right of the Saltdean Tunnel as you face the sea. Seven are exposed at times, though they can be completely covered. These cannon are 6ft long. Depth of water is 15m. There is enormous movement of the sea bed here, and it may be that only part of the site has so far been exposed. There are two more cannon lying across each other on the east side of the tunnel. These are identical to those raised in the area in the 1960s.

To see the cannon, come on to the main beach by way of the tunnel under the main road. Move to the east until the tunnel is out of sight so that you are nearly half-way towards the old sewer pipe. Three hundred yards out to sea, just where the yellow buoys are placed to keep the speedboats away from swimmers, you will find the two small (4ft) cannon lying across each other in 9m of water. You can check as you swim out if you are going the right way: at first the rocks go out in "fingers", then you cross a sand bar outside the rocks, and then you will come across a second set of rocks, on the outside southern corner of which (and still to the east of the tunnel) you will find the two cannon. An underwater metal detector search in this area has revealed a mass of metal under the sand.

To find the cannon lying among the wooden ribs of the old ship you must move to the west of the tunnel and go right until you can no longer see back into the tunnel. You will pass over an area of rock close inshore, then a sand bar, then a large stretch of rock and rubble with gullies, before the sand reappears and slopes steeply downward to 15m. It is here 80 to 100yds out at the foot of the bank (and ¾ mile from the shore) that you will find the cannon in 15m of water.

205 Spitfire This single-seat fighter is at 50 46 51N; 00 01 16W. First discovered when hit by a trawl, the aeroplane rises some 3m above the sea bed and was identified by divers called in by fishermen to remove the snagged netting. The remains are very close to the old sewage outlet.

206 Lobster Pot 50 46 36N; 00 00 12W. This is not one of those contraptions for catching shellfish, but the German equivalent of the RAF air–sea rescue refuges for ditched pilots in World War Two. The RAF versions were called "Cuckoos", and were moored along the Sussex coast (*see* Site **62**). The Germans called theirs "Lobster Pots" and they were moored along the French coast to assist Luftwaffe pilots and crew returning from raids on Britain. The British refuges were 30ft long, had a boat-shaped hull, and were painted bright red and orange. By contrast, the German versions were almost square, with a mast on the top, and a door in the side rather than the end.

Found by Brighton BSAC, this one is in line with the tip of Newhaven Breakwater and just slightly to the west of the monument marking the zero degree of longitude where it crosses the coast at Peacehaven.

Why a German air–sea rescue float lies on the sea bed off Peacehaven can only be guessed at. There was certainly an ex-German float (No. 23), which on 1 July, 1943, was in the RAF's possession and was moored at 50 46 18N; 00 08 20W, 3 miles south of Brighton. This float was serviced from Newhaven, but came under the overall control of the Royal Navy's Portsmouth Command. It may have broken adrift, as many other floats had done, and ended up in its present position, which is where a south-west gale would have driven it.

A Lobster Pot (Site 206) – the German equivalent of the
British Cuckoo (see Site 62).

207 Dragon This sloop of war was wrecked just to the west of Newhaven in 1799. The Newhaven section of the Lewes Journal of 1803 carries the following report concerning the wreck: "This morning one of our boats brought in two 24lb carronades, which had been discovered and dragged up during the low tide of last night a short distance on this side of Newhaven. The carronades it appears had formerly belonged to the *Dragon* sloop of war, which was wrecked on this part of the coast 3–4 years ago."

One possible site for the wreck is the place known to local anglers as Highest Conger Rock. This mark, almost exactly ½ mile to the west of, and in line with, the tip of Newhaven Breakwater, is not easy to find. Divers who have done so describe it as a small pinnacle about 20ft round. It rises from the sea bed in 7m, and comes close to breaking the surface at low tide. There are guns around it.

This may also, however, be the site divers believe to be that of the *Brazen* as some recovered material bears the Admiralty's broad-arrow mark. It is possible that this is Westmiss Rock, which figures in reports of the *Brazen's* loss (*see* Site **243**).

117

208 American bomber 50 45 19N; 00 00 19E. This aeroplane, believed to be a Flying Fortress, was said to be the cause of the death of a diver in 1975 when he was trying to clear a trawl. It is believed that a wing from the four-engined aeroplane collapsed on him, trapping him in 17m of water. Since the accident, Royal Navy divers have blown the wings off the fuselage. The wreckage stands only 1.5m off the sandy sea bed. On a recent dive it was discovered that there was still air in the landing wheel tyres!

209 Inverclyde This trawler had two doses of war service. In World War One she was on minesweeping and patrol duties under her original name of *Perihelion*. Once "demobbed", she was renamed *Gantock Rock*, becoming the *Inverclyde* in time to be called up again in World War Two.

Why the *Inverclyde* was under tow on 16 October, 1942, is unknown, but during that tow she sank at 50 46 28N; 00 03 38W. Now this 215-ton trawler is scattered over a wide area with her boiler 3m high off a sandy-mud sea bed covered by 12m of water. She was 121ft long with a beam of 22ft.

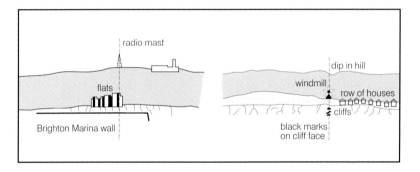

Transit marks for the Inverclyde (Site 209).

210 Ouse This 1,004-ton collier belonging to the LMS Railway Company was the first victim of an attack by E-boats on a small convoy of coasters making its way down-Channel on 8 August, 1940. Built in 1911, the *Ouse* was carrying a cargo of coal from Goole to Cowes. But though a torpedo caused her sinking, this did not occur directly from a torpedo hit. In fact, as she sheered away from a torpedo track, she collided with the British steamer *Rye* and went down at 50 44 12N; 00 08 24W. The *Rye* later saved her crew of 23.

211 Holme Force Caught in the same E-boat sweep as the *Ouse* and the *Fife Coast* (Sites **210** and **212**) on 8 August, 1940, the 1,216-ton *Holme Force* was carrying 1,000 tons of coke from the Tyne to Devonport when she was torpedoed "8 miles from Newhaven". She was built in 1930 and requisitioned by the Admiralty. She had four gunners on board as well as her crew of 13, but it is doubtful whether she had the chance to fire a single shot. She sank at 50 44 00N; 00 05 09W, and there were six men missing, including the master and three gunners.

212 Fife Coast This British coaster was the third victim of the E-boat flotilla ranging along the Channel on 8 August, 1940. A small steamer of 367 tons, the *Fife Coast* had been built in 1933 and was powered by an oil engine. When torpedoed she was bound for Plymouth from London with a cargo of 408 tons of refined sugar. She was attacked 15 miles west of Beachy Head and sank at 50 44 12N; 00 03 48W. She carried a crew of 11, including three naval ratings as gunners. Four crew and one naval rating were killed. Diving details are needed.

213 Wreck, name unknown This is a small trawler, lying almost north–south at 50 43 56N; 00 00 35W. She is about 105ft long, has a central hold, and her highest point is her stern, which stands 2m high in 20m of water.

214 City of Brisbane 50 44 33N; 00 00 50E. This 7,094-ton steamship was the last victim of Oberleutnant Lohs in *UB-57* before he and his entire crew were killed on 14 August, 1918, after hitting a newly-laid British mine in the approaches to his Zeebrugge base.

The *City of Brisbane*, 451ft long with a beam of 57ft, was riding high in the water on 13 August, 1918 – for she was travelling in ballast from London to Buenos Aires where she was to pick up a cargo of beef. Lohs' torpedo struck her in the port side aft close to No. 5 hold, and though she came to a dead stop very quickly despite her speed of 13 knots, she did not sink immediately.

Tugs from Newhaven were soon on the scene and tried to tow her close in to beach her for repairs. But just after midnight on 14 August it was clear that she was so full of water that she would never make it. The crew were all safely taken off before she settled, stern first. By the end of the month, her funnel (which was

Transit marks for the City of Brisbane (Site 214).

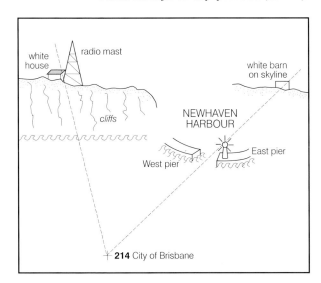

still above water where she lay in 20m) had collapsed and she was later swept clear "to 54ft".

The *City of Brisbane* is now upright in 23m, but broken clean in two. The bow is 5 to 6m proud where girder-work sticks up like a porcupine's spines. Elsewhere, massive plates stand 3 to 4m high. At the time of writing, there was a big net draped right across her and rising 6m above the wreckage. Take care.

The *Brisbane* is known to local divers as "the Anchor Wreck" because of the number of fishing boat anchors strewn around her.

215 Lancer II *Lancer II* lies at 50 44 10N; 00 01 09E – a long way from the spot where the collision that sank her took place. This happened off the Brighton Light Vessel (Site **222**) on 18 July, 1918, when HM Yacht *Vagrant* rammed this Admiralty trawler of 275 tons, which was heading for Newhaven.

The *Vagrant* took her in tow, but the trawler did not make it. When dived in 1970 she was found to be upside down in 21m and standing 7m proud. She is now very broken up, with her highest point, her bows, still pointing to the north-east.

216 Clan Macmillan The *Clan Macmillan* was an armed merchantman of 4,525 tons, built in 1901 by McMillans of Dumbarton. On 23 March, 1917, she left London for Glasgow in ballast but with a quantity of coconut fibre matting in her holds. At 1am on 24 March a torpedo from *UB-39* hit her in the starboard side amidships, the explosion bursting through the forward engine room bulkhead and the upper deck.

Captain George Young was sure she had hit a mine, and ordered all hands to the boats. As his own boat was full, he got into one carrying firemen. As the boats stood off the stricken ship, she showed little sign of sinking. The U-boat commander must have thought the same thing for suddenly another torpedo slammed into her, almost in the same place as the first, and sent a column of water "200ft in the air. Now the *Clan Macmillan* buckled and a fire broke out in the bow. Her back was broken and the masts began to bend towards each other. But still she did not sink.

Suddenly, the submarine came out of the dark and started asking among the boats for the Captain, who hid under the thwarts and told the firemen to say that he had been blown up with the ship. This they did, and when the U-boat had got the name of her victim from one of the other boats, she sheered off and was gone.

At 3am a patrol trawler picked up Captain Young and the crew. It was not until 6am that the *Clan Macmillan* broke in two and sank to the sea bed.

The *Clan Macmillan* was 396ft long with a beam of 48ft, but it is doubtful whether divers ever see more of her than a few feet at a time as the visibility is generally poor and there is much silt about. She lies in 20m of water, at 50 43 34N; 00 00 43E. Her iron propeller sticks up at a sharp angle and there is wreckage underneath it, which shows just how twisted she is. The remains of a trammel net link the two halves of the vessel together. This is a good wreck for lobsters.

217 Clodmoor This wreck lies close to that of the *Clan Macmillan* (Site **216**) and is often mistaken for her by divers. The *Clodmoor* lies at 50 43 40N; 00 00 30E. She was an armed merchantman loaded with 5,777 tons of wheat when she was torpedoed on 3 May, 1917. Built in 1902 by Doxfords of Sunderland, the *Clodmoor* was 3,753 tons, 243ft long, and had a beam of 47ft.

This big wreck is very twisted in 20m. The bow section stands proud with the chain lockers, but if you swim back from the bow for only 30ft, the wreck disappears. You then follow her outline along a sand ridge, which is probably caused by the ship underneath. Finally, the wreck emerges again and you end up swimming along the keel. The steel propeller is big, and lies proud of the sea bed on its shaft.

218 Wreck, name unknown This old steamer is upright in 24m of water, but is almost totally buried with only 2m showing above the sea bed. Most of her bow – the west end of her – is clear. She is now at 50 42 20N; 00 00 59W.

219 Wreck, name unknown 50 42 02N; 00 01 21E. This is a small ship, measuring some 44ft in length. She stands 2m proud of a sand sea bed in 25m. Diving information is needed.

220 Fortuna This Dutch steamship of 1,254 tons lying at 50 41 38N; 00 02 16W was carrying a cargo of cement when she ran into a mine on 22 October, 1916. The mine is believed to have been laid by the German submarine *UC-60*, which was one of the U-boats that surrendered at the end of the war and was used by Britain as a target before being broken up. The *Fortuna* was on voyage from Rotterdam to Cardiff, and 15 men died when she sank.

This near-intact wreck is considered an excellent dive. Divers say that it is possible to get all round the ship on one dive. The *Fortuna* is clearly Dutch, from the lettering on her portholes, and her beer bottles at the back of the wheelhouse. Until 1996 the doors were intact and one of them even still had the key in it! You can dive inside, but this is not to be undertaken without a reel and line, as silt can ruin visibility within seconds if disturbed.

The *Fortuna* is 251ft long, and most damage from the mine appears to be at the stern where it is possible to enter her through a large hole. Her cargo of cement is still in its paper sacks but solid, of course. It is possible to enter the stern of the ship from the well. Her highest point is her bow.

WARNING Inside the stern section this vessel is silted to within 3ft of the top. All bulkheads are gone, so if the silt is disturbed the visibility goes in the whole section. Take care!

221 City of Waterford This 1,334-ton British steamer built in 1921 was heading from Antwerp to Cork with 1,000 tons of general cargo when she ran into thick fog about 12 miles west of Beachy Head on 14 April, 1949. Unfortunately, in that fog and heading in the opposite direction was the much bigger *Marpessa*, a 5,500-ton Greek steamer. The ships collided, and the *City of Waterford* sank to the bottom at 50 40 30N; 00 06 38E.

Today, her single screw has been salvaged, but the *City of Waterford* is still upright with a slight list to port, and still points west. It is 20m down to her decks, and a further 10m to the sea bed. She is largely intact, and blue ceramic tiles are still in place on the floor of the galley together with lead-lined sinks. The cooking pots – some enormous and presumably for stews – are still hanging up, but are "welded" to the shelves. She is 270ft long, with a beam of 36ft.

222 Brighton Light Vessel This lightship was only in position during 1917 and part of 1918. She was established on a bearing of 188°, 7.6 miles from the charted position of the Marine Palace Pier Light on the current edition of Chart 1652. Her position was 50 41 19N; 00 09 36E.

223 Wreck, name unknown 50 38 41N; 00 08 16E. This small ship is lying in 45m and stands 5m proud of the uneven sea bed. She is upright with her bows to the south, and is 100ft long. Her back appears to be broken, though some of her superstructure is still in place.

224 Wreck, name unknown 50 37 45N; 00 04 54E. This 130ft wreck is becoming buried in 34m by rolling 5ft-high sand waves. She is broken in half and lies with her bows to the north-east. Though the sand into which she is sinking will eventually cover her, the stern section is still 6m proud.

225 Bombardon 50 38 30N; 00 01 48E. This seems to be a 480ft portion of the floating breakwater for the Mulberry harbours in France codenamed *bombardon*. Despite its length, this section is only 20ft wide. Though the west end is solid and 4m proud of the sea bed of sand waves in 34m, the east end of the second section (probably two sections joined together) is cracking up.

These bombardons broke the waves – even in Force 6 winds – and enabled small boats to unload supplies as soon as they were in position on the coast of France on the fourth day of the Normandy landings. Made of mild steel plate, with watertight buoyancy compartments, the breakwaters were moored in 12 fathoms of water to give sufficient depth inshore for Liberty ships to anchor behind them. Two miles of bombardon breakwater was used in the D-Day operations.

226 Dalhousie The *Dalhousie* lies in 35m of water and is well sunk into the soft sea bed. Sixty men, women and children died when this 800-ton fully-rigged sailing ship foundered at 50 40 00N; 00 02 48W in the early morning of 19 October, 1853. There was only one survivor.

The *Dalhousie* was built of Indian teak in 1848 and was one of the ships of the White Horse Line, which carried freight and passengers from London to Sydney. She went down laden with £100,000-worth of general cargo and commanded by the experienced Captain Butterworth.

In 1982, snagged nets by a Newhaven fisherman led to work on the site by the Salvamar salvage company, which is based in Jersey. They recovered pintles from the rudder, a section of the hull, mast bands, and other items. Later recoveries included part of the ship's wheel and the compass housing.

227 Girlvine 50 40 47N; 00 01 23W. This is the wreck of a small fishing vessel reported drifting and awash on 15 May, 1957. The ship, when finally she sank, settled well into the sea bed at 30m. Her hull is intact, but her decks have fallen in and she now looks like a big open boat.

228 Vasco A British armed merchantman of 1,914 tons, the *Vasco* was carrying 2,100 tons of general cargo when she struck two mines on 16 November, 1916, some 10 miles west-by-south from Beachy Head and 4½ miles off the coast. So quickly did she sink that 17 out of her crew of 26 were drowned. She was 280ft long and on a voyage from Hull to the Mediterranean. Locally called "the South Wreck" because of her position, due south of Newhaven, this 280ft ship lies in 33m at 50 39 31N; 00 02 00E. She is sitting upright with a very deep scour on her east side into which she will probably roll before too long. She is generally 5m proud with her bows to the south-east in an area where the sea bed consists of great waves of sand. She has three big holds with a deckhouse aft and was identified by Tim Bennetto from her china.

229 British Bomber Directly south of the *Vasco* (Site **228**) divers have found a World War Two bomber in 33m of water. Judging by the construction of the main fuselage, it is believed to be a Wellington.

The lighthouse at Beachy Head

AREA 6:

Newhaven to Beachy Head

This area runs from 00 02 00E to 00 15 00E, and includes Burrow Head, Newhaven Harbour, Seaford, Cuckmere, the Seven Sisters, Birling Gap and Beachy Head.

This whole stretch of coast is dominated – both visually and from a diving point of view – by the high chalk cliffs on either side of Seaford Bay, which produce long gullies running out to sea, mostly filled with sand. Further out, the soft sea bed and many flatfish make this an important area for trawling – especially for boats from Newhaven. From Newhaven, too, come the scallop dredgers, which work beds several miles offshore in deep water.

Hundreds of ships have been wrecked in the area, some recorded by name, many unknown. This becomes clear to any diver, who will find wreckage on practically every dive. Amphora shards and holed stone anchors have been found in the area, as well as pieces of Bronze Age weapons. Roman coins of silver and gold have been found by metal hunters buried in the cliffs at Seaford, suggesting sea traffic in the area.

Over the centuries gales from any southerly direction seem to have piled ships into Seaford or on to the chalk cliffs. Many were lost without written record, leaving behind only sea-bed puzzles.

What we do know, however, is that there was a sailors' prayer in the 17th century that included the words "God Keep Us from Seaford and its Shags". These sailors were not seeking protection from greedy sea birds, but were asking to be kept out of the hands of the smugglers and wreckers of Seaford, who were known as "shags" because they swallowed anything they could catch.

It would be wrong to exaggerate the number of ships lured to grief by the wreckers' wiles. More ships came to their end by natural causes than by the lantern hanging from the donkey's neck or the fire on the beach at Seaford which lured in ships to what they thought was the safety of the harbour at Newhaven. Many came to grief in storms on the beach at Seaford or close in to it. This makes Seaford one of the few places along the Sussex coast where interesting shore diving is a real possibility. The current record for shipwrecks at Seaford in a single night stands at seven (*see Harlequin*, Site **231**).

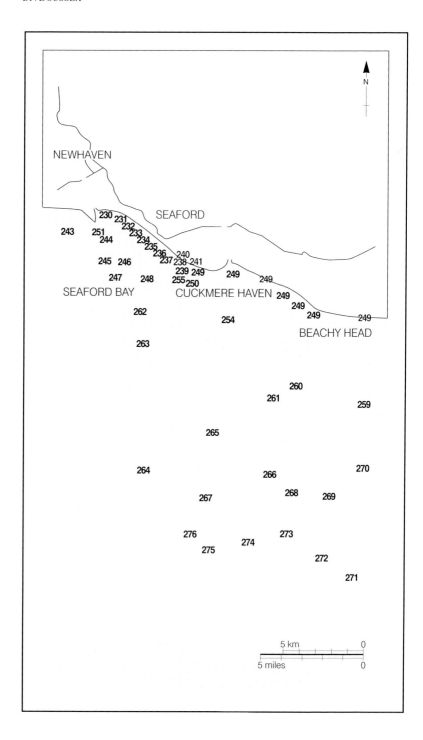

Wreckage is everywhere, and this – together with the large numbers of plaice to be found close inshore – makes Seaford and the surrounding area a magnet for divers, who on any calm day in summer are to be found in large numbers along the beach and sea wall or on boats heading out of Newhaven.

There is something magnetic, too, about the attraction of Seaford for wreckage. Some quirk of coastal currents brings a vast amount of floating wreckage into the bay. A classic example of this occurred in 1914 when a ship called the *Simla* was wrecked off the Isle of Wight, but her cargo – bales of paper, cases of whisky, boots, baby food, hams, cases of rum and brandy – drifted east and ended up on Seaford Beach.

Close in today are other more deadly cargoes that have been washed into the bay. Divers should be extremely careful what they touch, as World War One depth-charges have occasionally been seen on the bottom after the silt has been cleared by south-easterlies on spring tides.

Basically, the diver can be sure that westerlies bring in the silt and sand until sometimes the chalk gullies are full to the top and only the edges of the ridges show. South-easterlies are then needed for at least two days on spring tides for the silt and sand to be washed away again. Then up to 9ft of silt and sand can be stripped off the sea bed.

Some of the best visibility underwater comes after a long period of northerlies, when the visibility may reach 8m. A south-westerly, however, can ruin it in minutes. Diving here, then, in shallow water of 10 to 12m, needs careful buoyancy adjustment – one touch on the bottom and a cloud of silt can cover yards of sea bed.

Big plaice are attracted inshore by the mussel beds under Seaford Head and elsewhere. Dover sole, turbot and lemon sole lurk in the muddier places. Lobster and crab are found in the gullies.

A good deal of the offshore sea bed can be flat and featureless. Divers passing over such an area on a drift dive should look out for starfish – by putting the tips of their "fingers" together, they make themselves into a ball and let the tide bowl them along!

The Martello Tower on the eastern end of the sea-front at Seaford makes an excellent mark for boat diving. The tower is, in fact, the furthest west in a chain of 103 that stretched from Seaford to Aldeburgh in Suffolk and were to defend Britain against Napoleon. There are 74 between Seaford and Folkestone, and Seaford's is one of only 45 such towers still standing in England. The Martello Tower (No. 74) cost £18,000, but was only completed in 1809 when the danger of Napoleon's invasion had passed. It is 40ft high, and houses Seaford's Museum of Local History. The museum is run by voluntary helpers, and divers will find a good deal of shipwreck material there, including old wreck photos, two well-preserved cannon, and a huge anchor cathead from the wreck of the *Peruvian*, donated by visiting divers in 1984.

Seaford itself faces south-west and is very vulnerable to gales from that direction and from the south and west. Such storms create enormous seas in

Opposite: Dive sites in Area 6, Newhaven to Beachy Head. This area is covered by Admiralty charts 1652 (Selsey Bill to Beachy Head) and 2154 (Newhaven Harbour); Ordnance Survey Pathfinder maps 198 and 199.

The Martello Tower at Seaford now houses a museum.

the bay, and shingle from the beach is sometimes hurled right over the road and seawater forms pools on the low-lying land on the other side of the sea wall.

This low land is really the ancient course of the River Ouse, which centuries ago had its mouth at Splash Point at the foot of Seaford Head and miles from its present exit at Newhaven. It was a storm in 1579 that broke through the shingle banks of the river and gave it a new mouth at Meeching, not far from its course today. The place was then given the name of "New Haven" – as indeed it was – and Seaford, without a harbour or river mouth, dwindled in importance.

Until the great sea wall was completed in the late 1800s each great storm meant new floods – some so big that the inhabitants feared that the whole town would be engulfed. Each storm, too, brought fresh shipwrecks. There is a record, according to Seaford shipping historian Patricia Berry, of a wreck on Seaford Beach from which the local vicar, Robert Hyde, was suspected of looting £300 "in money". As he was the vicar from 1575 to 1638, that puts some date on the wreck, and shows that Seaford was a death-trap for shipping as far back as the 16th century. One estimate of the number of ships onshore between Newhaven and Seaford Head in the period 1700 to 1810 is more than 150. So it is no wonder that the Seaford shore and boat divers find themselves constantly among wreckage.

Divers should remember that cliff erosion in this area continues despite a great deal of coastal defence work. In certain places as much as 1½ft disappear every year, and there are sometimes 500-ton rock or chalk falls two or three times a winter. Just how much has disappeared in just over 100 years is surprising. The sewer between Brighton and Newhaven was laid from 1868 to 1874 under the cliffs some 250ft back from the coast. That sewer is now within 50ft of the sea. This, of course, means that any marks or details, such as caves where shipwrecked sailors sheltered, in reports written at the time of a wreck are now useless for location purposes.

NOTE Newhaven Museum lies on the West Foreshore and is run by volunteers of the Newhaven Historical Society. The museum has a good deal of wreck material and photographs of interest to divers and is open Saturday, Sunday and Bank Holiday afternoons from Easter to the end of October.

Launch sites

NEWHAVEN HARBOUR is on the River Ouse and an 8-knot speed limit is always in operation. The harbour is not well served by public launch sites suitable for inflatables and other small boats, but there is one site between Quay 10 and Quay 11 on the road called Riverside, which runs along West Quay. It is only suitable for use at or near high water. If you launch here, the harbourmaster advises care when threading your way through the numerous trawler moorings. Another do-it-yourself launching ramp lies at Meeching Boats, DENTON ISLAND. This is further up-river, but a concrete ramp allows launching from half-tide. A key to open the padlock to the ramp is available for a fee. Contact Meeching Boats (tel. 01273 514907) for further details.

If you like the easy life, Newhaven Marina will launch and recover boats daily in the marina, which is on the west side of the river nearer to the mouth. Overnight moorings for your boat are available. Divers using the marina facilities should ask at the office and will be given access to hot showers and toilets free of charge. Late-rising divers should, however, be warned that in times of exceptional demand such as hot sunny weekends and Bank Holidays, with the marina's two tractors launching boat after boat for hours in the morning, late-comers may occasionally be turned away. There is no booking system for launching, it is first come, first served.

Once launched, it is 3 miles from the harbour entrance to SEAFORD HEAD. Divers using the harbour should take care as the heavy traffic includes the Sealink ferry service to Dieppe. There are traffic signals at the entrance to the harbour on the southern end of West Pier, where the harbour control is situated. Signals used during daytime are:

RED TRIANGLE OVER RED BALL: entry permitted; RED BALL OVER RED TRIANGLE: departure permitted; RED BALL: free to move in or out; RED BALL OVER RED TRIANGLE OVER RED BALL: no movement permitted.

The river is silting, and dredging takes place almost continuously. The silt is dredged away, too, from the mouth of the river so there is no real bar there now. The shallowest depth of 4.5m where the silt does try to form a bar at the end of the breakwater can, however, produce a short, sharp sea.

Boat launching at SEAFORD can be undertaken almost anywhere over the steep shingle beach. There is no proper launching ramp, and all boats have to be carried down from the sea wall and heaved across the beach. This is all very well on the way down, but the return journey can be exhausting. Fortunately, car parking is easy on the roadway at the back of the wall. There is a toilet block near the Martello Tower.

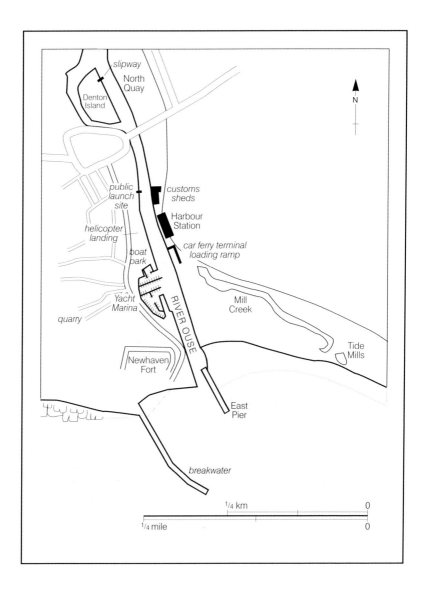

Newhaven Harbour.

Shore diving sites

Seaford Beach is one of the few areas along the Sussex coastline where shore dives are worthwhile. Here, just off the beach, is a fascinating tangle of wreckage, and the diver never knows what he or she will find. However, beach works in recent years to protect the sea wall have involved dumping 1.5 million cubic metres of dredged-up shingle and sand and some of the sites have been covered. Sites that were dumped on are recorded here in their original form as many of them are reappearing in their original condition from under the overlay.

Remember that this was where the French landed in 1545 only a few days after they had, they claimed, sunk the *Mary Rose*, and where they were driven back with heavy losses. Remember, too, that in World War Two the Dieppe Raid by Canadian troops and commandos set out from the area in 1942. There are rifles to be found off the beach, but as they are Lee Enfields Mark 6 they are more likely to be from accidents during the embarkation of troops for the invasion in 1944.

Divers should take care because evidence of war has been washed onto the beach too. There have been reports of World War One depth-charges. These are iron, about 2ft long, and 10 inches in diameter at the small end increasing to 16 inches at the middle. Wooden staves run down the whole length of the charge.

Lying to the east of the Buckle Inn is a depth-charge from World War Two. This is about the size of a 45-gallon oil drum. The ends are in place, with two bands around it. The brass depth-setting control is in place, but the main part has rusted badly, spilling pink explosive onto the mud. Do not touch!

Though positive identification of wreckage is often almost impossible, the following sites have been located and dived from the shore by Seaford divers.

The western arm of the breakwater at Newhaven shelters a popular diving site, easily accessible from the car park below Newhaven Fort. A short walk down the beach on the west side of the arm leads to the entry point. Follow the arm out until large rocks stacked against the breakwater are reached. Here there is much sea life, including flounders, plaice, wrasse, and pollack, as well as shoals of whiting and pouting. Crabs and lobsters are also found. Maximum depth is 12m with an average visibility of 6m. Best dived one hour before high water as there is a strong current after slack.

230 Catherine This brigantine was heading for Newhaven from the Channel Islands. On 13 March, 1914, in a south-easterly gale the captain decided to wait to enter harbour as it was so rough outside the entrance. It seems that while they waited the crew decided to splice the mainbrace, and when they did try to enter the harbour they missed it completely and became a total wreck on East Beach, Newhaven. The remains of the *Catherine* were found in 5m of water off the centre of the beach but slightly nearer to Newhaven than Tide Mills.

231 Harlequin (and six other wrecks) Dawn on 7 December, 1809, revealed a terrible sight. Seven ships were either smashed or in the process of being smashed. Hundreds of people lined the top of the shingle bank at Seaford Beach. Some men were down in the surf trying to save the stricken seamen. Others were about more deadly work – the "shags" were busy in the shallows.

An eye-witness of that unhappy dawn wrote: "There were some who, unmoved by the agonising shrieks of the exhausted and dying men, were only intent on plunder and rapine. Nor could the ghastly corpses that the tide sometimes cast among the objects of their covetousness suspend their iniquitous practices for a moment, or arrest them for glutting over the spoils acquired in the most shameless manner from the miseries of their fellow-creatures."

But the seven ships were not ashore because of the wreckers. At 3pm exactly on Tuesday, 5 December, 1809, the "Make Sail" signal fluttered from the yardarm of HMS *Harlequin* in Plymouth Sound and canvas dutifully blossomed on the 22 ships in the convoy. Shortly afterwards, with a fair wind, the *Harlequin*, a sloop of 18 guns, led the way down the eastern Channel under the guns of the Bovisand Battery and out to sea.

Though the *Harlequin* was hardly adequate protection for such a big convoy during the war with France, she was all that could be spared. There was much talk of Napoleon invading Britain, and Britain's naval might was thinly spread.

Lieutenant Anstruther, in command of the *Harlequin*, did not, however, feel inadequate in the least, and more than once on that first day's sailing he fired signal guns to order the fastest ships to drop back astern in his wake and keep as close as possible out of the way of any sudden attack by a French raider. In the night the convoy kept together, and all the next day sailed up-Channel towards the Downs where Lieutenant Anstruther had been ordered to hand over his convoy duties to other, larger warships.

A sudden storm from the south-west died away at 1am on the Thursday. However, the wind kept veering this way and that, and soon the convoy found itself in the middle of very strange weather – fog and steady sleet. The fog was so thick, even without the sleet, that a crew could scarcely see, even when holding a lantern a foot away from a particular object. For this reason, *Harlequin* kept firing guns to make her course clear to the following ships.

At 2am the sloop heaved-to and fired pre-arranged signals for the fleet to get between her and the land as this was a favourite area for French privateers to swoop on merchantmen. At 3am the gale came back from the south-west, but the fog stayed and so did the sleet. Now it was that the *Harlequin*'s captain made his big mistake. He knew he had passed the Isle of Wight at about midnight, and believed he was well clear of Beachy Head. So he ran in towards the shore and the other ships dutifully followed.

At 4am first the *Harlequin* and then the six ships immediately behind her grounded on the sea bed of Seaford Bay. The first thought of those on board was that they had run onto some uncharted rocks and they all fired what guns they could (the *Harlequin* fired rockets too) and the 16 following ships managed to stand off.

But there was to be no escape for the seven. A young midshipman aboard *Harlequin* later described what happened in a letter to his parents: "We struck about four o'clock on Thursday morning, when most of us were in our hammocks; but we were soon upon deck and cut away the masts, thinking we might get off; but the tide flowing in, our efforts for that purpose were unavailing. Little did we think at the time we were so near the shore; all of us thought we had struck on a rock; and we immediately fired our guns and burnt blue lights till all were expended; yet the convoy continued to follow us and six of them struck; the rest hauled their wind and got off safe: those on shore soon went to pieces. Ours being the first vessel that struck, and nearest to the shore, we lost only two lives, but many poor souls belonging to the other vessels perished..."

The young sailor did not say so, but the two men they lost were killed when the masts came down. The *Harlequin's* guns soon followed the masts overboard.

Now, for the first time, despite the fog and darkness, those on board the stranded ships realised that they must be close to the shore. They could hear what one of the crew described as "a murmuring of voices". As the time passed those who still clung to ships could hear more … "The cries of the poor mariners as they were washed from their only ground of safety, their vessels, mingled with the roaring of the storm, and added poignancy to the misery we endured. The confused sounds from the beach now became more distinct and powerful, evincing that the concourse of people continued to increase."

Come the dawn, the true situation could at last be seen. The shore was black with people, including the 81st Regiment of Foot, stationed at Blatchington Barracks in the town ready for any attempted invasion by Napoleon. The troops were marched to the shore by their officers to take part in any rescue work. The on-lookers lined the top of the shingle banks, parting and scurrying back every now and then when a particularly big wave crashed down close to them.

The *Harlequin* had come in closest and was the centre ship onshore. We think we know the exact spot she struck, right opposite the place where Buckle's Service Station now stands on Marine Parade. To the west, and immediately next to *Harlequin*, was the *Unice*, a 174-ton brig from New York, carrying cotton, potash and wooden staves. Thanks to the efforts of the 81st Foot, who formed lines with linked arms out into the sea, Captain W. Bowers and his nine crew were all saved.

Still further west was the *February*, a Prussian ship of 460 tons, in ballast. She dropped her anchor when she struck, and this stopped her from being swept in when the tide turned. Instead, she rolled on to her side and the sea ran right over her. The 16 men on board got on to the mainmast, but it soon broke and only one of the crew reached the shore alive.

Further west of all was another Prussian ship, the *Midbedach*. Weighing 350 tons, she was loaded with wine, brandy, sugar and coffee. Of her crew of 13, only two were saved. Her captain, J.G. Shultz, was not one of them.

Furthest away in the other direction – to the east – was the *Weymouth*, of 180 tons. She had only recently been recaptured from the French, and was carrying a cargo that included tobacco and cork. She was under the command of her mate, as Captain Llewellyn had remained in Plymouth to sort out all the paperwork of her capture and recapture. Now the *Weymouth* lay right in under the low cliffs at the start of Seaford Head and though four of the crew successfully launched a boat, it was quickly overwhelmed and they were all drowned. Seven of her crew of 11 were saved, however, by means of a line down to the ship from the cliffs above.

Closer to the newly-completed Martello Tower on the sea front was the *Traveller*, a brig loaded with fruit. All eight of her crew were saved.

Next to the *Harlequin* to the east was the *Albion*, a schooner of 128 tons, under the command of Captain J. Jermond. She was carrying brandy, saffron, cork, wood, and almonds. All nine of her crew were saved.

As ship after ship was smashed to pieces, all attention from the shore fastened on the *Harlequin*. At high tide she was washed closer to the shore by the incoming tide, but the seas were so enormous that any attempt to swim for it would have been fatal. So they tied a hawser to an empty wooden cask, and it was, luckily, washed ashore. Some people at least on the beach were not concerned with loot, and grabbed the hawser. One by one the crew of the *Harlequin* made their way along it, as did the one passenger on board.

When all were onshore, it was suddenly discovered that the wife of the passenger and his two small children were still aboard. At great risk, two of the *Harlequin's* crew launched a small boat and somehow got out to the ship, grabbed the woman and the children, and made it safely back to shore. They had no sooner landed than the hull of the *Harlequin* broke up.

By 10am it was all over. Seven ships had gone, 32 men had died, and the survivors were being offered "every hospitality" at the New Inn (that you will now find renamed as The Wellington just at the foot of The Causeway off The Esplanade).

The 81st Foot had worked wonders, and their lines out into the sea were largely responsible for the fact that the loss of life was not greater. A few minutes after 10am, Lieutenant Michael Derenzy, who had been at the forefront of the rescue operations, walked up the beach to collect his uniform coat, which he had taken off earlier. It had gone. So had the gold watch in the pocket. The "shags" of Seaford let nothing go to waste!

To locate the wreckage of these ships on the shore is not easy, because much of it must be jumbled among the sites of other shipwrecks or buried under the sand. But to find the *Harlequin's* guns, you should swim 60yds out from the end of the big groyne directly in front of Buckle's Service Station on Marine Parade (*see* Site **232**), and go slightly to the west. In the sandy-bottomed gullies in a low reef lie three cannon. The remaining 11 guns – 6-pounders and 12-pounders – are 250yds further out on another reef with gullies. This might be the place where the *Harlequin* jettisoned her guns as the cannon are all close together. The big anchor there may well be *Harlequin's* too.

However, as with much of Seaford's wreckage, it is impossible to be certain which ship the wreckage, even cannons, came from. This site is the same one (or very close to it) on which swivel guns of the early 1400s were found. And just to add to the confusion, a diver is said to have found the bell of the *February* on the sea bed just two groynes to the west of the Martello Tower. That would make the *Harlequin's* loss much further to the east.

232 Buckle Garage Cannon Site This is one of the sites affected by the beach works and shingle dumping as it lies 300yds offshore almost directly in front of the Buckle Service Station on the Seaford front. There were three cannon exposed closer in only 60yds from the end of the big groyne directly in front of the garage and slightly to the west, but the main wreckage area is further out.

There were some gullies close in and this is where the "Plate Anchor" (Site **233**) lies; but a strip of sand separated this inshore reef from the other one further out.

A sure sign that you are getting close is if you swim over a very bomb-shaped bomb, but a safer mark is a 6ft anchor, upright and leaning against a chalk ridge. It was close to this anchor that two swivel guns were found. One is now in Newhaven Museum. The other, which was raised by Doug Barnard of Billingshurst, underwent conservation treatment at the *Mary Rose* laboratories.

To the north-west of the anchor is an area of lead shot. There are thousands of musket shot and garland shot here. Garland shot was made up of pellets of lead

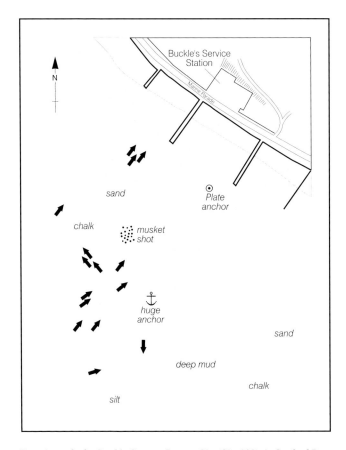

Transit marks for Buckle Garage Cannon Site (Site 232), in Seaford Bay.

shot, each piece having a hole to allow it to be threaded on to copper wire and wound round a shaped wooden block. When fired, the wood fell behind, and the wire unwound and finally snapped, leaving a swathe of musket shot to cut through rigging and men, 500 or 1,000 shot at a time. Here are the holed shot and the copper wire. Though garland shot was usually fired out of 24-and 32-pounders and upward, the cannon here, 14 in all, are 6-and 12-pounders. One cannon was raised from the site in August 1989.

These cannon may be from the *Harlequin* (Site **231**). But if so, they are lying on an even older site, for among these gullies have been found bronze dividers dating from 1630 and Dutch silver coins from 1720. These artefacts can now be seen at the National Maritime Museum at Greenwich.

All in all, this site is extremely confusing, as marks on the swivel guns are Portuguese from the early 1400s.

233 The Plate Anchor This has not yet reappeared. It is made of very old iron, and is circular with a 4ft diameter. It is not more than 60yds offshore (at mean low water), and about 75ft to the west of a line drawn straight out from the first groyne past the Buckle garage to the east.

The "anchor" is made of inch-thick iron with a 4-inch by ¾-inch thick band going round the outside edge. In the centre is something like a big washer with five to six rivets in it and a swivel for a big ring. The ironwork seems completely smooth underneath. It is too heavy for divers to move without lifting bags.

234 Margharita On 19 September, 1894, a blazing ship came ashore close to the Buckle Inn on the Marine Parade. She was the French steam trawler *Margharita*, which had been fishing within the 3-mile limit when she was spotted by the local revenue cutter, which gave chase. In the scurry of getting under way on the French ship, someone knocked over a lamp. This started a fire that spread swiftly. The crew took to their boat and rowed to shore opposite the Esplanade Hotel. The *Margharita* burned out and sank.

235 Peruvian This sailing barque was bound for Hamburg from Esmeraldas in Ecuador with a cargo of ivory nuts (the seeds of a South American palm), and logwood. She was heading up the Channel when a south-westerly gale drove her on shore close to the front of the Esplanade Hotel on the morning of 8 February, 1899.

The first rocket lines from the Coastguards were blown wide, so strong was the wind, and the Newhaven lifeboat, the *Michael Henry*, was almost blown across the

Crowds start to gather as the Peruvian (Site 235) begins to break up off Seaford in February 1899.

bay. Eventually, the lifeboat worked in between the wreck and the shore and brought off nine men. After these men had been landed at Newhaven, it returned to the wreck for the rest of the crew.

In the meantime, the rocket team had managed to drift a line across the *Peruvian* and hauled the two remaining crew through the surf. One got safely ashore, but the second had no sooner climbed out of the breeches buoy than a huge wave knocked him over and he was washed back into the foam and lost.

The *Peruvian* was a steel-hulled ship and appeared to be little damaged by the time the wind dropped. Work was started on unloading her, before trying to pull her off, but three days later the wind came back even stronger than before and the ship began to break up. High tide was at 10pm that night, and the waves broke right over her and the friction of her broken steel plating caused sparks to fly high in the air. A large crowd watched, and by the morning all that was left of her was wreckage on the beach.

For years after the wreck the ivory nuts of her cargo were washed up on the beach and local craftsmen carved scenes showing the wreck on their hard white interior. Some of these carved nuts can be seen in the museum at the Martello Tower.

The *Peruvian*'s main wreckage, mostly steel plates, could be found offshore in less than 10m off the steps a little way to the west of the Esplanade Hotel. Before the beach works, a group of divers raised one of her catheads with a fine metal lion's head decoration on it. This large piece of wreckage is now in the museum too.

To help you locate her grave, the Esplanade Hotel is now just a gap in the row of buildings along the front. The hotel stood at the top left-hand corner of The Causeway as you approach the sea.

236 The Union This big American sailing ship came ashore in 1872 off the Salts Recreation Ground, which is at the back of Marine Parade, Seaford. The ship is remembered more for her cargo than anything else, so presumably the crew were saved. Her cargo was tins of pineapple, sewing machines (parts of which are sometimes uncovered in shallow water after storms), and barrels of lamp-black. These barrels burst when she broke up, and the blacking was whirled on the wind and turned a whole flock of sheep black in seconds.

237 Gannet This 1,824-ton steamship did not intend to put into Seaford. She was bound for London from Calcutta, and Captain White had set down his passengers at Southampton. His cargo of tea, coffee, wheat, linseed, cotton, indigo, hides, stags' horns and wood, however, had stayed with the ship as she made her way on towards the London docks.

The day of 14 February, 1882, started badly. A cloud of misty rain cut visibility down to a matter of feet, and the *Gannet* was blinded and lost. She ran right onshore just to the west of Martello Tower, and as the surf made it impossible to launch boats the crew were taken off by breeches buoy.

As soon as the weather calmed there were several attempts to float the *Gannet*, but the shingle had banked up around her and even four powerful tugs could not move her. The next move was to get the cargo out of her. To do this a wooden bridge was built from sea wall to ship, and railway lines were laid across it for "French Wagons", or trolleys, to run on. Once a piece of cargo came ashore it was

The Gannet (Site 237) ran aground near the Martello Tower at Seaford in 1882. Most of her cargo was recovered before she broke up in a gale.

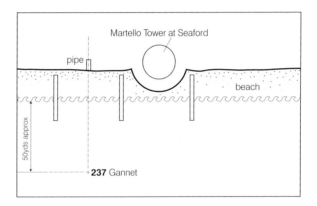

Transit marks for the Gannet (Site 237), off Seaford.

taken by farm carts to the station. Most of the cargo was out of her three weeks later when a great gale came out of the south-west and smashed her to pieces.

Today, you may be able to find the *Gannet* at 50 46 00N; 00 06 20E spread over an area of 150 square yards. The wreckage is mostly the steel plates from her 302ft hull. To find the wreckage, you must first find the large drain in the sea wall mid-way between the two groynes just to the west of the Martello Tower. A swim of about 50yds in a direct line from this drain-hole will put you in the area of the bow.

238 Sagatun This Norwegian barque was bound for Newhaven with a load of timber and arrived off the port on the morning of 24 September, 1900. However, an onshore gale made entrance impossible. The *Sagatun* anchored in the bay and prepared to ride it out. For two days she did so, but in the afternoon of 26 September she broke from her anchors and drove hard for the shore. She struck almost exactly halfway between the Martello Tower and Seaford Head, and quickly became a total loss. The Captain, his 15-year-old daughter and the crew of nine were taken off by breeches buoy after the rocket team had put a line over her.

239 The Mary Davis and the Ehren Christmas Eve, 1888 saw yet another boat smashed to pieces on the shore near the Martello Tower. The *Mary Davis* was a small schooner loaded with Portland stone. She tried for Newhaven Harbour during an onshore gale, but began leaking so badly that the captain decided to run her ashore, which he did between the Martello Tower and Seaford Head. The rocket team were soon on the job and all the crew were saved. The Seaford fox-hounds were out on the hill and the huntsmen were able to give the rescued crew the contents of their flasks. The sailors must have welcomed this; they were described at the time as "having had a rough time". The *Mary Davis* was matchwood only ¾ hour after she first struck, but some of her cargo of stone was later used in the building of the Surrey Convalescent Home at Blatchington.

The *Ehren*, another small schooner, did the same thing exactly a year later in almost identical circumstances to those of the *Mary Davis* – onshore gale, rocket rescue of all crew, breaking up shortly afterwards. The location was also the same.

The crew of the Sagatun (Site 238) were saved when it foundered off Seaford in 1900.

240 The Bronze Age wreck This wreck may be from the Bronze Age. Bromley BSAC have been searching under Seaford Head and close to the sewer exit for more evidence of a Bronze Age wreck to add to the two axe-heads they have found so far.

If there is such a wreck at Seaford, it would not be surprising because at one time the River Ouse formed a large, shallow lagoon behind the huge shingle banks that blocked its direct access to the sea. These banks turned it parallel along the coast until it finally made its escape at Splash Point under the towering heights of Seaford Head. On the other hand, the Bromley finds may have come from the ancient settlement on the Head where Caesar's Roman legions camped later.

241 The Colossal Cannon Right at the east end of the bay, past the Martello Tower and on past the sewage pipe, there is a little beach with a small arm and sea defence blocks. Here there is a wooden groyne. Swim down this, and 15yds off it is a very large cannon. It is over 9ft long, the touch-hole can be clearly seen, and the muzzle appears to be broken off. Is this a cannon from the Martello Tower defences? Or evidence of another shipwreck?

242 Lead Ballast Gully 50 44 24N; 00 12 12E. After coming down the steps from Birling Gap car park, stagger or swim 300yds east towards Beachy Head (Site **258**). Here, even at low water, there are 3m of water in the deep gullies – like all those along this stretch, these are floored with a mixture of sand and mud and are often visited by roving bass. In some of these gullies are 6-inch by 6-inch timbers with 3ft moulded blocks of lead ballast. These lead slabs have cut-outs in the edges for keel timbers and ribs. It is clear that these are part of a shipwreck.

Boat diving sites

243 Brazen This Royal Navy sloop of 18 guns and 363 tons was lost with all hands except one on 26 January, 1800. Part of her wreckage was located in 1984 after many fruitless searches for her in previous years, though no positive identification has yet been made.

Brazen was under the command of Captain James Hanson. Not that he had commanded her for long, for the ship was formerly the French privateer *Bonaparte*, which was taken by the Navy's *Boadicea* on 9 December, 1798, and renamed and refitted in Portsmouth in April 1799.

Jeremiah Hill, the man who was soon to be the only survivor of the wreck of the *Brazen*, was drafted into the ship from the frigate *Carysfort*. He was one of the last men to be put aboard, and on 16 January, 1800, the *Brazen* sailed for Channel patrol duties and was immediately despatched towards Newhaven to deal with some "insolent attacks" by marauding French vessels.

The *Brazen* was small – 105ft long with a 28ft beam – was flush-decked, and only 14ft deep. But even so, 106 men were crammed aboard and lived in extreme discomfort. The only thing to offset such misery was the fact that it was ships like the *Brazen*, fast and free-ranging, that gave the crew a good chance of prize money. On 24 January she captured a French merchantman and sent her to Portsmouth with a prize crew.

The sloop Brazen (Site 243) was lost in 1800.
This painting by Ted Shipsey show her under sail.

On the night of 25 January, Jeremiah Hill came on watch at 10pm during a period of strong winds and heavy rain. Now the wind built to a full gale from the south-west, and though Hill was relieved at 2am, it is a sure sign of what conditions were like below that he did not go down to his hammock until 4am. At five in the morning, a rending crash sent him racing up on deck with his jacket and "trowsers" in his hands. He had no time to put them on and was, within moments, part of a team under the carpenter cutting the weather shrouds to let the main and mizzen masts go by the board. This had little effect, and soon the ship was right on her side. Hill got to the stump of the mainmast and hung on desperately.

Meanwhile, on land, the stricken vessel had been spotted, and two extraordinary machines were being pulled by horses close to the edge of the cliffs. These rescue machines had been made for just this sort of emergency. An arm of wood could be swung out over the sheer drop, and from a rope through a pulley-wheel a wooden cage could be lowered down to the shore. As soon as it was ready, two men from the rescue team stepped into the cage and were lowered down to that part of the shore not yet covered by sea.

On seeing this, two officers on the *Brazen*, both strong swimmers, left the wreck and struck out the ½ mile to the shore. They did not make it. Another man tried and got close to the cage, but drowned before he could be grabbed by the men in it.

Despite this, Jeremiah Hill, a non-swimmer, launched himself towards the shore on one of the sliding carriages of the ship's carronades, which had drifted close to his perch. This solid block of wood carried him right in to shore where he was grabbed by the men in the cage and dragged inside. It was only when Jeremiah could finally speak that they knew the name of the ship, which soon broke up. The stern with two of the guns was carried on to the shore, and timber was washed up on the other side of the harbour.

Ninety-five bodies were recovered and buried in the churchyard of St Michael's, the parish church of Newhaven. A large monument was placed on the spot, and you can still see it there today with lists of the officers' names and details of the wreck.

Documents of the time describe the wreck as being on the Ave Rocks or Westmiss Rocks, and a great part of divers' difficulty in finding the wreck site has been owing to the fact that no chart appears to list these names; nor can the Navy Hydrographic Department find any record of them. However, recent diving on the rocks off Old Nore Point, which is the first point to the west of Newhaven Harbour breakwater where a reef called the Fricker, Friggle or Frigger Rocks (all spellings appear on maps) sticks up from the sea bed, has produced some results.

Discoveries so far include a short bronze pin bearing the Admiralty's broad-arrow mark, a sword blade, a 5ft anchor, a 20ft section of mast, massive timbers 17ft by 2ft and a cast-iron 4ft swivel gun.

There is so far no positive identification of this site, which is heavily silted, as that of the *Brazen*. It might just be that of the *Dragon* (Site **207**).

WARNING Divers report nets for sole and plaice being laid in this area.

244 HMS Ocean Sunlight 50 46 09N; 00 04 04E. Built in 1929, this 131-ton drifter was requisitioned by the Admiralty for service in the World War Two, but did not last long, being sunk by a mine on 13 June, 1940. She sank within 800yds of the end of Newhaven Harbour arm and was dispersed by explosives in 1959 – so enthusiastically that this clearance was stopped because of the damage being done ashore!

She is now very broken up in 10m of water. The wreckage is in three main parts. The bow section is on a bearing of 141° 800yds from Newhaven Light, the midships is 20yds away on a bearing of 139.5° and the stern is 120yds away on a bearing of 137.5°. Little of it stands more than 2m above the sea bed, and it is a very silty dive.

245 Leven This 775-ton dredger was mined on 15 February, 1917, at 50 46 03N; 00 04 08E. She was 185ft long with a beam of 39ft, but there is little left of her now because she was so close to the wreck of the *Ocean Sunlight* (Site **244**) that the over-liberal use of explosives in that dispersal also blew the dredger wreck to pieces. The wreck lies in 10m of water, and is very spread out.

246 Saint Ronaig 50 45 51N; 00 04 45E. This British MV of 509 tons was, like *Ocean Sunlight* (Site **244**), a victim of a mine in June 1940. The *Saint Ronaig*, 167ft long, was sunk on 11 June and was dispersed with explosives in 1959 until the locals complained about the damage the explosions were causing ashore. Her remains now stand only 1m high. She lies a mile offshore on a bearing of 75° 30' from the Martello Tower on the front at Seaford.

247 Jean B A small fishing vessel at 50 45 36N; 00 04 12E. The *Jean B* sank on 3 June, 1976, in 13m of water after a collision with another fishing vessel, the *Escallonia*. All the crew were rescued. The vessel is broken up.

248 Venus This one too is very broken. She lies at 50 45 27N; 00 05 30E. A British MFV of 22 tons, the *Venus* was 44ft long, and now lies in 12m of water where she sank while under tow on 27 May, 1981, after taking in water. All the crew were rescued.

249 Seaford Head This area is mainly interesting to the diver for the gullies that continue all along the coast to Beachy Head (Site **258**). Starting at 50 45 18N; 00 06 48E, the gullies are similar all along the coast to the east. Close in to the towering white cliffs they are usually about 2 to 3m deep and the same distance wide. With walls that are of chalk and floors of mud or sand, they wind along as though training to be canyons when they grow up. Black patches of mud are common. Close to the head there are extensive mussel beds. Some ancient cannon are present and very old wooden timbers appear to have grown into the walls of the gullies. There are lobster too, as well as crabs and many big plaice. Large turbot have been seen. The gullies tend to peter out as they move seaward onto a bed of soft sand mud, where Dover sole are often found in summer.

Almost off the Head – less than a mile away – there have been a number of finds of 4.7-inch brass shellcases, some bearing the date 1941. The cases (no shells are present) have not been fired. The number of these discoveries – they stand out like bright green logs on a drab brown sea bed – suggests a wreck in the vicinity, possibly that of an ammunition barge. So far, however, there has been no positive identification or position for it.

250 The Amphora Site While diving between Hawks Brow and Yellow Falls and almost opposite the ancient settlement site on Seaford Head, John White of Holborn BSAC found the neck of an amphora on the top of one of the gullies that run out to sea from the chalk cliffs. He was in 11m of water. The piece of amphora was later dated as from the first or second century AD, and probably came from Spain. A later search of the area in 1970 produced a holed stone, the holes made by a stone-headed bow drill. This was possibly an ancient anchor.

A similar stone was found in July 1975, by the then Diving Officer of Thurrock BSAC, Terry Mitchell, in exactly the same area. At first he feared it was a bomb, so encrusted was it. His drawing of the stone is almost identical with those stones found by the author in the Mixon Hole, though these had no holes through them (*see* Site **17**).

More recently another piece of amphora has been found off the Head.

251 Landing craft One of the pre-invasion casualties, this LCM is nearly completely buried. It lies 1 mile directly out from the Buckle Inn (when you can just see right up the river, you are over the wreck). Beware of the harbour traffic.

252 Polynesia This German steamer went aground just to the west of Beachy Head (Site **258**) on 24 April, 1890. She was towed off, but as she was taking in water fast she was beached at Cuckmere, where part of her cargo of fertilisers was off-loaded. Before the operation could be completed, a gale sprang up and she became a total wreck.

It is likely that the area of obstructions charted at 50 45 16N; 00 09 06E have something to do with this wreck. A steel mast at 50 45 08N; 00 08 51E may well be part of the *Polynesia* too. Her boilers are in less than 10m to the east of the Haven.

NOTE The area of obstructions noted above as the *Polynesia* was said, in years past, to be the remains of a submarine.

253 Coonatto

In a little cove to the west of Flagstaff Point under a monument marking the gift of the land to the National Trust lies the remains of this famous wool clipper. The *Coonatto* ran ashore just before dawn on 21 February, 1876, homeward-bound from Australia.

The *Coonatto* was 633 tons, 166ft long with a beam of 46ft, and was built in London by Thomas Bilbe in 1863. She was named after an Australian township and made over a dozen fast runs before being wrecked while in the ownership of the Orient Line.

Her last voyage began on 14 November, 1875, when she sailed from Adelaide laden with wool and copper ingots. At 2.20pm on 19 February, 1876, she was recorded as passing the Lizard under the command of Captain John Eilbeck Hillman, a Londoner who got his master's ticket in 1868. At 4.15am on 21 February she was ashore at "Crowlink" – on the rocks in a strong onshore wind.

Though salvage continued until the end of March and most of the valuable cargo was recovered, the *Coonatto* was totally broken. All her crew, however, were safe and walked ashore one low tide. Captain Hillman's master's certificate was suspended for three months and there was much talk, none of it proven, that she had been run ashore for the insurance. Hillman went back to sea as Master of the *Inch Kenneth*, but died when she foundered in October 1877.

Today, the remains of the *Coonatto* lie in less than 2m of water, and she is owned by Mr John Wareing of Seaford. She can be approached at low spring tides by walking along the cliffs to the west from Crowlink Gap, but the descent to the water can be tricky. The best position to look at her is from the sea. She is lying with her bows to the south-east and her remains stretch back for 100ft towards the cliffs where some teak still stands up 1m or so clear. Some iron-work can still be seen on the starboard side as well as some planking.

254 Devon Coast

Known locally as "the Stone Boat" because her cargo of cement has become just that, this three-masted British steamer of 668 tons was going from Swanscombe to Liverpool when she was in collision with the *Jeanie*, another steamer, from Cardiff, 5 miles south-south-east of Newhaven on 4 November, 1908. The *Devon Coast* came off worst, and the *Jeanie* took her in tow and headed for Newhaven. But she sank at 50 44 25N; 00 08 50E, directly off Cuckmere Haven.

The wreck was finally identified as the *Devon Coast* by the builder's plate, which was recovered by a diver in 1981. Today, she is well broken up and sunk into the mud-sand sea bed so that she is less than 2m proud of the bed at 15m. In her prime, she was 200ft long with a beam of 29ft. Her winches can still be seen. When she was built in 1909 by Harness on the Tees she had two holds, four winches, and six derricks.

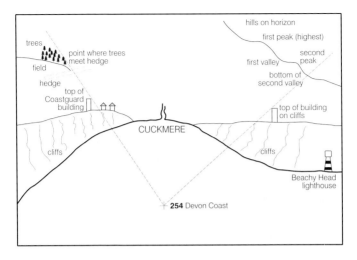

Transit marks for the Devon Coast (Site 254).

255 The "Big Ship" Most wreckage off Seaford Beach is a complete tangle, with items from one wreck intertwined with those from another. But there is a group of items that must have come from a very big ship indeed. In line with the last groyne to the east of the Martello Tower straight out until you can just see the first two of the Seven Sisters, there is an enormous anchor, called perversely by local divers "the Roman Anchor". It has a 12ft shaft, and a ring on the end about 2ft in diameter. One of the huge iron flukes is well-buried in the sea bed. It looks large enough to hold something the size of HMS *Victory*.

An anchor can, of course, be lost without losing a ship. However, in line with the groyne and slightly closer in are huge pieces of oak with 2½-inch diameter bronze pins, some of which are 5ft long. Elm deadeyes in the area have iron banding round them, and they too compare well for size with those on HMS *Victory*. There are cannon there too. So far three 32-pounders and two 24-pounders have been found, as well as a very long bow-chaser like those on frigates used for ranging shots.

As if this were not enough evidence of a big wreck, offshore (so you just cannot quite see the Seven Sisters) and slightly to the east of the last groyne between the Martello Tower and Seaford Head is an enormous yard, 128ft long and so fat that divers can only just get their arms around it. On each end are lignum vitae wheels 5 inches in diameter for ropes about ½-inch thick, used to swivel the yards. This, together with other big timber-work, lies at the foot of a big gully running out to sea and half-covered with silt.

NOTE Divers who find enormous cannonballs off Seaford should not get too excited. Halfway between the Martello Tower and the Buckle were two 68-pounder gun emplacements. They never fired a shot in anger, but obviously they did practise and as a result that size of shot has been found less than a mile offshore by divers.

256 The Nympha Americana and the Mercury Pool This is one of the earliest recorded wrecks in the area, but *Nympha Americana* is not this vessel's real name at all. She was, in fact, *La Nuestra Señora de los Remedios*, and she came ashore at 11pm on 29 November, 1747. The place where she struck was said to be Crowlink Gap, the fourth dip in the line of the Seven Sisters between Cuckmere Haven and Birling Gap.

Built in 1730 in South America, she was a 400-ton ship, carrying 23 large cannon and six small swivels. But even with that armament her crew of 280 put up no resistance when stopped by British privateers under the command of Commodore George Walker off Cadiz in March 1747. For some reason it was when the ship was escorted into the port of Lisbon that she began to be called *Nympha Americana*. Once in Lisbon, the British privateers discovered the full extent of the riches of their prize. She carried a cargo of silks and velvets, barrels of oil, brandy, wine and lemon juice – all bound for Veracruz in Mexico from her home port of Cadiz. But that was nothing compared with what lay deep in her holds: £40,000 worth of quicksilver – better known today as mercury and wanted by the Mexican mints to refine silver. It was a very valuable cargo indeed, and Commodore Walker decided to send it and the *Nympha Americana* home with a prize crew as part of a convoy to Portsmouth.

The convoy made good time to Portsmouth, stayed there three days, then set out on the final leg to London where the ship and the mercury were to be sold by auction. The convoy hugged the coast, but on the first night a gale sprang up from the south. In the darkness and snow flurries, the *Nympha Americana* lost the convoy, but thinking she had raced ahead of their shortened sail, she slowed down to let them catch up. In fact, the convoy was ahead of her and her waiting game had taken her far too close inshore.

Through the murk, the lookouts could suddenly see the great white faces of the Seven Sisters, and down went her anchors. But it was too late. The wind drove her hard, and the ship struck the low reefs just offshore of the cliffs. So great was her speed that, with her high stern acting as a sail, she carried on going even after her whole bottom was ripped off. Finally the upper part of her hull came to rest near the base of the cliffs and above the low-tide mark.

At this moment, all 150 men of the prize crew were safe; but soon the pounding waves broke her in half amidships and those in the bow section were flung into the sea as it overturned. Thirty men drowned.

By dawn the news was well and truly out and people from miles around raced to share in the shipwreck spoils. As the news spread the few became hundreds, and by noon there were thousands on the beach fighting over the wreck and her cargo. Troops were called in and the *Sussex Weekly Advertiser* of 7 December, 1747, reported: "Never was known such a multitude of people at a wreck before, many of whom were drinking too plentifully of a Cask of Very Strong Brandy, which they found on the beach, were intoxicated and afterwards perished by Death. While numbers of others loaded themselves and some of their horses with goods that were thrown up by the tide from the said Wreck tho' there is a party of soldiers sent to prevent so Abominable a practice and notwithstanding they have shot one Man dead, yet People will continue to venture."

It took all the soldiers in Sussex to restore order, and then all attention turned to the salvage of the most important part of the cargo, the mercury. It appears to have been in earthenware jars packed into chests, and some of these were

146

The Nympha Americana (Site 256) is one of the earliest recorded wrecks off the Sussex coast. There was much looting and loss of life when this ship was wrecked in 1747.

fished out at the next low tide, some more by boats with hooks from the place where her bottom was ripped out. But most of it they could not reach.

The *Sussex Weekly Advertiser* reported in January: "There is a Great Quantity lies in deeper water and cannot be got without a diver, for which Reason there is one come down from London, who purposes to undertake it by the ton weight." It seems he kept his boast, for in the issue of 1 February, the paper reported: "This last Tide we have been very lucky to take up a great many chests of Quicksilver to the great Joy and Satisfaction for the Worthy Gentleman, Owners and Insurers." By the end of April 1748, all salvage finished, and by then they had recovered mercury worth £31,210. But we know that was not all of it!

Some say it was in 1972, but the author believes that it was, in fact, in 1974, that a small group of divers were working along the gullies under Brass Point looking for plaice. One of the divers spotted a big one and stabbed it with his hand-spear. To his surprise, the fish disappeared under the sand in a silvery splash and, as he plunged his hand down after it, he found that trapped in the gully was a pool of mercury!

One might dismiss this as just another diver's tale were it not for the details of what followed. The divers who found the mercury puzzled over how they could raise it and finally came up with a real brainwave. Making sure that they could return to the exact spot, they hurried off to Newhaven and bought up one shop's entire stock of rubber hot water bottles. Apparently they filled 20 of these from the mercury pool, then sold them for £250 each!

Is it true? The basic story probably is, especially as you can see a jam jar half full of mercury in the Local History Museum in the Martello Tower at Seaford. Is that the last of the mercury from the *Nympha Americana*? Probably not – that is why divers should keep their eyes very much open when diving in that area!

257 Anna Amelia This Swedish galliot going from Bordeaux to Lubeck with a cargo of wine was a total wreck at Birling Gap on 16 May, 1796. The captain was Gottfried Vocking, and he could do nothing to prevent the looting of his cargo – in which even troops from Eastbourne Barracks took part. The wreckage of this ship may be in a gully to the east of Birling Gap (*see* Site **242**).

258 Beachy Head An awesome sight looking down or up, this 534ft chalk headland has the remains of its old lighthouse on the cliff 1½ miles to the west. It was known as "Belle Toute". During 1998 it was being slid back from the cliff edge on hydraulic jacks, to save it from falling into the sea.

The present Beachy Head lighthouse is down on the rocks at the foot of the head. It is 142ft high, and clearly marked with a big red band to make it stand out against the chalk background when viewed from out at sea.

WARNING Though the gullies close in are very full of marine life, divers should take great care when in this area. Tidal currents around the Head are tricky and strong.

259 Wreck, name unknown 50 41 54N; 00 14 14E. This wreck has been located on echo-sounder; it lies in a general depth of 23m and stands 6m proud. Diving details are needed.

260 Obstruction, identity unknown 50 42 39N; 00 10 32E. All we know is that this is a 69ft metallic lump on the sea bed in 21m and standing only 2m proud of it. There is another small metal object 100yds to the west.

261 Millgate Though no positive identification of this wreck has been made, it seems likely that it is the *Millgate* of Manchester, which completely capsized and foundered in a south-westerly gale on 2 November, 1905, when 4 miles from Newhaven at 50 42 19N; 00 09 55E.

The Newhaven lifeboat found the *Millgate* in huge seas with a severe list to port, her cargo having shifted. After standing by for ½ hour, the lifeboat coxswain sensed that the list was getting worse and moved in to take off the 10 people on board. Fifty minutes later the steamer turned completely over and sank.

Today the wreck is in 22m, lies with her bows to the south-east, is 130ft long, and it is clear that her cargo was cement. She is badly rusted and holed. The stern, at 4m, is the highest point. She is upright, though the sand is spreading over her.

262 Wreck, name unknown This small ship – 92ft long with beam of 38ft – is often called the *"Celtic"* by local fishermen. That, however, is not her identity (*see* Site **263**). She is partly buried in the mud in 21m and is broken up. There is a mast lying alongside her at 50 44 07N; 00 03 49E. Her boiler and steam engine remain proud and their type and the recovery of parts of a candle-lit semaphore lamp suggest a World War One casualty.

263 Celtic This Belgian trawler sank while under tow at 50 43 36N; 00 04 03E on 9 April, 1958. The crew of four were rescued by Newhaven lifeboat. She is now very broken up in 23m and many of the pieces left after both salvage and clearing operations are now buried in the sandy sea bed.

264 T.R. Thompson Another victim of Oberleutnant Lohs of *UB-57*, who sank her without warning on 29 March 1918, at 50 40 10N; 00 05 38E with one torpedo at 3.50am. So swift was her sinking that the master and 32 of her crew went down with her. Only three men were saved.

The 3,538-ton *T.R. Thompson* was 360ft long with a beam of 47ft, and was armed with a 4.7-inch gun on her stern. At the time of her sinking she was carrying 5,600 tons of iron ore from Algeria to Middlesbrough.

The *T.R. Thompson* now lies in 30m of water with her bows to the east and partially buried. Her superstructure has collapsed, and the highest point is the stern, which is 14m proud. Shell cases lie in an overturned box by the gun. She is upright with a bad break almost halfway along her length. Her bell, weighing nearly a hundredweight, was recovered by Bromley BSAC in September 1989.

265 Mira This 3,700-ton early British oil tanker, which was built in 1901, was sunk by a mine laid by *UC-50* on 11 October, 1917. She was fully loaded with 5,226 tons of fuel from Port Arthur, Texas, for Dover. The mine exploded at 12.25pm on her starboard side just forward of the bridge and released oil at once, but there was no fire and none of her crew were seriously hurt.

However, the *Mira* was badly holed and her steering gear was jammed, so she went round in wide circles as she sank. After Captain John Davies managed to stop the engines, one of the convoy escorts, HMS *P-45*, took the tanker in tow but soon had to slip the towing hawser and let her sink at 1.15pm, starboard side first.

The *Mira* is at 50 41 11N; 00 08 24E, and is easy to locate because of the large "boil" over the wreck site. She is on her starboard side, and so much on her beam-ends that the deck is vertical. Sand waves on the sea bed at 30m are building up around her, and the hull seems to be cut completely through about one third of her length from the bow, which is pointing to the north-east. She was 345ft long with a beam of 47ft.

WARNING The *Mira* is apparently so corroded that parts are extremely shaky and dangerous. The large holes in the side-plating have razor-sharp edges. Take care.

Transit marks for the Mira (Site 265), off Beachy Head.

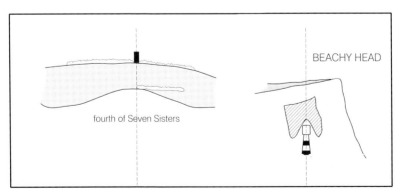

BEACHY HEAD

fourth of Seven Sisters

266 E-Boat Or so they say. This "unknown" at 50 40 28N; 00 09 45E has had both naval and civilian divers on it and the argument about whether it is an E-boat or not still rages. She is 51ft long with a beam of 26ft, lies north-east to south-west, and is metal. That much we do know. The most recent divers on her say that this was a collection of pipes in a girder-like construction in 27m. More diving information is needed.

267 Wreck, name unknown She lies in 30m at 50 39 00N; 00 07 48E, but is not charted, so the position must be regarded as approximate.

268 Ashford This 1,211-ton British steamer was registered in Sunderland. She is now at 50 39 44N; 00 11 25E, lying north-east to south-west and upside down. The highest point of the hull is 6m proud of the bottom at 30m. There is a badly-damaged area near the cast-iron propeller. This might suggest that she was a mine victim, but in fact the *Ashford* collided with the German barque, *Pirat*, of Hamburg, on 25 June, 1906. The *Ashford* was going from Seaham to St Nazaire with a cargo of coal. After the collision she was taken in tow by the tug *Dominion*, but sank 2 hours later. The *Pirat* got safely to Hamburg where she had her bow and 40 plates replaced.

269 Wreck, name unknown 50 39 35N; 00 12 50E. This is the wreck of a very battered ship. She lies on a soft silt sea bed with her bows towards the south-south-west, and salvage experts estimate her to have been about 2,500 tons. Her bow is twisted almost off and lies on its starboard side about 6m proud of the sea bed at 29m. The midships is a mess; the stern is the highest point at 8m.

270 Blanefield This vessel is the centre of a confusing cluster of wrecks, but diver Michael Keane has finally confirmed that the ship at 50 40 24N; 00 14 42E is the *Blanefield* by raising her 84lb 15-inch-diameter bell. He was lifting a large crab out of a hole under one of the ship's fallen steel plates near the bow and found that the crab had been sitting in the bell!

The *Blanefield* which was chartered by the Government to carry supplies to Cape Town for the Boer War, was built in 1898 for the Seafield Shipping Company of London by Short Brothers of Sunderland. The 3,411-ton ship was intended for the nitrates trade. She was 352ft long with a beam of 45ft and draught of 17ft, and her three-cylinder engine with twin boilers could produce 313hp to give her a top speed of 10 knots.

She was carrying a cargo of sodium nitrate from South America to Dover on 1 May, 1906, when she was in collision with the big four-masted steel barque *Kate Thomas*, homeward bound down the Channel for Liverpool, and running before a north-easterly Force 4. The steamer sank swiftly, killing six men out of her crew of 29. She settled upright on the sea bed in 28m with her deck some 17m below the surface. Her masts stuck up out of the water at all states of the tide. The *Kate Thomas*, despite heavy bow damage, managed to reach port. She was later repaired and finally sank in another collision in April 1910.

Salvage divers were soon put down on the *Blanefield*, but they reported that she was so badly damaged on her port side that there was no chance of raising her. When her masts finally collapsed, she was forgotten.

Today the triple expansion steam engine is the highest point, 6m proud of the 30m sand and gravel sea bed. The third cylinder, measuring some 5½ft across, is a fine sight. The wreck stands 2m high with a 3m scour around the stern itself. Ahead of the engine the collision damage brings the wreckage level with the sea bed then it rises again to 4 to 5m at the bow, whose starboard side is collapsed. It was on this side of the bow that the bell was found.

There is another wreck, inside the *Blanefield*, said to be so close that you can swim from one to the other. This is probably the wreck visited by divers from HMS *Bronington*, Prince Charles's first Naval command, in May 1976. They then described her as a small coaster some 100ft long, lying north-south in 28m. She was in two halves, upright but in poor condition with her superstructure collapsed. Her cargo appeared to be railway lines and sleepers.

Local fishermen call this wreck the *Adventurine*, but they may be confusing this with the *Avanturine*, an Admiralty requisitioned trawler of 296 tons built in 1930 and sunk by E-boats "off Beachy Head" on 1 December, 1943.

There is yet another wreck close by, also in two halves, but partially buried in the sandy gravel. The boiler is the highest at 6m proud. This one is sometimes referred to as the *Mid Surrey*, but the steamer of that name, built in 1870, is reported as sinking off North Foreland following a double collision, first with lighters and then a tug, in August 1908.

271 Wreck, name unknown 50 37 53N; 00 13 16E. This is a ship of about 120ft lying almost north–south in 37m on a flat sand sea bed. It has not, to my knowledge, been dived.

272 Nyon This Swiss motorship of 5,364 tons now lies at 50 38 04N; 00 12 22E in 43m of water following a collision with the Indian ship *Jalazad* of 6,199 tons on 15 June, 1962.

But she is not half the ship she used to be! For the *Nyon* ran aground off St Abb's Head in Scotland in November 1958, was badly holed, and was stuck so fast that tugs could not haul her off. So the salvors cut her in half and pulled free the important stern section containing all the valuable machinery. This was then towed to Rotterdam, where a new bow section was built on to her. In July 1959, the *Nyon* was back in service. In 1962 she was on her way from Antwerp to Montreal with a cargo of cars and 7,000 tons of high grade steel when the collision took place.

Now she lies east–west, with her bows to the west on a sea bed of soft sand. She is well broken, but her bridge is still her highest point at 14m. Her bow is 10m off the sea bed. Not only is she deep, but even more care than usual should be taken as the *Nyon* lies in a trawling ground and is festooned with nets.

273 Braunton This 4,575-ton British merchantman was torpedoed by *UB-29* at 50 38 54N; 00 10 45E on 7 April, 1916, while on the last leg (to Newport from Boulogne) of a long voyage with a cargo of 1,800 tons of shells and shell cases. Her cargo had been loaded in Halifax, Nova Scotia. All the crew were saved, but the 380ft ship with her five holds crammed with ammunition sank stern first to a sandy sea bed 30m down.

Today the *Braunton* lies with her bow and stern intact, but listing about 60° on her port side. In 1983 there were still thousands of shells and shell cases in her

The Nyon ran aground off St Abb's Head in Berwickshire in 1958, as this picture shows. The stern section was saved, and the Nyon was rebuilt. In 1962 she sank off Beachy Head following a collision (Site 272).

holds, but salvage work since has obviously spread some of that deadly cargo out on to the sea bed around her. She lies with her bows to the west, but the highest point of the wreck is her stern, which stands some 13m proud.

274 George Sutton This 105ft steel brigantine sailed from Newcastle for Cork on 27 August, 1883, with a cargo of coal, and was never seen again – until dive-boat skipper Tim Bennetto found her at 50 38 33N; 00 09 17E. The transverse deck beams are still in place and the clipper bow is a fine sight. She is mostly intact and upright at 33m. Tim Bennetto confirmed her identity by finding her name engraved on the hub of her wheel together with the launch date of 1 May, 1866. She had been repaired after springing a leak before she sailed, but there is no evidence of what happened to her. Her crew were all lost when she disappeared.

275 HMS Keryado 50 38 34N; 00 07 43E. This 1920-built, Admiralty-requisitioned trawler was sunk by a mine on 6 March, 1941. HMS *Keryado* was originally a French minesweeper before being taken over by the Navy on 5 July, 1940. Her 252-ton hull is now very broken up in 35m, and she is becoming buried. She lies north–south.

276 Inger This Swedish steamer was carrying a cargo of Welsh coal from Swansea to Sundsvall on 31 May, 1930, when she collided with the Italian steamer *Literno* 6 miles south-west of Beachy Head (Site **258**) at 50 39 07N; 00 07 47E. It seems likely that the *Literno* hit the *Inger* on the starboard bow judging by the damage seen there by divers who have visited this intact ship on the sea bed at 35m, from which she stands up some 12m. Her bridge is amidships, and there are two holds on either side of it containing the coal. She has an iron four-bladed propeller with a spare stowed in the aft hold. Highest points are the winches on the bow, which points to the east.

AREA 7:

Eastbourne to St Leonards

This area runs from 00 15 00 E to 00 32 00 E, and includes Eastbourne, Pevensey, Norman's Bay, Bexhill and St Leonards. It is not an easy area to dive because of a shortage of dive boats. However, some fishermen are now prepared to take divers out instead of angling parties. Fishing boats at Eastbourne are kept on the beach.

It is also true – despite protests from devotees of Rye diving – that the further east you go the greater the problems of silting and poor visibility become, particularly close inshore. Yet wreck diving off Eastbourne in the area around the Royal Sovereign Shoals and Light Tower is superb, and offers a variety that cannot be surpassed anywhere along the Sussex coast. The boat problem comes up again here, and Eastbourne divers take their inflatables out to these wrecks despite the distance. Visiting divers should not try to do the same without local knowledge.

Eastbourne divers warn that with dive sites more than 4 or 5 miles out, they are likely to be in coastal shipping lanes. Small coastal shipping also comes close inshore around Beachy Head. These ships pass both sides of the Royal Sovereign Light Tower, and appear to have scant knowledge of, or regard for, the "A" Flag! Eastbourne BSAC members welcome visiting divers (see Appendix 1) and suggest that divers intending to dive the area ring a member of the branch a few days before the projected dive to check on the underwater visibility.

Shore diving at Eastbourne is almost non-existent because of the sandy sea bed in the area. There are a few rocky patches accessible from the beach towards Beachy Head, but these are generally covered in too much kelp, and are too shallow for comfortable diving – though they do provide Eastbourne BSAC with a chance to give novices a "wetting" when all else fails.

Tides in the area around Beachy Head are often erratic compared with the tables, and local knowledge should be tapped whenever possible. Some tides have been noted to be as much as 2 hours adrift either side of listed times!

Marks are difficult to find in this area when well out at sea, and any haze obliterates them. Local divers often locate wreck sites by timed runs from the Royal Sovereign Light Tower.

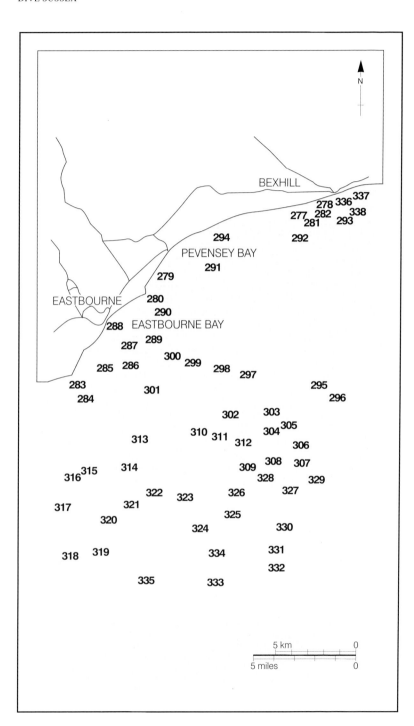

Two wrecks are entered here, but not as wreck sites as neither can be dived – being under the beach!

Resolution This 68-gun ship of 885 tons and 120ft long was driven ashore in Pevensey Bay during the Great Storm of November 1703. It was this storm that destroyed Henry Winstanley's Eddystone Lighthouse with him inside it, in addition to sinking 13 men o'war with the loss of 2,000 lives, and smashing hundreds of merchant ships onshore or to the sea bed. It was such a great disaster that Queen Anne decreed that 19 January, 1704, was to be a day of public fasting in memory of those who had lost their lives in "The Storm".

Ownership of the *Resolution* has been transferred by the Ministry of Defence (Navy) to the Nautical Museums Trust. But even if there is little chance of diving on her remains, according to the experts who believe she now lies right under the beach, anyone diving close to the shore here would do well to investigate any object that looks like a cannon!

Les Trois Drus This was a French brigantine wrecked on the rocks at Galley Hill, Bexhill, in 1779. This is a now-you-see-it-now-you-do-not wreck, appearing and disappearing according to the whims of the highly-mobile coast. She was carrying silks and some gold coin – some of which disappeared when she was first exposed in 1925. In recent years she has become more deeply buried in the sand, but appeared briefly in 1974 when her bows showed above the surrounding beach.

Archaeologists treat this wreck with great caution – mainly owing to the fact that the last time they were called out to the ship's reappearance, it turned out not to be the ship at all but part of an old groyne! There must, however, be a wreck close inshore at Bexhill. Silver coins are found on the beach, but are so worn that they have become little more than silver discs.

There is another surprise in this area, too. Not far away from the place where the silver coins are found are other discoveries that are much, much older! They are dinosaurs' footprints and they can be seen on the sea bed close inshore between Hastings and Bexhill. This area features several large expanses of sandstone slabs, and it is in these slabs that the dinosaurs' footprints and fossilised bones have been found. The slabs are believed to be the remains of a sandy delta of a river that once flowed down from the north. The footprints and fossils found so far have been in the sandstone of the between-the-tides level, but it would do no harm for divers in the area to keep their eyes open for other traces of these long-extinct monsters.

Launch sites

There are four public launch sites at Bexhill where you can get boats across the shingle strip that runs down to sand at low water. There is no ramp at Herbrand Road, but boats can be launched straight off the road onto the beach. At Brockley Road, where it enters West Parade, the launch is down a wide – 16ft in fact – concrete ramp. No cars are allowed, so the return can be a hard pull.

Opposite: Dive sites in Area 7, Eastbourne to St Leonards. This area is covered by Admiralty chart 536 (Beachy Head to Dungeness); Ordnance Survey Pathfinder map 199.

There is another wide concrete ramp down to the water at BOLEBROOK ROAD (or rather between Middlesex Road and Bolebrook Road), just by My Lord's Rock. No cars are allowed. At the foot of GALLEY HILL and to the east of the Angling Club is a large car park from which a narrow walkway leads to the beach. Boats can be launched down this walkway. If you want to park close to the launch site, this is your spot.

Shore diving sites

277 Bexhill Reef This rock reef is largely mussel beds and gullies with sandy bottoms. The mussels attract plaice, and there are small congers and dogfish. As it is only 40yds out, at right angles to the beach, it also has the remains of old wooden groynes impacted into the sea bed. The reef stands 2 to 3m proud in 7m and is directly out from the Sackville Apartments and Mermaid Restaurant in De-la-Warr Parade.

278 Goat Ledge, St Leonards This rock ledge is 3m high and visible at low water in a maximum depth of 7m. It runs diagonally from the end of the shingle beach south-east towards Hastings Pier. Popular with photographers for sole and small fry of all kinds including eelpout, rockling, blennies, and weevers. Is opposite the dive centre in Marine Court.

279 Barn Hill This 5,439-ton British steamer laden with copper and other, more general, cargo from Halifax, Nova Scotia, for London, was caught in the moonlight 3 miles south-south-west of Beachy Head at 10.30pm on Wednesday, 20 March, 1940, by a lone Dornier 17 of Oberst Fink's Kanalkampgruppen.

Colonel Fink had been appointed Channel Battle Leader, given the task of clearing the Channel of all Allied shipping, and used his Dorniers to that effect. Known to British air crews and ground gunners as the "Flying Pencil" the Do-17 specialised in shallow diving attacks at speeds exceeding 370mph, which would rip the wings off most other aircraft. And that is the way this particular Dornier attacked the *Barn Hill*. Two bombs arced home as the Dornier pulled out. One went down the *Barn Hill*'s funnel. The other hit her astern, and she burst into flames.

Four of her crew were killed at once. Another was so severely injured that he died in hospital shortly after they got him ashore. Seven more were badly hurt. The Captain, Michael O'Neill, was blown from the bridge and crashed to the deck unconscious. He rolled under some debris, and looking at the shambles that had been the bridge the survivors of the crew assumed he was dead in the tangled metal.

The first vessel to reach the blazing, drifting ship was the Eastbourne lifeboat, which took 28 men back to shore. No sooner had they done so than a message was received to say that the bell was ringing on the burning ship, which was now drifting towards Eastbourne. Out went the lifeboat again.

On board, Captain O'Neill had regained consciousness only to find that he was the only man alive aboard a blazing ship. He had a double fracture of one arm, a broken collar-bone above the other and five broken ribs. In intense pain, he nevertheless managed to crawl and roll along the deck to the bell, but found he could not move his arms to ring it. He solved this by seizing the rope with his

A German Dornier bomber attacked the steamer Barn Hill (Site 279) in March 1940. She sank after grounding off Langney Point, Eastbourne, and is a shore dive.

teeth and shaking his head violently. Then he collapsed amid the roaring noise of the fire, which seemed to have taken an even firmer hold on the stricken ship.

By now the sea was up, and when the lifeboat came alongside it was almost impossible to board her. One of the lifeboatmen said: "One moment the ship would be towering right over and showering sparks and molten lead on the water, the next we would be up on the waves almost level with her deck." Despite this, two of the men in the lifeboat, Alec Huggett and Thomas Allchorn, leaped aboard and found the Captain. For their bravery, the two men were later awarded the RNLI bronze medal for gallantry. At dawn, hundreds of Eastbourne residents watched as the ship, still burning fiercely, drifted across the sea front and finally grounded off Langney Point, where she now lies at 50 47 23N; 00 20 20E.

It took Eastbourne firemen several days to put the fires out. On the final day of their fight, two of the firemen were on the afterdeck and five were below at the bilge pumps when the *Barn Hill* gave a sudden lurch as she broke her back. The men were taken off by a fireboat just as she broke in two.

A month later, heavy seas began to break her up. Her cargo – or some of it – started to be washed up on the beach. The news spread rapidly, and just as in those shipwrecks of old, hundreds of people gathered on the shore and began to scoop up the harvest from the sea – tins of food of all kinds, including meat stew and baked beans. Men, women and children waded into the icy sea to collect them. Some proper salvage of the copper was later carried out, and today the *Barn Hill* is rated as a good second dive – at high water only, for her boilers show at very low tides and the depth over the rest of her is only 4m.

The shore diver will find that the *Barn Hill* is spread about in what amounts to a small bay, and at low spring tides you can wade out to the first part of the wreckage. Even so, a shore dive on the best of her will entail a 500yd snorkel. She belongs to Metal Recoveries of Newhaven. There are three boilers left, plus bits of the engine and a lot of plating. Marine life is prolific as she is the only shelter on a flat sandy sea bed for some distance. As a result, she is infested with congers, and there are crabs, lobsters, sole and plaice as well as bass in the area too.

280 Oneida This brigantine of 198 tons had Aberystwyth as her home port. She was going from Hull to Trieste with a cargo of railway iron when she was totally wrecked on Langney Point on 12 September, 1869. The actual wreck site is 300yds to the west of the point, but divers have found little left today, except for some of her iron cargo.

281 Jenny's Stool 50 50 00N; 00 30 00E. Jenny's Stool is a strange name for the inner rocks of Bexhill Reef. There is evidence of an ancient shipwreck here with a pipe and a sword scabbard being raised. Chelmsford BSAC are working the area.

282 The Claystones This is really part of Jenny's Stool (Site **281**) and the Bexhill Reef, and is to be found close to the end of the Bexhill sewer pipe. In front of a really big block of flats there are mussel beds. Big plaice are to be found on them in autumn among the "claystones", which are big boulders of compressed clay. Though this site is close inshore and can be a shore dive, it is best reached by inflatable.

Boat diving sites

283 Head Ledge This reef runs out for about ½ mile to the south-east of Beachy Head (Site **258**). Tide races and overfalls are common in the area, which is why shipping is advised to give the Head a wide berth of some 2 miles in all but the calmest weather. The Ledge does provide some excellent gullies, but it is fair to say that there is always a swell on it. Tide tables are not always right: Eastbourne divers say that if you follow them to the minute you will always be late on the ledge. Rocks here show at very low tides. Inside the ledge and moving to the west there are some superb gullies over 4m deep, which seem to be a nursery ground for juvenile crustacea.

284 Pioneer This small collier, whose master was Charles Denyer, was bound for Shoreham with 460 tons of coal when she ran onto Head Ledge on 28 June, 1888, in broad daylight and on a windless sea. This calm did not last long enough for her to be re-floated, and she soon became a total wreck. Her wreckage can be found around the ledges, but is so broken that it is impossible to identify any single part of the ship.

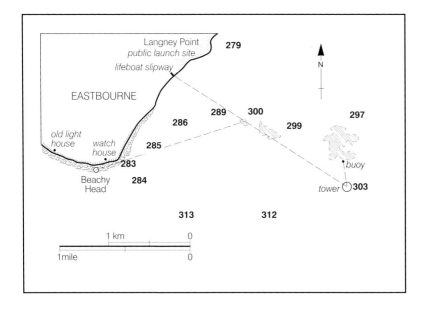

Beachy Head and Eastbourne, showing Head Ledge (Site 283), Elphick Tree (Site 300), Horse of Willingdon (Site 299), Royal Sovereign Shoals (Site 297) and the locations of the Pioneer (Site 284), the Sitakund (Site 185), the Marian (Site 286), the Liberator Bomber (Site 289), the Charles M (Site 313), HMS Ariadne (Site 312) and the Gambri (Site 303).

285 Sitakund Salvage debris at 50 44 41N; 00 17 12E is all that is left for divers of a massive supertanker. The 15,567-ton 605ft Norwegian supertanker caught fire while she was in ballast in the Channel. Three crewmen were killed in the subsequent explosions. She was beached in the lee of Beachy Head (Site **258**) on 21 October, 1968. The fire was put out on 23 October.

The *Sitakund* was beached exactly 1.16 miles from the Beachy Head Lighthouse. She was cut in half by salvors and both halves were eventually towed to Spain for scrapping.

Lying just to the north-east of the Holywell Bank, this is a low neap-tide novices dive in 7m of water. One or two plates and girders can be seen, and the diver will be surrounded by shoals of fish, mostly pouting, for this can be a very sheltered spot. However, at certain states of the tide, it whips around from Beachy Head and should be treated with respect.

286 Marian Although quite a large yacht when she sank on 25 November, 1925, at 50 45 10N; 00 18 35E, later dispersal operations and a sandy sea bed have left little of this vessel visible.

287 Endeavour *Endeavour* was one of the small salvage boats working on the Greek steamer *Germania*, which ran aground in April 1955 after being in collision in dense fog with a Panamanian steamer *Maro* off Beachy Head (Site **258**). The *Germania* was later re-floated, but the *Endeavour* sank at 50 45 36N; 00 18 24E on 6 June that year and is now largely buried.

288 Davenport The wreck of this small fishing boat lies at 50 45 57N; 00 18 20E, but is almost completely buried under the sand. The area where the *Davenport* sank is, in fact, now considered to be a safe anchorage, which is a clear indication of how little shows.

289 Liberator Bomber 50 45 48N; 00 20 42E. This US Liberator four-engined bomber is not marked on modern charts, but is in 10m of water and is upside down. The fuselage is flattened but intact, and only the wings and engines are holding it up from being buried in the sand on which it lies. A simple mark for her is to motor straight out square-on to the Eastbourne lifeboat station until Beachy Head Lighthouse (*see* Site **258**) just appears.

290 Alan Dean A sailing barge at 50 46 30N; 00 20 51E. The little that is left of the *Alan Dean* is sunk into the silty sea bed and was dispersed shortly after her sinking at the beginning of May 1932. Depth is 10m.

291 The 1944 Spitfire 50 48 00N; 00 23 00E. This British fighter, which crashed in 1944, is very broken up and only small bits are left. In 1975, permission was given to salvage her, but the tail was left behind several miles offshore in Pevensey Bay. Depth is 6m.

292 The 1941 Spitfire This Spitfire lies on the sea bed at 50 49 36N; 00 28 30E and is well broken up. It crashed here after aerial combat on 27 October, 1941.

293 Spitfire (Hastings) Close to the site of the *Amsterdam* (Site **337**) but ½ mile out is the wreckage of yet another spitfire. To find her, position your boat so you can look straight up Harley Shute Road, which comes down near the old Shunting Sheds on the sea front. The aeroplane is very broken up.

294 Lancaster Easy-Dog This Mark III version of the famous RAF bomber was one of a main force attack on the third largest synthetic oil refinery in Germany at Gelsenkirchen in the Ruhr on the night of 9/10 July, 1943. Today *Easy-Dog Four Seven Five*, to give her full markings, lies half-buried in gravel on the sea bed in Norman's Bay at 50 49 00N; 00 23 24E.

This Lancaster was one of 50 Squadron RAF Bomber Command based at Skellingthorpe near Lincoln, and the aircraft stationed there had a large number of Australians among their crews. On 9 July with Sergeant J. Clifford at the controls, *Easy-Dog* became airborne at 11.40pm, and the crew settled down to the long trip to the target, but all of them knew that Gelsenkirchen, near Essen, was bound to be heavily defended. All the crew aboard were sergeants, except for Flying Officer J.A. Butt, the navigator.

Flying Officer Butt seems to have been spot-on with his navigation too, because almost exactly on his estimated time of arrival, there was no doubt in anyone's mind that they had reached their target despite the fact that the air below 18,000ft was covered with 10/10ths cloud. RAF aircraft at the head of the bomber stream had already turned for home and flares warning of enemy aircraft still hung high in the night sky.

Those were not the only flares to be seen, and as heavy anti-aircraft fire burst all around them Sergeant Clifford was pleased to see the red marker flares of the aiming point. He started his run-in immediately and, once his bombs were gone, turned for home. But he was still over the target when the whole aeroplane juddered and shook as the port outer engine was hit in the petrol induction system and spun to a standstill.

As if this was not bad enough, the next AA shell hit the starboard inner engine and petrol tanks. Something had hit the starboard outer engine as well, for it too started playing up as the Lancaster limped home. For hours the gunners strained their eyes into the night. They were without doubt the target that every German night fighter would love to find, damaged and almost unmanoeuverable. Sergeant Clifford dropped into the cloud as often as possible and followed Butt's "straight home" course as best he could with his crippled aeroplane.

Easy-Dog caught fire, but almost reached the British coast before being forced to ditch at sea at 4am after one crew member, the mid-upper gunner, had baled out and was lost at sea. However, her distress call was picked up on shore. One of the fast air–sea rescue boats stationed at Newhaven was sent to rescue the remaining crew members, but even at top speed on a calm sea it was a long run, and the men from the Lancaster were not picked up until 5.20am. The air–sea rescue launch was logged back to base at 6.45am, but by then both *Easy-Dog*'s pilot and engineer were in hospital being treated for their burns. In the engineer's case, there was little that could be done and he died of his extensive burns in hospital the next day.

How much of Sergeant Clifford's *Easy-Dog* is left today it is difficult to say. She is in 10m of water, but the heavy gravel bottom moves and the gravel is piled 8ft high to the underside of the wings. Two engines were hauled up about 10 years ago, but members of Chelmsford BSAC, who have been working with Mr Alf Cave of the local aircraft preservation society, believe that much of the fuselage and other engines are buried under the gravel.

The Chelmsford divers – who found the wreck when clearing nets for a fisherman from a fastening that was said to be an old boiler – are still working on the site. The aircraft was identified by an emergency oxygen set and a fire-extinguisher from one of the engines, one of the bottles of which was found to be still full of freon. The Chelmsford divers have been in contact with some of *Easy-Dog*'s crew in Australia.

295 The Duchess 50 43 57N; 00 29 42E. This former railway steamer built at Troon in 1899 used to have the grander title of the *Duchess of Fife*. But either way, her noble career was brought to an end by a collision with a destroyer on 1 July, 1917. At the time, the *Duchess* was carrying Government stores from Newhaven to France. She sank so swiftly that nine of her crew were lost. The *Duchess* is 177ft long with a beam of 27ft, and now lies in 17m on a sandy sea bed from which she stands 6m proud.

296 Wreck, name unknown 50 43 36N; 00 30 13E. In 20m of water and 3m proud of hills and gullies lies this broken wreck of an old steamer. There is much ammunition lying around, but this vessel has not yet been identified.

297 Royal Sovereign Shoals 50 44 42N; 00 26 00E. This area is marked to the south by the Royal Sovereign Light Tower (Site **300**) and closer south by the Royal Sovereign Buoy, but it is still necessary to head north away from the buoy keeping it in line with the leg of the Tower for several minutes to find this site. Water disturbance and overfalls can usually be found in the centre of the shoals. The rocky sea bed here undulates up to about 7m, though there is one spot on the shoal's western edge where it comes up to within 4m of the surface at low water. There is a wealth of marine life here, varying, of course, according to season. Big plaice are to be found.

NOTE Oddly enough, no-one seems sure of the reason for the name of the shoals. There was no *Royal Sovereign* wreck here.

298 Long Shoal 50 44 54N; 00 24 18E. To the east of the Horse of Willingdon (Site **299**) and separated from it by the channel called Kinsman's Nab is Long Shoal, which does not rise so close to the surface as the rocks of the Horse. There are mines from HMS *Ariadne* (Site **312**) on this shoal jammed in gullies in the rocks. Also there is a large ship's anchor and 200yds of chain capable of holding a really big ship. Divers who have followed the chain to its end expecting a wreck have been disappointed. The chain comes to an abrupt halt with nothing attached to it.

299 Horse of Willingdon 50 45 00N; 00 22 30E. This is a rocky outcrop nearly a mile in length. There is usually a large disturbance over this site as at low water there is only about 4m of water over the rocks, which fall down most steeply on the south-west side to the flat sandy sea bed characteristic of the area at 12m. It is a further mile out on the same bearing as Elphick Tree (Site **300**), and divers say that the Horse is more interesting to dive and has more plentiful marine life.

Not such a welcome sight as the lobsters and crabs in this heavily-potted area is the presence of sea mines. These are believed to be from HMS *Ariadne* (Site **312**), and are proper mine-like mines with horns. One found recently by Eastbourne BSAC divers was standing a good 4ft high, but was full of sand. In most cases these mines are only cases with the inspection plates off, but they are best avoided as some might be live.

300 Elphick Tree 50 45 12N; 00 21 36E. This, the nearest area of rock diving to Eastbourne, lies about 2½ miles out from the shore. The depth at low water is 9m, falling to 12m. There is quite a quantity of marine life on this rocky outcrop. Plaice can sometimes be found on the surrounding sandy sea bed.

This area can be located by following a compass bearing of 130° magnetic from the lifeboat slipway to the Royal Sovereign Light Tower (Site **302**) out on the horizon. There is usually a disturbance over this site. Another method of finding Elphick Tree is to steer for the light tower until Beachy Head Lighthouse – the functional one under the Head (*see* Site **258**) – is just showing. This site is usually heavily potted for lobsters, with many marker buoys in evidence.

301 Wreck, name unknown Though a wreck is charted here at 50 44 25N; 00 21 07E in 12.8m, local divers have not been able to locate her and believe that she is completely buried.

302 Royal Sovereign Light Tower Completed in 1971, this tower replaced the light vessel that had marked the shoal since 1875 (except during World War Two). It is made of reinforced concrete, and was built in two sections in a basin hollowed out of the beach behind its storm crest at Newhaven. Work began in 1967, and despite the sea breaking through in a southerly gale and bringing shingle that took three months to clear out, the work was completed late in 1968. The divers involved in preparing the foundations for the tower had a rough time – literally. On average, weather permitted work on only 8 days per month. Though it was expected that some boulders would have to be removed from the chosen site, the first divers – in the spring of 1968 – found the area was entirely covered with large boulders, the result of a collapsed stratum of oolitic ironstone not found before in the English Channel. The divers – working in poor visibility and restricted to a few hours of slack water – had to chart each boulder, guide a grab from a ship to move it, and then level off gravel dropped from a barge to make a suitable foundation. It is not surprising that this part of the work was not completed until the early summer of 1970.

The next step was to float out the base and vertical pillar section and sink it down on to the levelled area. Then the upper cabin section and the superstructure were floated over the pillar section. The pillar had an inner telescopic section – once it was attached to the cabin, it was jacked up 45ft and locked into position. Now the underside of the cabin was well above maximum wave height, and the navigation light was 112ft above sea level. The cabin section had accommodation for the principal keeper and his two assistant keepers, with a modern all-electric kitchen, sitting room with television, a hobby room, laundry and a freezer.

The tower became fully automatic in 1994 and is visited once a month for maintenance. The roof of the cabin serves as a helicopter landing pad. The fog signal gives uniform sound radiation over 360° and has a range of about 5 miles. The signal is two blasts each of 2 seconds every 30 seconds. The lantern gives one flash every 20 seconds with an intensity of 3,500 candelas, giving a range of 12 miles. Should the main lamp fail, an automatic lamp-changer brings a second lamp into focus.

There is some good diving around the tower itself, particularly among those boulders that the construction divers did not have to try to move. The sea bed is interesting from the actual base to about 250yds away.

303 Gambri This hired naval steam trawler of 274 tons was lost after she hit a mine on 18 January, 1918, "off the Royal Sovereign Light Vessel" (Site **304**). Her wreck is now at 50 43 23N; 00 26 32E. This 126ft vessel lies in 19m, is 3m proud, and lies north-west to south-east.

304 Royal Sovereign Light Vessel This light vessel was at 50 42 39N; 00 26 48E for all of World War One and afterwards, and was returned after World War Two from 1946 to 1971, before being withdrawn when the present tower (*see* Site **302**) was made operational. The light vessel's position was about ¾ mile south-south-east of the tower.

305 F.D. Lambert 50 42 42N; 00 27 40E. This 2,195-ton British merchantman was unarmed when she had her first brush with the German Navy in World War One. She was shelled by a German warship on 25 April, 1916, when 5 miles

163

east-south-east of Gorleston Pier and south of Great Yarmouth, Norfolk. Though damaged by gunfire, the *F.D. Lambert* escaped without injury to her crew.

There were still no casualties when the *F.D Lambert* was attacked by a German submarine while following a zig-zag course 1 mile east of the Royal Sovereign Light Vessel (Site **304**) on 13 February, 1917. She was carrying a cargo of coal from Newcastle to Savona, Italy. Though no-one died, the ship was not so lucky. Her master, Mr W.C. Lamb, said later that the torpedo caught her on the port side level with the foremast. It blew a huge hole in her side and she started to settle so quickly that he ordered abandon ship immediately. The submarine was seen on the surface by the men in the lifeboats. Today, the 200ft ship stands 4m proud of the sea bed at 23m but is very broken and silted.

306 Wreck, name unknown 50 42 19N; 00 27 52E. The sea bed here is bumpy and is the site of a 100ft wreck (which is badly broken and probably by now completely in two as the latest information dates from 1975). More diving information is needed on this one. Her highest point is 19m.

307 Wreck, name unknown 50 42 01N; 00 28 01E. This is the wreck of another one of the old ships in this area that is sinking deep into the soft sea bed. Echo-sounder traces show her at 24m in a general depth of 28m.

308 Rio Parana 50 42 20N; 00 26 52E. This British steamer was carrying coal from Tyneside to Italy, when she was torpedoed by *U-8* on 24 February, 1915. All the crew were saved. The *Rio Parana* was a 4,015-tonner, 346ft in length with a beam of 48ft. She now lies on a bumpy sea bed in 23m and is 4m proud at her highest point. The coal is still to be seen. Her stern section is the most complete, and she is well broken elsewhere with lots of plates lying flat on the sand and many girders scattered around. The iron propeller is still there.

309 Oceana They say that there is still £3,000-worth of silver bars somewhere in the tangled wreckage of this 6,610-ton P&O liner, but the author cannot confirm it. Local divers say that a single silver ingot was recovered in 1996 by a member of a visiting club. The wreck is at 50 42 19N; 00 25 45E in 22m and is "well blown" as one Eastbourne diver described her.

The story of the sinking of the *Oceana* and her gold and silver cargo, worth £750,000, begins on Friday, 15 March, 1912. On that day the P&O liner – 468ft long with a beam of 52ft – sailed from Tilbury with 40 passengers, a crew of 210 and a lot of general cargo in addition to all those gold and silver ingots. Her destination was Bombay. Her Captain was T.H. Hyde, RNR, and her engines could give her 16 knots from their 7,000hp.

The second day of the voyage dawned clear but windy. *Oceana* was going well. She was cruising only slightly below her maximum speed, and she was little affected by the head-wind because the sea was calm.

Beating up the Channel on that March day was the *Pisagua*, a famous four-masted steel barque, and a great ocean-racer of the Laeisz Line. The *Pisagua* that morning had the wind behind her, was under full press of sail, and was travelling along at nearly 20 knots. She was nearly home, heading for Hamburg from Mexillones with a cargo of nitrate.

The 468ft liner Oceana (Site 309) was bound for Bombay in 1912 when she collided with the Pisagua and sank.

Aboard the *Pisagua*, the *Oceana* had been seen, and her master was confident that the liner would soon give way to his sail; but just to make sure, as the ships drew closer, he burnt a warning flare. In the *Oceana* the Chief Officer saw the flare and gave the order to port the helm. At this, the pilot who was still aboard, a Mr Penny, came out of the charthouse. One glance was enough to tell him that the turn was the wrong way and not big enough. "Hard aport!" yelled Penny, and as Captain Hyde hurried to his bridge, the *Pisagua* struck. All 2,850 tons of her travelling at nearly 20 knots was like taking a steel tin-opener to the *Oceana*'s side – and a gash 45ft long opened up below the waterline.

The two ships bounced apart. The *Pisagua*, with her foretop mast shattered and her bow stove in, drifted away to leeward. The *Oceana* was in a worse state, and though her watertight doors were swiftly closed, some of the passengers had to wade through flooded companionways to reach their lifeboat stations. There was no panic, and all went well until one lifeboat was lowered too soon, and seven passengers and two crew were drowned when it capsized.

Most of the rest of those on board were safely taken off by the cross-Channel steamer *Sussex*, which had picked up the radioed distress call. Now it was the tug's turn. The Newhaven tug *Alert* took the first tow, stern first, at 8am.

But soon the *Oceana* developed a list, which increased so much that the stern with her propeller began to show above the water. Captain Hyde and the officers plus those crew who had stayed to help with the tow now had to abandon ship and were taken off by the *Alert*. The towing cables were cut, and at 10am on Saturday,

16 March, 1912, she started to sink. It took her a full 20 minutes to go down, and finally she settled on the sea bed with her masts and the tops of her funnels showing. The *Pisagua*, meanwhile, was towed safely to Dover for repairs.

At dawn the next day the salvage divers were at work. The first dives were into the Captain's cabin to get the keys of the strongroom. Then three of the room's five locks were opened with the keys, but two would not open and had to be smashed off with hatchets.

Today's divers are well aware of how strong the tides are in the area. Those old hard-hat divers were swept about all over the place. A report of the time says: "Owing to the amount of debris on her deck and the chaotic state of things below, it was difficult and, in many places, impossible for the men to work upright. They had to crawl on hands and knees, squeeze through hatchways, and overcome all sorts of obstacles in their progress through the wreck."

The operation took only 10 days, and there are indications that all the gold and silver was recovered, though one report does say (probably optimistically) that £3,000-worth was never found. Common sense tells you that if the salvage divers were prepared to work through all states of the tide then it is hardly likely that they would have left behind a fortune after only 10 days' work.

Today's divers will, of course, wait for slack. This sometimes only lasts for 30 minutes on the wreck, of which no superstructure remains. The boilers, standing 6m proud, are the most prominent feature. All around the boilers is a tangled mass of wreckage of masts, timber decking, and winches. Visibility after a long spell of calm weather can reach 14m. The sandy sea bed is liable to encroach on the wreckage, which appears to be in the middle of an area of shifting sands.

310 Wreck, name unknown 50 42 31N; 00 25 24E. Nothing much is known about this wreck. She lies there in a depth of 26m, and she stands some 4m proud. Diving information is needed.

311 Wreck, name unknown 50 42 47N; 00 24 29E. Another victim of the soft sea bed in these parts is this wreck, now almost completely buried at 20m.

312 HMS Ariadne This wreck is spread over a wide area at 50 42 52N; 00 23 29E. Great care should be taken when diving her for reasons explained below.

HMS *Ariadne* was built in 1898 and at the time she was planned it was thought that there would be a place in sea warfare for a fast, heavily-armed commerce raider. So she was built at John Brown's with 18,000hp engines and huge Belleville boilers, which were intended to make her one of the fastest cruisers afloat. Unfortunately, the weight of the armour plate fitted to this 11,000-ton ship slowed her down a lot.

Speed trials shortly after her commissioning at Portsmouth in June 1902 showed that she could only manage 20.75 knots flat out. Even so, she became the flagship for Admiral Sir A.L. Douglas while he was Commander-in-Chief of the North American and West Indies station. After those moments of glory, however, she was, by 1908, relegated to be tender to the *Barfleur*. Just before the outbreak of World War One she was further demoted to the training service.

The *Ariadne* was, in fact, obsolete almost as soon as she was launched, and it was the building of ships like the light cruiser *Emden* of 3,600 tons by Germany that made her so. The *Emden* was so much faster that while the *Ariadne* was

There are unexploded mines around the Ariadne (Site 312).

relegated to odd jobs during the first years of the war, the *Emden*, captained by Karl von Muller, caused untold damage to Allied shipping.

In a cruise lasting from the outbreak of war until 9 November, 1914, the *Emden* captured or sank some 23 merchant ships totalling 101,182 tons in the Indian Ocean, before being sunk at Cocos (Keeling) Island by the Australian cruiser *Sydney*.

In July 1917, the *Ariadne* was finally allowed to adopt a belligerent role – but then only to lay mines across the 240 miles of sea from the Orkneys to Norway. It was on the 26 July that the *Ariadne*, laden with 400 mines, lumbered down the Channel towards the Royal Sovereign Light Vessel (Site **304**). If she had been crewed as planned she would have had 677 officers and men packed into her 462ft hull. But as she was only to operate as a mine-layer, there was 304 crew aboard to do just that and to man her reduced armament of four 6-inch and one 4-inch guns. Her two torpedo tubes were unmanned, and there were no torpedoes on board. But there were some close by! Itchy fingers in the German *UC-65* were ready to send them across to the *Ariadne* directly Captain Otto Steinbrinck gave the word.

But Steinbrinck was in no hurry. To get the *Ariadne* in his sights he had just completed the longest-ever submerged run through the heavily-defended Straits of Dover during the early hours of that July morning in 1917. He now watched carefully as the two M-class destroyers, HMS *Peregrine*, on the port bow of the cruiser, and HMS *Norman* to starboard, forming the *Ariadne*'s anti-submarine screen, passed him.

Captain Steinbrinck fired only one torpedo at the big cruiser. At 2.21pm, it struck home amidships on her port side – and the resulting explosion was enormous. Some of the mines on board the *Ariadne* went off at once. Thirty-eight men were killed instantly. Nine more were badly wounded. If the *Ariadne* had been carrying her normal complement the number of casualties would have been much higher. She sank in 19m of water and stayed upright long enough for her escorts to take off all the other crew members. Not long after the last man, Captain Harry Hesketh-Smyth, left the ship, she rolled over and sank down on her starboard side.

Though the cruiser was badly broken by the explosion of the mines aboard, she was further broken up in 1923 and 1925 by the explosive charges used by the Ocean Salvage and Towing Company to disperse her under contract to Trinity House. By 14 September, 1925, they reported nothing now standing more than "45ft above the sea bed" in a general depth of 20m. In 1975 the wreck was bought by Metal Recoveries (Orkney) Ltd, and by 1981 the sea and the salvaging had dispersed her widely.

One report of the time said that there was nothing standing more than 4m above the sea bed. Salvage work started again in 1984, and the ship is now broken into two sections (although it is difficult to know where one ends and the other begins), with the bow section pointing to the Royal Sovereign Light Tower.

WARNING Salvage work at one time was done by grabs, and as a result of their use the mines that did not explode at the time of the torpedoing are now broken open and gun-cotton is exposed. These mines are scattered around the area, so divers should take great care. Eastbourne BSAC also warn that anyone diving this distance out must keep a constant watch for coastal shipping. Tides are very strong and wreckage sharp. One diver is said to have been picked up several miles away after his SMB line was severed by the wreckage.

313 Charles M This is a small but modern collier of 403 tons lying at 50 42 44N; 00 18 48E. This 150ft motor vessel was damaged in a collision on 31 March, 1949 and sank while under tow. She was identified by her bell. She lies east–west with her bows to the west. Her bow and stern stand about 6m proud of the sea bed at 31m.

314 Mount Stewart An iron steamer of 679 tons, the *Mount Stewart* was sunk in a collision on 19 December, 1890 with the Norwegian wooden barque, *Dinorah*, which also sank. The *Mount Stewart* now lies close (at 50 42 39N; 00 18 14E) to that other more modern collier, *Charles M*. This one was identified by her ship's bell too. She sits upright in 28m with her bridge her highest part at 7m. She has settled with her bows to the north-east. Her bow is 5m proud.

315 Avanturine Local fishermen say that this is the wreck of the *Adventurine*, a large coastal trawler, but they may well be confusing the name with that of the *Avanturine*, an Admiralty-requisitioned trawler of 296 tons built in 1930 and sunk by E-boats "off Beachy Head" (Site **258**) on 1 December, 1943. This wreck, at 50 41 35N; 00 15 08E, is upright in 22m and stands 6m proud of the sandy sea bed.

316 Unidentified German submarine This wreck of a U-boat at 50 41 35N; 00 15 08E is upright in 22m and only 60yds away from the wreck of the *Avanturine* (*see* Site **315**). At one time this was thought to be the *U-40*, but a dive by Bob Peacock of Thanet BSAC on the Sandettie Bank at 51 07 47N; 01 48 07E has almost certainly located *U-40* there. At present the identity of the submarine has not been confirmed, though a Newhaven salvage company is said to have worked on her.

317 UB-130 Launched on 26 June, 1918, *UB-130* was one of the last of the U-boats to get into the war. The 510-ton boat carried 10 torpedoes for her four bow tubes and one stern tube. She had a 10.5cm gun on her deck, could cruise 3,500 miles on the surface at 6 knots, or 50 miles at 4 knots submerged. In 30 seconds she could take her three officers and 31 crew below surface in an emergency crash dive.

But none of this potential was ever used. Even though her captain was brought back to command her from his activities in the Mediterranean (where, while in command of *UC-54* and based in Yugoslavia, he had sunk many ships and behaved in a distinguished manner), he had little chance of fresh glory. In fact, when Kapitän-Leutnant Prince Heinrich 37th – better known as the Prince Reuss – took *UB-130* down the Kiel canal and out into Helgoland Bay on 25 October, 1918, to join the German High Sea Fleet for one of their last enterprises, it all ended in something near to farce. For something went wrong with the steering gear, and the Prince had to take his U-boat back into Kiel by steering using the propellers only. On 4 November, 1918, he was back in Kiel. On 11 November the war was over. During the division of the spoils after Germany surrendered, the French took over the boat called *UB-130*. But they did not keep it for long. For some reason the French decided that she should be broken up in a British breaker's yard; and she was on tow towards that fate when she lost the tow and sank at 50 40 30N; 00 15 18E.

UB-130 was first dived by Hounslow BSAC in September 1975. They found her on a bottom of fine sand in 38m with her bows pointing to the south-west. The gun pointed forward along her 182ft hull, and the conning tower was open. The conning tower was damaged, though, with part of the outer skin lying on the sea bed beside her. One periscope was in the raised position, and her steel propellers were still in place. That report – and one from Peter Cornish and his BSAC Special Projects Group stressing that attempts to enter the submarine via the narrow conning-tower hatch were very dangerous – is in striking contrast to a more recent report from divers that says she is very broken and in three pieces. The wreck has been confirmed as *UB-130* by numbers stamped on her propeller.

318 Seven Seas *Seven Seas* is the romantic name for one of the early victims of German submarines in World War One. Nine men, including the master, died when this steamer, in ballast from London to Liverpool, was torpedoed without warning by *U-37* on 1 April, 1915. Today, this 1,194-ton ship, 250ft long by 32ft beam, lies in 35m on her starboard side with her bows to the south-east. Her position is 50 38 53N; 00 15 33E. She appears to be sinking into the sea bed and her bridge is her highest point, some 7m proud. She has two forward and two aft holds, which are heavily silted. She appears badly damaged near the forward holds, probably from the torpedo strike.

319 Mohlenpris 50 39 18N; 00 18 06E. This 175ft Norwegian collier of 638 tons was carrying a full cargo of 691 tons of coal from Llanelly to Le Treport, when she was captured by *UB-40* on 15 April, 1917, and sunk by explosive charges placed by a boarding party. She now lies on a sandy sea bed at 30m and is upside down. The highest point is her stern, which is 9m proud, and her bow points to the west. She is badly damaged amidships.

320 Lalen Mendi A Spanish steamer of 2,138 tons and laden with 3,110 tons of unscreened coal for Bilbao and Barcelona from Middlesbrough, the *Lalen Mendi* was torpedoed amidships on 17 November, 1917. Now this 290ft steamer lies north–south at 50 40 21N; 00 17 58E in 26m of water. Her bow lists to starboard from the badly-broken midships section. Her stern is her highest point some 6m proud of a rocky sea bed dotted with "pools" of silt and sand.

321 Wreck, name unknown 50 41 06N; 00 20 30E. This is a small coaster sitting upright but well sunk into the soft sea bed. Her bows point to the north-west, she has four holds, and her bridge – which is the highest point at 9m off the 33m sea bed – is amidships.

322 Wreck, name unknown 50 41 30N; 00 20 42E. This wreck lies in 30m of water and stands 6m proud. She is only 50ft long. Diving information is needed.

323 The 1906 This is what local divers call her, but despite knowing the year in which she sank no one has yet put a name to her and she is officially classified as "unknown". We know the date of this old 262ft ship because a Trinity House report of 1906 stated that the ship's mast stuck up 2ft above the surface. By 1923 she had been swept. When the wreck was first dived in 1981 she was found to be an old steamer with an iron propeller sitting upright on an even keel in 23m. The stern, the engine, and the bow all stand 5m proud, but she is well sunk into the sea bed and heavily silted. She lies at 50 41 02N; 00 22 58E.

324 Two-gun Trawler 50 39 40N; 00 23 50E. As the name implies, this is a well-armed trawler of about 500 tons lying with her bows to the south, upright, and 8m proud of the 27m sea bed. She appears to have a diesel engine, and she was carrying a quantity of coal. Divers also say that she looks as though she was rammed on her port side forward. This might make her the *Linnet* – a trawler that was sunk in collision on 4 December, 1925 – if it were not for the puzzling guns. This is a mystery wreck that needs more diving to identify it.

325 Phoenix D1 50 40 39N; 00 25 39E. This 174ft Mulberry harbour unit is a Phoenix D1 type made of concrete reinforced with rods. She lies on a rough bottom with a maximum depth of 24m.

326 Grabwell A victim of weather during massive movements of ships along the British coast during World War Two, the *Grabwell* lies at 50 41 16N; 00 26 00E. She sank on 6 May, 1942, while on tow. Today this dredger of 251 tons lies north-east to south-west on a flat sea bed at 22m. She is 196ft long and stands 5m proud.

327 Alaunia The biggest wreck in Sussex waters, this 13,405-ton Cunard liner was built of steel in 1913 and was intended for the Canada run. On 19 October, 1916, however, when she was coming from New York and bound for London with her holds full of 8,000 tons of general cargo (she had dropped mails and 180 passengers at Falmouth), she hit a mine laid by *UC-16* and sank in 36m of water at 50 41 03N; 00 27 17E. Two of her crew of 187 died in the explosion.

The German mine-layers of the Flanders Submarine Flotilla were giving the Allies many problems in 1916 – and sinking a great number of ships. Despite the fact that the mine-laying submarines could only carry a maximum of 18 mines per trip, they established minefields in areas as far apart as Flamborough Head, Yorkshire, and Waterford in the south of Ireland. Mines were sown off Falmouth, Dartmouth, Portland, and Portsmouth. In 1916 alone the submarines laid 212 mines off Dover, 100 off Dunkirk, 100 off Calais, and 60 off Boulogne.

At 4.30am, very soon after the explosion, and the *Alaunia*'s distress calls, the Eastbourne and Newhaven lifeboats were launched. But boats of the Dover Patrol got there first and soon there were two patrol boats and five destroyers around her taking off the crew and a few remaining passengers. The liner still didn't sink and a naval officer and seven ratings went on board in an attempt to prepare her for tugs to beach her. But the sea pouring into the hole in the ship's hull soon showed the boarding party that this was impossible, and they were taken off by the Eastbourne lifeboat. The *Alaunia* sank at 9.20am when she rolled over and went down by the stern.

Today, heavy swirls in the water down-tide of the ship give away the presence of this big wreck. She is on a sand-and-shingle sea bed at 36m, and lies almost due east–west with her bow to the east and 12m proud. Her superstructure has been swept, and she now lies at an angle of 45° on her port side with all her

The 520ft Cunard liner Alaunia (Site 327) is the biggest wreck in Sussex waters.
She hit a mine in October 1916 and sank in 36m.

superstructure lying in a heap of twisted metal at the foot of her steeply-sloping decks. Everything detachable seems to have slid down the decks. She is infested with congers, and is home to shoals of fish, mostly pouting. She is regularly visited by fishing parties.

Though the wreck of the *Alaunia* has been swept, she is nevertheless remarkably intact, and her full 520ft can be explored by the careful diver. The bow is the highest part, and the first 100ft of her from the bow is almost perfect; but she is broken up amidships and towards the stern. The wheelhouse, more or less intact, lies 10m from the main wreckage on the port side. Do not confuse this large piece of wreckage with a smaller one further towards the bow and also well away from the ship's side. Photographers, looking for a good opportunity, should follow the anchor chain draped over her bow and they will find a huge 20ft tall anchor hanging from the end of it. Another large anchor is on her deck further back. Visibility can be as much as 18m on a good day. The wreck is charted at 13.1m to her highest point, but big scours – there is one of over 3m on the north side, which is the side she is lying on – accentuate the depth of the sea bed.

NOTE There has been a diving fatality on the *Alaunia*. Great care should be taken when diving this very big, old wreck.

328 Balfour This hired naval steam trawler of 285 tons lies at 50 41 34N; 00 26 49E, but is sinking deep into the muddy, uneven sea bed on which she rests. She is 134ft long with a beam of 23ft, built of steel, and was lost after a collision on 13 May, 1918. The depth is 23m and she stands only 1 or 2m proud of that.

329 Wreck, name unknown 50 41 41N; 00 28 01E. She lies south-east to north-west, but is so broken that it is difficult to work out which end is the bow. The wreckage is on a rough sea bed of hills and valleys varying from 25m to 30m in depth. The minimum depth to the wreckage is 18m.

330 Glenartney This 5,201-ton merchantman was torpedoed by *U-34* on 18 March, 1915, when she was 4 miles south of the Royal Sovereign Light Vessel (Site 304). One of her crew of 40 was killed when the torpedo struck. The *Glenartney* was inward bound from Bangkok to London with 7,661 tons of rice. She sank stern first and is now at 50 38 48N; 00 25 32E.

The wreck is lying on her starboard side, concealing the hole made by the torpedo about 10ft from her sternpost, on a flat sea bed of sand at 31m, and was swept to 19m in 1976. Her bow is to the east, and she is very broken with only the bow section and the boilers being clearly defined and standing some 6m proud.

331 Caleb Sprague The E-boats came roaring out of the dark to the south-east of Beachy Head (Site **258**) at 2.45am on 31 January, 1944, and hit the small convoy left, right and centre. Within moments, HMS *Pine* (Site **95**) had 10 dead and was listing from a direct torpedo strike. The *Caleb Sprague* of 1,813 tons and full of 2,305 tons of steel and timber took a torpedo in the port side and sank so swiftly that she took 25 men out of the crew of 27 and four gunners on board down with her. The next ship in line was the *Emerald* (Site **332**), and she was the next to go. Within minutes the E-boats had vanished back into the night.

Today, the 250ft *Caleb Sprague* lies with her bows still to the west – she was bound from London for Newport. She is upright, and the highest point is her bridge amidships – some 11m off the 46m sea bed. There has been some salvage work on her cargo of steel, but that does not account for the damage to her port side to holds No. 3 and No. 4 – no doubt the place where the torpedo hit her. She has been positively identified by her bell as being at 50 38 15N; 00 25 29E.

332 Emerald 50 38 18N; 00 25 35E. The *Emerald* was another victim of the E-boats that hit HMS *Pine* and her small convoy on 31 January, 1944 (*see* Site **331**).

This wreck is shallower than the *Caleb Sprague* at 37m, and stands 10m proud of a flat sea bed that rises in a long bank to the north of the wreck. The 806-ton *Emerald* was bound from Middlesbrough to Poole with a cargo of coal. She was 202ft long, with a beam of 30ft, but the wreck has now been swept. Her entire crew of 12 and the three gunners on board at the time of the attack were all lost.

333 Western Coast 50 38 24N; 00 23 28E. This small steamer was on her way from London to Liverpool via Plymouth with 1,200 tons of general cargo when she was torpedoed on 24 February, 1915, by the German submarine *U-8*. The torpedo struck her on the port side at No. 2 hold.

The crew of the *Western Coast* all managed to take to the boats without loss. Then all 240ft of the ship went to the bottom in 34m. This 1,165-ton steamer is largely intact, but is rarely dived.

NOTE *U-8* was destroyed when caught in explosive sweeps in the Dover Straits on 4 March the same year. Her captain, Kapitän-Leutnant A. Stoch, was captured.

334 Wreck, name unknown 50 39 16N; 00 24 15E. This one is lying on a rough sea bed in 32m and stands 5m proud. She is heavily silted. More diving information is needed.

335 Mulberry Unit Though most of the Mulberry units wrecked off the coast of Sussex are concentrated to the west, this one is at 50 37 36N; 00 18 14E. But at 44m to the sea bed and only 5m proud, the wreckage is hardly worth a diver's time.

336 Bo-Peep Rocks 50 50 42N; 00 31 42E. Said to be named after the Custom House that was hereabouts, these rocks also take their name from the customs men who figure so prominently in that old nursery rhyme. What has Bo-Peep got to do with customs men? Surely the rhyme is all about a woman who lost her flock of sheep? Well, no. Remember how it goes:

> Little Bo-Peep has lost her sheep,
> And doesn't know where to find them;
> Leave them alone and they will come home,
> Dragging their tails behind them.

The rhyme takes on a new meaning when you know that Bo-Peep refers to the customs officers, who had their post by the rocks, and that the sheep are the smugglers, and that the tails they dragged behind them were barrels of contraband brandy!

This is also said to be the place where William the Conqueror landed, just to the east of the hamlet of Bulverhythe. At the approach to the Pier in Hastings itself you can see the flat rock called the Conqueror's Stone on which, legend says, William had his first meal in England.

The site now has another reason for being famous. For this is where the protected wreck site of the Dutch East Indiaman *Amsterdam* (Site **337**) is being dived.

337 Amsterdam This big Dutch East Indiaman, which came to grief on the shore near Hastings on Sunday, 26 January, 1749, is one of Sussex's protected wreck sites. She has – when the tide came in and diving was possible – been excavated by a combined British and Dutch team of diving-archaeologists in the hope that she may later be taken back to Holland, finally completing her voyage after some 250 years on the beach! All diving, except for the archaeological team's work, is prohibited in an area within 100m of grid reference TV 778 083 (see Ordnance Survey Landranger Map 199). This Protection of Wrecks Order came into operation on 5 February, 1974.

The *Amsterdam* was commanded by Captain Willem Klump. He was 33 and this was his second command. She weighed 700 tons, was 150ft long, and had a beam of 35ft. She was heavily armed with 54 cannon on two main gun decks.

On 15 November, 1748, Klump took the *Amsterdam*, a brand-new ship, out into the North Sea with 12,000 miles of voyaging ahead of her to the East Indies. But it did not work out like that. The wind swung to the north-west and Klump had to anchor or be blown onshore. For four days they rode it out. Then, seizing the chance given by a temporary calm, the *Amsterdam* sailed back to Holland. Two days later the wind swung back to the east, and Klump tried again. When the wind went against him again it was two weeks before he could get back to an anchorage.

Finally the storms passed, the wind settled in the east, and Klump got the *Amsterdam* out of the Zuider Zee for the third and last time on 8 January, 1749. One man had already died aboard but he had probably been ill before he signed on. What deadly illness he had already passed on to the crew, nobody could then know. But as the *Amsterdam* ran head-on into one of the worst south-westerly gales of the century, the crew had little time to worry about such things. Ships raced for shelter wherever they could. But Klump had gone too far to turn back again. The *Amsterdam* went first onto one tack and then the other. One of the Dutch East Indiamen, which had left Holland only the day before the *Amsterdam*, ran ashore between Eastney Point and Southsea Castle. Mountainous seas swept men overboard from the *Amsterdam*, but now Klump had another worry. In 12 days of tacking he had 50 men dead – the illness that the first man to die on board had brought with him was now in full flood. Each day of the gale five men – dead of some tropical fever – were flung overboard.

By 20 January the *Amsterdam* had still not passed Beachy Head (Site **258**) and Klump decided to take refuge in Pevensey Bay, a well-known spot in which to shelter from south-west winds. But before he was properly into shelter, the ship grounded on a shoal and lost her rudder. Her anchors went down and she finally came to a stop off Bexhill.

There she stayed until 26 January, when either her anchor cables parted or they were cut by someone who feared the plague aboard more than the billows on the shore. The crew had had enough. They broke into the ship's wine store and soon most of them were drunk. At 3pm someone aboard managed to get her guns fired as a signal of distress. Finally she beached in the spot where she lies today.

Then the looting began. The Hastings authorities safely removed practically all the silver she carried with the help of troops, but wine from her cargo was openly on sale very soon at one shilling a bottle. Even the Mayor of Hastings was selling it! But the ship had sunk onto a patch of shifting sand and mud, and she gradually sank into it. Soon it was up to her deck level, and nothing more of her cargo could be stolen. Then the sand covered her except at very low tides and she was more or less forgotten. In fact, under the beach at Hastings, or rather Bulverhythe, lay an almost intact East Indiaman and a complete slice of history as it was in January 1749.

There the vessel remained until a local man who was greatly interested in the history of the area and who was the site agent for a firm building a sewage outfall decided to use an excavator machine to probe the old wreck site. To universal amazement up in the bucket came fine horn combs, an ivory fan, brass candlesticks, full wine bottles, shoes, and stoneware jugs. And up, too, came the most fantastic find of all – five bronze cannon, still wrapped in the sacking that had covered them when they were loaded with the rest of the cargo! Furthermore, the ship appeared to be intact from the deck down.

The site was quickly designated as that of an historic wreck under the 1973 Protection of Wrecks Act.

In 1984, a diving tower was built just to one side of the wreck site and diving started. To the British and Dutch divers' surprise, even when they were diving in the below-decks area they sometimes had visibility of 3m – this, despite the fact that at low tide the area appears to be almost solid sand.

The recoveries in 1984 and 1985, under the direction of archaeologist Peter Marsden, were fabulous. They range from dress material decorated with hearts and flowers, to bottles of wine still corked and packed in straw, to giant lead-covered barrels of butter that seem to be our ancestors' first attempts at tin cans. Hundreds and hundreds of items underwent conservation procedures in the old ballroom of the Hastings Holiday Centre. Some of these items, including cannon and an anchor, are on display in the Hastings Shipwreck Heritage Centre, but the majority have been returned to Holland.

Sadly, the *Amsterdam*, which was the best preserved Dutch East Indiaman wreck in the world, has fallen victim to international funding difficulties and plans to raise and return her to Holland are at a standstill. The old ship is now being heavily attached by teredo worms, and chances of a successful recovery are fading fast.

338 Prehistoric Forest Just offshore, close to the *Amsterdam* (Site **337**) and near Bo-Peep Rocks (Site **337**), divers have found large quantities of waterlogged wood. These are the remains of trees, and when dated by carbon-14 tests they show that there was a forest on this site almost 5,000 years ago.

Part of the beach at Hastings, with the cliff railway in the background. The remains of the Amsterdam (Site 337) lie under the beach.

AREA 8:

Hastings to Broomhill Sands

This area runs from 00 32 00E to 00 51 24E, and includes Hastings, Fairlight, Pett Level, Winchelsea, Rye, Camber, and Broomhill Sands.

The town of HASTINGS has been associated with the sea and seamen from the beginning of recorded time. Whether William the Conqueror landed at Bulverhythe, or further west, as some people say, in Pevensey Bay in 1066 (*see* Area 7) we shall probably never know. But we do know about even earlier activity of ships and shipping – for stone anchors have been found all along this stretch of coast. Recently a fisherman from Hastings trawled up a big stone anchor some 3ft high and 6 inches thick, which may indicate the presence of a really ancient wreck some 2 miles out to sea from the town.

Hastings used to be a powerful member of the Cinque Ports, providing ships and men to defend England against the French; and today their descendants, the modern fishermen, still winch their boats up the shingle near the tall black-painted net-drying sheds. And – be warned – they launch them down the beach again with a rush and with the engine going to get them clear of the close-in breakers.

Among the attractions for divers in the town of Hastings is Hastings Library in Claremont, off the sea front near White Rock. This library holds an enormous amount of wreck material for the area and any diver researching his favourite wreck should consult the card-index there first. A large number of old newspapers and documents have already been wreck-searched and the work is going on all the time.

In Rock-a-Nore Road, at the rear of Hastings Harbour and next door to the Fishermen's Museum is the Shipwreck Heritage Centre. This centre, under the guidance of archaeologist Peter Marsden, houses an exciting collection of Sussex shipwreck material.

The Hastings area is generally served by the dive boats from Rye, but there are also boats in Hastings itself that will take out divers.

Divers should be alert for nets, large numbers of which are set in the area. Another problem is the visibility. Inshore, long periods of calm are required for the material in suspension to settle.

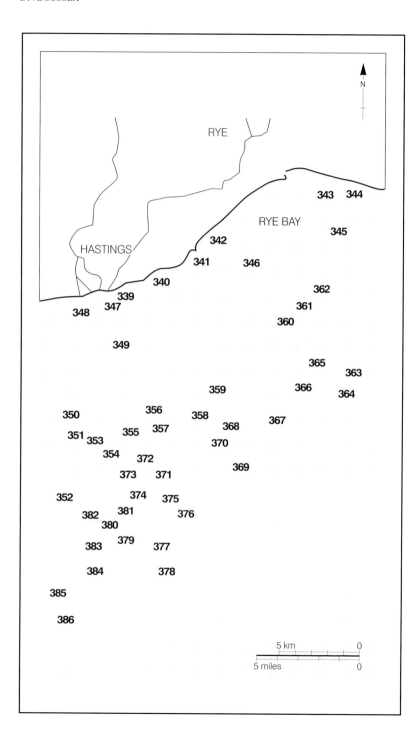

RYE

RYE BAY

HASTINGS

343 344

345

342

341 346

340

339

348 347

349

362

361

360

365

363

359 366 364

356 358 367

350 368

351 355 357

353 370

354 372

373 371 369

352 374 375

382 381 376

380

383 379 377

384 378

385

386

5 km 0

5 miles 0

N

The Shipwreck Heritage Centre at Hastings.

Further east, the mud begins to mix with sand inshore, and RYE BAY is really where the mud takes over. Moving along the coast, the presence of mud becomes obvious after FAIRLIGHT CLIFFS – and more particularly at PETT LEVEL round the site of the *Anne*. This inshore area of poor visibility continues right up to Rye.

Though you might find divers admiring the narrow cobbled streets and old buildings of the medieval town of RYE, their real interest lies down the River Rother to RYE HARBOUR and beyond where the river finds its way to the sea in Rye Bay. For this is wreck-diver country. Rye itself is now some 2 miles from the sea, which has retreated since the 16th century when the town was one of the Cinque Ports.

But Rye still does a lot of business with the sea. Timber comes in from Russia and Finland, mostly in German ships. And a useful piece of information with which to impress people on the diving boat is that most of the talcum powder used in Britain also comes into this country through the port of Rye.

From the fishing point of view, Rye is trawler country with Rye Bay the home of plaice, sole, turbot, and other flatfish. Rye Harbour – which is within ¾ mile of the entrance – dries at low water. Near the mouth of the river the bottom is sandy, but the river-bed becomes more muddy upstream. Though most diving is done from hired hard-boats, the diver-coxswain should be warned not to cut corners or bends in the river as the water shoals there dramatically.

Opposite: Dive sites in Area 8, Hastings to Broomhill Sands. This area is covered by Admiralty charts 536 (Beachy Head to Dungeness) and 1991 (Rye Harbour and Approaches); Ordnance Survey Pathfinder maps 199 and 189.

179

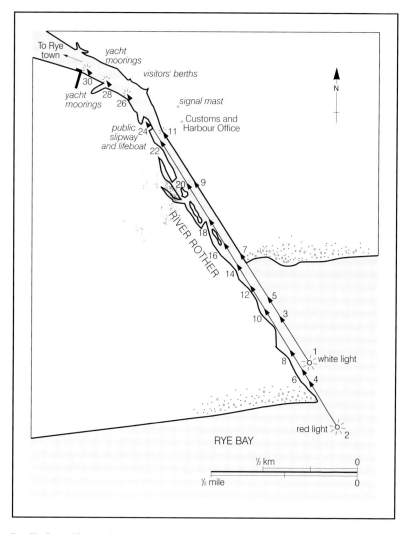

Rye Harbour. The numbers 1 to 30 locate the navigation lights detailed on page 182.

The tide runs fast in the narrow river channel, with the flood stronger than the ebb. The entrance is 30m wide at its narrowest point and lies between the east and west piers.

On the west side there is a long training wall, with a groyne that extends out to sea and has a red light on the end of the arm. The river is navigable from 2 hours before to 3 hours after high water.

Rye is being increasingly used by large cargo ships, and all vessels must give way when such a ship is moving in the harbour (that is, the area from Strand Quay in the town of Rye down to the sea). When such a vessel is on the move a black ball (or balls) will be shown on the Signal Mast near the harbourmaster's office in Rye Harbour itself. At night, an amber, quick-flashing light is shown.

Launch sites

Launching at Hastings is straightforward. There are no restrictions, and launching can be carried out over the beach almost anywhere – although you should keep away from the pier and avoid both sides of the harbour. The west side of the harbour arm in particular is not safe because of the sea defence works, or stabbits, that are exposed at low tide. These, you will see, have spikes and other nasty protrusions, which could well do an inflatable mortal damage.

It is also wise to keep clear of the fishermen's boats when launching as they do not take kindly to other vessels being launched off "their beach". The fishermen are known locally as "chopbacks" because in some dispute at sea a Hastings man in the late 1700s split a Frenchman nearly in two with an axe!

At Rye, the only official launching site for divers' boats in the area is the slipway at Rye Harbour village. There is a charge. Approach Rye Harbour by turning off the Rye to Winchelsea Road (A259) at the Martello Tower just outside the town of Rye and head for the sea.

The slipway is of concrete with stones near the water's edge. During the summer it becomes quite busy, especially at weekends, during the possible launch times, which are 2 hours before to 3 hours after high water. A slipway controller is usually there to collect dues and organise orderly launching. As the inshore lifeboat also uses this slip, the controller will stop all private launching

The concrete slipway on the River Rother at Rye.

during any rescue emergency, and will make sure the lifeboat gets away swiftly. The launching site is near the William the Conqueror pub; 200yds from the slipway there is free parking for 500 cars.

Once launched, the diver-coxswain should know that beacons and light numbers along the banks are even on the port side and odd on the starboard (see map on page 180). Light No. 1 shows a white flashing light. Red flashing lights are at 2, 6, 10, 46. Red flashing lights and beacons are at 18, 24, 26, 28, 30. Green flashing lights are at 3, 7, 9, 19, 25. At 11, there is an occulting green light with white sector showing 326½° to 331½° and a beacon.

Once out at sea, look out for trawlers from Rye Harbour as the local fishermen trawl for scallops as well as flatfish. Beds of queen scallops, the smaller variety, are also fished from Rye. There are many obstructions on the sea bed in Rye Bay, and even the trawlermen are amazed at the number of huge anchors that foul their nets in the area. A good example of this can be seen near the Lifeboat Shed at Hastings. This 5-ton monster was raised by diver Alan Kennard of Rye with lifting bags after he had found it lying on hard ground 1 mile north of the *Australier* wreck. The fact that it was on hard ground is, in itself, unusual for the area.

Rye is one of the Meccas of wreck divers and this book has only been able to concern itself with those wrecks up to the end of the coast of Sussex, though a large number of other wrecks lie just over the "border" to the west of Dungeness and well within Rye dive-boat range.

Shore diving sites

The visibility in the area is often poor and shore diving is usually only worthwhile after long periods of calm. However, the following sites can be interesting.

339 Rock-A-Nore, Hastings This is a large rocky area east of Rock-A-Nore beach below the cliffs next to the East Hill lift. Water entry is at the eastern arm (the small one) and the rocks are to the south-east in around 7m with an average visibility of 4m. In summer there are cuttlefish here and all year round there are large plaice and flounder. This area is a nursery for many species and is regularly visited by staff of the local sea life centre to collect specimens.

340 Fairlight Cliffs Launching is easy at Pett Level at the cliffs, eastern end. Under the cliffs are gullies and a boulder-strewn sea bed, which has plenty of life.

341 Hook Ledge This rock ledge drops down to 7m immediately off the shore and, in good visibility, has a great deal of marine life to offer. The position is 50 52 36N; 00 41 00E.

342 Anne Listed here because she is literally on the shore – though all diving on her is banned – the *Anne* is another of the protected wrecks inside Sussex boundaries.

The 70-gun *Anne* was a victim of the Battle of Beachy Head in 1690. What is left of her now lies at 50 53 22N; 00 41 46E, and all diving is prohibited within 75m of this point. Although the *Anne* was deliberately beached and it is possible to wade out to the site at low water, this is also prohibited.

The Battle of Beachy Head on 30 June, 1690 started badly, went badly and finished badly, as far as the English were concerned. London gossip at the time said that "the Dutch had the honour, the French the advantage, and the English the shame." *Anne* was not part of that shame.

Launched at Chatham in 1678, she was just short of 151ft long, had a beam of 40ft, and carried 26 32lb guns on her main deck, 26 12lb cannon on the upper deck, 10 6-pounders, called sakers, on the quarter-deck and four more on the forecastle. Four 3-pounders guarded her poop, and the ship was fought by 460 men.

During the battle, the *Anne* was commanded by John Tyrrell. She was part of a combined English fleet under the orders of the Earl of Torrington, who had 56 ships. Meanwhile, the French, commanded by the Comte de Tourville, had 70. The French fleet came out of Brest and started up-Channel with the intention of blockading the Thames.

The Dutch, who were in the lead of Torrington's fleet, were in action within an hour of the start of the battle at 8am on 30 June. The French attacked in a crescent-moon formation, and this meant that Torrington and his squadron in the middle of the line could only fire at long range. The *Anne*, however, was fighting French ships close to by 9.30am, though she did not open fire until she was within a musket shot of the enemy.

At 2pm the breeze dropped and the *Anne* was one of several English ships that were becalmed in the middle of a slugging match with the French. By 4pm, the *Anne* was so riddled with shot that she had to be towed out of danger into the middle of the Allied fleet.

The next day, Torrington held a council of war and decided to retreat. He really had no alternative. The French had lost no ships at all. The English and Dutch had lost – or seemed likely to do so because of the damage they had sustained, which amounted to seven ships. Any ship that could not keep up was to be abandoned.

Captain John Tyrrell did not like this, and rather than abandon the *Anne* he wallowed along behind the main fleet up-Channel. Seeing Tyrrell in trouble, the captains of the *York* and the *Swallow*, both his personal friends, took the *Anne* in tow. Finally though, with the French edging in, the towlines had to be abandoned and Tyrrell struggled on alone.

On 3 July, the *Anne* was dropping further and further back, and Captain Tyrrell had no comfort from the sight of four badly-damaged Dutch ships being scuttled or burned near Hastings.

The next day dawned calm, but the light breezes did not help the *Anne* to catch up. Her position was now clearly hopeless. Captain Tyrrell fired a gun, and Torrington sent his yacht back to find out what the signal was for. Tyrrell sent a message to the Admiral saying that unless his ship could be protected she was in great danger of being captured. Torrington replied that no help could be given. Tyrrell had fought a good fight and now he knew what he had to do. The *Anne* altered course and slowly made her way inshore.

The French were closer now, scenting an easy kill. But Tyrrell still had time to select a good spot for beaching. Finally, the *Anne* slid to a halt on a deep mud beach close to the little hamlet of Pett Level. Now everything that was portable was taken out of her and the next day, when the French gave every indication of landing troops to take her, the *Anne* was set on fire.

When she finally guttered out, her lower parts sank into the mud and she was forgotten. Until, that is, early 1974 when, spurred on no doubt by the discovery of the *Amsterdam* (Site **335**), someone took a bulldozer down to the wreck site of the *Anne* at low spring tides. The diggers raised iron cannonballs, grenades, musket balls, clay pipes, spoons, a pewter plate and damaged timbers that were sticking up from the beach. The Protection of Wrecks Order was rushed through as a result. A trial excavation in 1997 has shown that much of the ship's hull – the bottom 14ft of it at least – lies under the mud together with many artefacts of the period. These will all be revealed when the wreck is excavated and lifted from her muddy grave by the Nautical Museums Trust, which now owns the *Anne* and has plans to place her in a specially built museum on a site at St Leonards opposite the grave of the *Amsterdam*.

Boat diving sites

343 The Big Anchor Lying at 50 55 30N; 00 48 54E at the east end of Camber Sands, this is a big old anchor, a fluke of which dries at low spring tides. It has been known to damage fun boats, and is a nuisance to swimmers at times.

344 HMS Caulonia This requisitioned trawler of 296 tons was built in 1912. Today she is a stranded wreck 50 55 15N; 00 50 14E. Buoys usually mark the site. The *Caulonia* was in Rye Bay on 31 March, 1943, when she ran aground, foundering when she could not get off. She was then only 600yds due south of the Coastguard lookout post at Jury's Gap on Broomhill Sands. Despite being so close in, she can be a worthwhile dive, with visibility of 6 to 7m.

Amazingly, there is another small wreck between her and the shore. This one, which is 25yds closer in, consists of a tangle of plates and ribs. The author can find no name for her.

345 Robin Hood This is a bit of a mystery at 50 53 24N; 00 50 18E. Here, undoubtedly, is the wreckage of a big old wooden ship. Great foot-square wooden beams stick up 3m out of the mud, and there are other larger timbers, a keel and a stern-post. The wreck seems to be at least 100ft long overall, and is in 10m of water. Local divers believe that there is much more buried under the mud, and on one exploration an iron cannon was exposed. This site is often dived when it is too rough to get out to the deeper wrecks, but no clue to her identity other than the fishermen's name of *Robin Hood* has so far been found. Archaeologists who have dived her recently confess to being just as puzzled about her identity and date.

346 Flying Fortress Probably a victim of German fighters or anti-aircraft fire on one of the mass daylight raids carried out by the American squadrons of the US 8th Air Force based in Britain, this bomber did not quite make it back to England – crashing into the sea just 1½ miles offshore at 50 52 30N; 00 43 00E.

Today, the aeroplane is mostly buried, with just part of a wing, an engine and the undercarriage showing. Three propellers have been salvaged, but there are many small items scattered around, and machine-gun bullets and radio valves were picked up recently.

347 Thistle This steam trawler was working the grounds off Hastings on 11 September, 1948, when she sprang a leak. She was taken in tow for Newhaven, but sank close inshore at 50 50 52N; 00 34 48E. Her remains are now completely covered by sand for most of the time.

348 Flying Fortress Just 200yds straight out from Hastings Pier is the wreckage of a Flying Fortress of the US 8th Air Force, which crashed while returning from a daylight raid on Germany during World War Two. This is a wonderful dive for novices, with much fish life and a depth of 12m. The aeroplane covers and uncovers, but there are usually two engines to be seen along with part of the fuselage.

349 Eagle Sunk in May 1945, this steel barge was for transporting fresh water and was one of those fitted out for the Normandy landings when it was thought that the troops might be so held up before breaking out of the beach-heads that supplies of all essentials would have to be brought in by sea. The wreck is at 50 49 10N; 00 36 26E, and is some 3m proud of the 14m sea bed. The barge itself is 80ft long with a beam of 26ft. In the barge is the water tank – a steel cylinder some 15ft in diameter.

The wreck is known for the fish life around it, and is an excellent dive for novices. There are bass to be seen there in summer, and a permanent cloud of pouting. The bow is just like that of a Thames barge, and it is possible to get right down under it.

The pier at Hastings. Just 200yds out is the wreck of a Flying Fortress bomber (Site 348).

350 The Engine At 50 46 56N; 00 34 19E this is simply the engine and boilers of a steamer that seems to have almost entirely disappeared. Lying on a sandy sea bed at 20m, the wreck appeals to photographers because of the abundant fish life. The site is changing, probably due to nearby dredging. The sea bed appears to be sinking away from the wreckage revealing plates, ribs and the propeller shaft. Perhaps it is not too late for some diver to find a piece to identify her.

351 HMS Agate This hired trawler is at 50 46 15N; 00 34 03E, where she sank after hitting a mine on 14 March, 1918, "off the Royal Sovereign Light Vessel" (Site 304). Her position then was given by the Dover patrol boat, which rescued all aboard as 50 45 00N; 00 32 00E – so it seems likely that she drifted for some time before finally sinking at her present position. Of 248 tons and 122ft long, this wreck has been swept to 11.9m, and as the sea bed is at 13m you can see that there is not much showing today. Divers report that she has all but disappeared into the sandy bed.

352 Wreck, name unknown A small ship at 50 44 23N; 00 33 31E. Lying on a slope that runs down to 22m, this one is less than 4m proud. Diving information is needed.

353 Sir Robert Wigham A big name for a little motor vessel. This former target-towing ship is at 50 45 48N; 00 35 46E. She sank on 3 December, 1956, in 18m of water and has now almost disappeared into the sea bed.

354 Wreck, name unknown Very little is known of this ship. Lying at 50 45 48N; 00 36 43E, she is 82ft long in 21m on a wavy sea bed of sand. She stands 3m proud.

355 Broderick This British steamer of 4,321 tons was 365ft long with a beam of 47ft. She was sunk by *UB-57*, commanded by Oberleutnant Lohs, on 29 April, 1918. She was in ballast, but was carrying some 50 prize cattle breeding stock as she headed from London and Dunkirk for Venezuela. The first torpedo hit her in the port side by No. 2 hold. But she did not sink and her master, George Copper, made a run for the English coast. Lohs' second torpedo 30 minutes later also exploded on her port side. This time she sank in 20m, but her two masts showed at all states of the tide, making her a very definite hazard to navigation. In fact, as late as 1921 the master of the steamship *Sebu* reported hitting something underwater in her position. Some dispersal followed then, and again in 1959. But it is possible that this wreck accounted for another ship before the later dispersal work took place, for a 60ft small wreck lies close by the main area of wreckage among the sand dunes around the site.

The *Broderick* is now very broken up at 50 46 16N; 00 37 47E. She stands little more than 4m proud. There is, however, a great deal of marine life on her and around her. Codling and pouting swarm around, and plaice and turbot can often be seen on the sea bed.

356 Umba This former German war prize – then called the *Utgard* – was torpedoed by the German submarine *UB-57*, which the day before had sunk the *Broderick* (Site **355**). The 2,042-ton merchantman sank almost immediately after she was hit and now lies at 50 46 37N; 00 38 36E. Out of the crew of 25, 20 including the master died in the sinking at 1.40am.

The 291ft *Umba* was in ballast going from Dunkirk to Barry when she was torpedoed on 30 April, 1918. She is now broken in two on a humpy sea bed, and lies north-east to south-west. The bow section is the largest piece and is to the south-west. It is also the tallest – being some 10m high.

It is 24m to the Russian-made 6lb gun on her stern, which has shells underneath it. But divers should be warned that the mid-ship break is deceptive, and the forward section in fact slopes down to 37m.

357 The Gun Wreck This one lies at 50 46 12N; 00 38 58E on a bumpy sea bed at 23m. "Gun Wreck" is purely a local name, of course, and we do not know her real one. She is 6m proud of the sea bed, lies east–west, and is 280ft long. Her centre section is heavily broken up, and the wreck, which is on an even keel, is dominated by the big gun mounted on the stern.

358 Wreck, name unknown 50 47 34N; 00 42 14E. This wreck has been dispersed and is now in two halves. She is very well broken also, and is scattered over a sandy sea bed at 17m. The largest part is 4m proud.

359 Actuality This 945-ton British collier was in collision with the steamer *Betty-Ann* in fog on 27 October, 1963. The crew of 12 were all saved, but the *Actuality* now lies on the sea bed in 18m at 50 48 54N; 00 43 42E. She has been dispersed and swept, and as a result is very broken up. Plenty of wreckage of this 202ft ship can, however, still be seen as well as much of her coal cargo. Some of the remains stand 6m proud.

360 Lepanto At one time it was thought that this wreck at 50 50 13N; 00 47 02E was the steamer *Australier* of 3,687 tons, which was torpedoed on 29 April, 1918, by the German submarine UB-57, but she lies further to the east. Local fisherman have always called this one the *Lepanto* or "Panto" and they may well be right as a bell recovered in recent years had "lepanto" on it.

There was a *Lepanto* of 2,310 tons, built at the Earles of Hull shipyard in 1877. She was 305ft long with a beam of 36ft and was owned by Wilson and Sons, also of Hull. This might have been our ship except for the fact that she was sunk off St Catherine's Point on the Isle of Wight, on 7 January, 1898 after colliding with another British steamer, the *Knight of St George* in thick fog. Lloyd's report that when divers found the ship she was in 15 fathoms and there was a large hole from the collision on her port side.

This is clearly not our *Lepanto*, but there was a British ship called *Lepanto* in World War One. She was much bigger (6,389 tons) and was armed with a large gun, which she used to good effect to escape from a surface attack by gunfire from a German submarine in the Channel on 15 March, 1917. She next appears in official records on 23 October that year when she was torpedoed 3 miles off Dartmouth by another U-boat. Although two of her crew were killed in the explosion, she managed to get into Dartmouth for repairs. She seems to have survived the war as no ship of that name is reported sunk by enemy action; yet our wreck was first reported to the Admiralty at Dover on 4 September, 1918 and as having 9.5 fathoms over her.

The wreck has been swept and is on her starboard side lying south-east to north-west. She is 328ft long and is on a flat sea bed from which she stands some 10m proud. When visibility is good, this is an excellent dive with cabins, portholes, ladders and companion-ways all in place. The ship's telegraph has been raised but gave no clue to her identity. Can any diver help?

361 Ella Sayer A 2,549-ton collier sailing from Penarth, near Cardiff, to Dunkirk with 3,900 tons of coal, the *Ella Sayer* was in the swept channel on the British side before moving out to cross to France when she was "submarined" on 29 April, 1918.

Though the torpedo took the *Ella Sayer* in the port side amidships and killed two men at once, it took the ship an hour to sink at 50 50 30N; 00 47 59E. It is possible that she was a victim of the U-boat that sank the *Australier* (*see* Site **360**) on the same day.

Where the *Ella Sayer* lies now, it is 28m to the very silty sea bed (owing to a scour of 5m that the ship has made in the 23m sea bed). She stands some 8m proud, and the slightest touch by a diver will send clouds of silt up to ruin the visibility. She is lying across the tide from north-west to south-east, and is broken in two.

The *Ella Sayer* was 313ft long with a beam of 45ft, and was built in 1898 for the Tyne Iron Steam Boat Company. The steam whistle has been recovered from the upright midships section. This wreck is sometimes called the *Cape Jubilee* by local fishermen. She is owned by three Hastings divers – Stuart Farquahar, Nick Marley and Carl West.

362 Swale 50 51 12N; 00 49 03E. This 3,400-ton London steamer was run down by another steamer, the *Portslade*, in fog on 18 March, 1906, and quickly sank to the sea bed at 21m. She is still sinking into the mud and silt of the sea bed, and her highest point today is 4m proud. This wreck is, like others in the area, heavily silted; and the sea bed is soft. The wreck is very old, so take great care with the rusting plates.

363 Argonaut One of the first package tours came to an abrupt end when this luxury steam yacht, bound for a Mediterranean cruise with 113 passengers on board, was rammed at 8.30am on the foggy morning of 29 September, 1908, and sank at 50 48 33N; 00 50 32E. All on board were saved.

Today, the *Argonaut* is owned by divers John Nightingale, Ian O'Riley and Malcolm Ilott. She is a good dive despite some salvage work done on her. Her condensers are gone and so is a lot of large copper piping – much to the surprise of her owners. The first hard clue to her identity was the recovery of a fork bearing the name *Argonaut*. After that, as if her shape and dimensions were not enough, more cutlery and crockery bearing her name clinched matters.

The *Argonaut* is on an even keel with her bows to the south-east. Her iron hull is clearly screw-driven, but there were at least two masts of steel rigged for sailing. She is 334ft long with a beam of 40ft, and is in remarkable condition despite her age. She sits on a hard gravel sea bed at 32m and is at least 10m proud. The stern is very pretty and intact with 4ft-square windows all round giving a castle effect to the poop deck. Though the bow is intact, the figurehead is gone, and little remains of the bowsprit.

All those on board the Argonaut (Site 363) were saved when she sank in fog in 1908.

The wreck is silty, and scallops gather round her. The silt comes from somewhere else and the visibility is generally good, with about 12m commonplace. The ship's wheel has been recovered, as have many plates bearing her name. Divers should remember, though, that this is a trawling area and, as if to remind them of this, there is usually at least one large net draped over some part of the wreck. Take care!

364 Maxwell This British ship was on her way from San Francisco to Hull when she sank after colliding "off Dungeness" with another steamer on 3 April, 1902. The ship in collision with the *Maxwell* was described in reports at first as the *Patanenia*, then as the *Patagonia*. The *Maxwell* took long enough to go down for all her crew to be saved, and now lies at 50 48 14N; 00 49 31E.

The depth is 31m. The ship was swept to 17.5m in 1976, but is still upright with a slight list to port though sunk quite deep into the sandy sea bed. The deck is gone, and it is possible to see right through three decks in places. In fact, divers can swim from stern to stem inside the hull ending up at her bowsprit, which is still in place and makes a most impressive sight.

There are still some portholes on her and the boilers and a winch are clear. Many divers have found cups and saucers on her. They have also commented on the green tint in the water around the wreck and attribute this to the copper ore she was reported to be carrying at the time of her sinking.

365 Wreck, name unknown 50 49 05N; 00 48 31E. This is a very small wreck in 25m of water. The highest point is 3m and the broken wreckage appears to be sinking into the sea-bed sand-waves. More diving information is needed.

366 Rundø 50 48 02N; 00 47 01E. This 262ft wreck was listed as "unknown" for many years and was reported to be carrying a cargo of shell cases. A dive at the beginning of 1985, however, revealed that she was lying on her port side, that she had a hole in the bow, which could well have been made by a torpedo, and that her iron propeller was still there, though her condensers had gone. The holds were full of mud, but there was a clear indication that she had been carrying nitrates, not shell cases. One of the divers recovered the bell, which bears the name *Rundø* (the name suggests that the ship was Norwegian as Rundo is a cliff, known for its nesting birds, off the town of Aalesund in Norway). However, the only Norwegian steamer named *Rundø* was built in 1903, was renamed *Terje* when sold in 1916 and was broken up after being wrecked in 1934 in Norway. So the wreck is still a mystery, lying north-east to south-west in 30m and in a dip between two sand ridges some 5m high.

367 The Admiralty Boat 50 47 20N; 00 45 20E. That is the local name for her. In fact, her real name is not known, even though we do know quite a lot about her. She is, for example, probably a World War One casualty, some 200ft long and upright on an even keel on a flat sea bed at 35m. She was carrying 3-inch shell cases bearing the broad-arrow mark of Government arsenals, so she is probably British. Her bows point to the west. She is broken in half amidships. She has winches fore and aft. Her anchors are properly stowed. Her decking is gone in many places and you can see through almost to her keel. There is a 2m scour on her port side.

368 Wreck, name unknown This wreck is at 50 47 17N; 00 44 21E, and some people claim that this is the *Carlisle Castle* (Site **377**), but she is too small for that. She is about 200ft long and stands upright on a flat sea bed at 30m. Poor visibility is common in this area, and this may account for some of the confusion over identity. Certainly this wreck is old (her ribs are showing near the forward hold). Her bridge – aft of the second hold – stands some 6m proud.

This wreck might be the 3,109-ton *Euphorbia*, which was carrying 4,700 tons of rice, as it lies close to the wreck of the *Rydal Hall* (Site **369**). Both these ships were going up the Channel in the early morning of 1 December, 1917, the *Rydal Hall* following almost in the wake of the *Euphorbia*, when the *Euphorbia* was torpedoed by *UC-75* between No. 3 hold and the engine room, killing several men there. Some of her crew managed to get into boats and head towards the *Rydal Hall*, but she too was torpedoed amidships by *UC-75*. The explosion blew a hole about 80ft long in her side. Fourteen of the *Euphorbia*'s crew of 35 were killed in the incident.

369 Rydal Hall Twenty-three men from the crew of 59 died when this 3,314-ton armed British steamer carrying 4,300 tons of manganese ore, jute and linseed oil, from Calcutta to Dunkirk, was torpedoed by *UC-75* on 1 December, 1917 "14 miles east by south of the Royal Sovereign Light Vessel" (Site **304**). The explosion blew an 80ft hole amidships. Today she lies at 50 44 54N; 00 44 51E on a flat sea bed at 34m. She is canted over to her starboard with her bows to the east, and is 11m proud. She has four holds, with her bridge amidships. Her plating is now very thin, so great care should be taken when entering any part of her 350ft hull.

370 Hoheweg This 1,088-ton German steamer with a general cargo was in collision with the steamer *Sunny Prince* on 14 February, 1955, and sank at 50 46 09N; 00 43 03E. Her mast caused problems for a time, and she was buoyed until she was dispersed in June 1962. Now her 226ft hull lies on a flat mud-sand sea bed at 32m and stands some 10m proud.

Called "the German" by local fishermen and divers, it is possible to look in through the portholes and see some of her cargo of big tractors with iron seats, and Volkswagen cars.

371 Skerryvore This 3,371-ton British steamer built in 1892 had her holds full of iron ore when she collided with a German barque, the *J.C. Vinnen*, on 15 May, 1910. The *Skerryvore* sank so swiftly that 22 of her crew drowned. The only survivor was picked up by the *J.C. Vinnen*. The *Vinnen*, a steel-hulled sailing ship of 3,166 tons, was badly damaged in the bow area, but made port with little trouble.

The 341ft *Skerryvore*, which was going from Villaricos to Rotterdam at the time of the accident, now lies in an area of extremely strong tides and has her 15ft-diameter iron propeller still in place. She is in 33m, and leans into the edge of a great sandbank on her port side. She has settled into a north-east to south-west position, and though sand and silt are encroaching she is still 10m proud. Divers have positively identified her by her bell.

372 Wreck, name unknown 50 45 15N; 00 37 09E. This small wreck lies in a deep hollow and does not even peep over the edge into the surrounding sea bed. The general depth is 28m.

373 Wreck, name unknown 50 44 35N; 00 36 14E. This wreck has been dispersed and little remains standing very high off the sea bed at 21m. The wreck is in two definite parts – close, but completely separated.

374 Dona Isabel This 1,179-ton steamer was caught by a torpedo during the same E-boat sweep – on 2 November, 1943 – that sunk the *Storaa* (Site **381**), and was not long in following her to the bottom. Another ship, the *Foam Queen*, was sunk by the same flotilla on the same day.

The *Dona Isabel* is intact and lies on her port side along a great bank of sand with her bows to the north-east. Her iron propeller is still in position, and her central wheelhouse is intact. Her cargo is coal. She is in 30m at 50 44 00N; 00 37 48E and is owned by Sussex Marine Salvage, the firm of which Geoff Parsons and John Short are partners. Their message is: look, but please do not touch.

375 Wellpark That is the name on the bell recovered by divers from this large old shipwreck of some 354ft lying north-east to south-west at 50 43 48N; 00 38 30E. Despite it being reported that she was a World War One Ministry of Transport ship, as there is no trace of her among the war casualties under that name, the author can only assume that she survived the war and was a victim of weather or some other disaster. On the other hand, she may have been sailing under a different name at the time of her sinking.

The wreck of this vessel is 17m high, but since she lies in a deep 13m scour in the 40m sea bed a dive of 36m is needed to reach her.

376 Jan Brons This small (400-ton) Dutch motor vessel lies close to the *Wellpark* (Site **375**). She was sunk on 12 October, 1945, after being in collision with the Greek steamer, *Panaghis*. Now she lies in 39m and stands some 7m proud, though the sand is building up on her port side and will soon overwhelm most of her decks. She was carrying a general cargo at the time of her sinking, and the most recent dive on her revealed that she was full of tyres and lorry wheels. She is at 50 43 47N; 00 38 40E, and has two pom-pom guns. A larger gun, which the pom-poms flanked, has now been lifted.

The armament of this vessel makes some salvage divers convinced that this is not the *Jan Brons* but the *Storaa* (Site **381**).

377 Carlisle Castle With American "doughboys" fighting in the trenches in France, the great arms arsenals of the United States were opened to the Allies. The 4,325-ton *Carlisle Castle* was one of several British ships that were used to ferry these materials of war to Britain and on to France. She was coming up-Channel from the United States on 14 February, 1918, and was "eight miles east by north from the Royal Sovereign Light Vessel" (Site **304**) when Oberleutnant Lohs in *UB-57* spotted her. Lohs had been given command, of *UB-57* on 29 January. He used just one torpedo, which struck her in the starboard side, killed one man in her engine room, and sent this, his first "kill" with his new command to the bottom very quickly. It was amazing that the whole ship did not blow up, so packed was she with shells and shell cases. She also carried a large quantity of grain. She sank down to the sea bed in 38m and at low tide the tip of her mast just showed. Today, her bows still point north-north-east, and she has been swept to 23.2m; but she is still upright at 50 42 28N; 00 39 10E.

Though many salvage firms have been interested in this 460ft wreck, the last amateur group to dive her reported that there were munitions by the ton still inside her. The shells are packed in separate boxes from the shell cases.

378 Wreck, name unknown 50 42 04N; 00 38 58E – and deep. The sea bed here is very lumpy and dips down to 41m. This wreck stands 8m proud in places, but is clearly sinking into the sea bed. No further information is available, though this appears to be a small wreck of about 100ft.

379 Wittering Formerly known as the *Framptondyke*, this British motor vessel of 1,599 tons lies at 50 43 01N; 00 36 36E. On 25 February, 1976, while bound from Rotterdam to Cork with a cargo of wheat, the *Wittering* was in collision with the 999-ton German ship *Odin*. A deep-sea tug was swiftly on the spot, and all the crew of the *Wittering* were safely taken off before the tug started trying to tow the British ship. But the *Wittering* soon capsized and the tow ropes broke away.

When divers found the vessel she was in 40m of water, lying on her port side with her bows to the west. More recent diving has revealed that she has swung so that her bows are now nearly due south-west, and that some of the tow lines are still in place and floating clear of the wreck. From being on her port side she is now nearly completely upside down and her highest point is 14m off the shelving sea bed.

380 Confederate Gun-runner This brig, laden with rifles (probably a consignment of arms for the Confederate States in the American Civil War) was also carrying an inscribed tombstone, which gave the diver who found it quite a shock!

The brig was believed to have sunk in about 1862 because the tombstone was for the grave of a woman and her baby who had died in childbirth at St Thomas in the Virgin Islands in 1858.

This wreck was worked by a commercial company who hoped to find gold among the cargo but did not. What the brig's cargo did contain were machetes for the sugar plantations, hundreds of gin and brandy bottles (the latter full but undrinkable with lead caps inscribed "Vieux Cognac"), Paris perfumes and the rifles – French flintlock muskets of the 1820s.

What remains of the ship is at 50 43 22N; 00 35 56E. The depth is 43m. The Nautical Museums Trust have a substantial collection of objects from this wreck for display in their Hastings Shipwreck Heritage Centre.

Divers who visit the "gun-runner" now will find little of her hull remaining (although the lowest section, which had been copper clad, is rather more solid, and the rudder is still on the stern). There are a few boxes of rifles left and some bottles – and untouched are piles and piles of sheets of window glass sufficient to build a multitude of greenhouses!

381 Storaa This Danish steamer of 1,967 tons was seized by Britain when Denmark was occupied by the Germans on 9 April, 1940. The *Storaa* was in port at the time, and her Danish crew scuttled her. She was raised and repaired and sailed for Britain until 2 November, 1943, when she was caught by an E-boat sweep and went down after being torpedoed by one of the 50-knot boats. Her position then was given as 50 43 39N; 00 37 18E and the depth somewhere close to the 20-fathom line (120ft or about 37m).

The *Storaa* was 282ft long with a beam of 42ft. Her position today is believed by some divers to be that charted as "possibly" the *Jan Brons*.

382 Gold Coin This 279ft Greek ship of 1,957 tons was originally called *Eos*. But she had been renamed the *Gold Coin* by the time she and the MV *Duhallow* collided on 4 December, 1972. The *Gold Coin* had her holds full of maize and was bound for Dakar.

Now she lies at 50 43 55N; 00 34 47E on her starboard side with her bows towards the north. The fish have made sure that her holds are empty. The depth of 18m is not the reason that she is so broken up; this is owing to a dispersal carried out in 1974. Nothing now stands more than 2m proud.

383 Wreck, name unknown This is almost certainly a World War One victim of a mine or torpedo judging by the big hole near the bows. At 50 42 50N; 00 34 55E, this is a large ship on its port side in 33m. She stands nearly 10m proud of the coarse sand sea bed at her highest points amidships, but her bow and stern are starting to sink into the sea bed. Her bows are towards the west.

384 Wreck, name unknown Another World War One victim. This one, at 50 41 42N; 00 33 48E, almost certainly sank because of a mine – her stern is almost completely blown off, though the rest of this 2,500-ton vessel is reasonably upright. She has been swept to 22m on a sea bed at 38m. Recent dives confirmed that she lies east–west.

385 Freighter, name unknown 50 41 13N; 00 32 20E. This wreck of a freighter of about 1,700 tons is upright on the sea bed at 34m. She is about 350ft long and her bows point east-north-east. She stands 10m proud, and is in remarkable condition – so much so that her anchors are still in place. They appear to be of 1914–1918 vintage. The wheelhouse, though collapsing, is still visible amidships. Her holds are empty and the engine room is aft. There are winches at bow and stern, and during a recent dive, despite poor visibility, the divers concerned felt sure that damage to her port side indicated a torpedo hit.

386 Samwake There were 88 Liberty ships with the prefix Sam. Some said that this stood for Uncle Sam, others that it meant Superstructure Aft of Midships, but a British source was always responsible for the remaining part of the ships' names.

The 7,176-ton *Samwake* was launched in April 1944, and was sunk by an E-boat's torpedo when she was travelling in ballast back from the Normandy beaches to the River Thames during the night of 31 July, 1944. The crew of 43 and 15 gunners, plus a military policeman, were all saved. She was 441ft long with a beam of 57ft. She now lies in deep water of 48m, and her position of 50 40 06N; 00 33 18E is only approximate.

APPENDIX 1:

Dive Services

Dive boats

Boats available are listed in order from east to west. Diver Magazine is the source of information for other operators.

Bracklesham Bay Wittering Divers, 6.5m RIB, 10 divers, all electronic gear (tel. 01243 672031/ 673494).

Littlehampton Marina *Jonathan Seagull* (diver-skipper Ray Lee), 10m, 12 divers, all electronic gear (tel. 01903 783541).
  Huntress Four (diver-skipper Bernie Attwood), 8m, 8 divers, all electronic gear (tel. 01903 783541).
  Michelle Mary (diver-skipper Ivan Warren), 11.5m, 12 divers (tel. 01903 739010; boat 0850 503812).

The Ship and Anchor Marina, Ford, Littlehampton
  Les Ann (diver-skipper Vernon Parker), 9m, 6 divers, all electronic gear (also *My Joy,* 10m, 10 divers), (tel. 01243 553977; boat 0850 312068).
  Blue Dolphin (diver-skipper Cyril Gubby), 10m, 10 divers, all electronic gear (tel. 01243 551371; boat 0378 045388).

Shoreham *Blue Smartie* (diver-skipper Sam Coles), 10m, 12 divers, all electronic gear (tel. 01273 440940).
  Colgan (diver-skipper John McLoughlin), 10.5m, 10 divers, all electronic gear (tel. 01273 624351; boat 0860 925941).

Brighton At Brighton Marina, Pontoon 32:
  Girl Gray (diver-skipper Mike Snelling), 13m, 12 divers, all electronic gear (tel. 01273 693400; boat 0973 386379).
  Grey Viking (diver-skipper Alan Young), 10m, 12 divers, all electronic gear (tel. 01273 300388; boat 0421 865212).

Spartacus (diver-skipper Tim Bennetto), 11m, 12 divers, all electronic gear (tel. 01273 586445; boat 0860 209367).

Channel Diver (diver-skipper Steve Johnson), 12 divers, all electronic gear (tel. 07970 674799).

Newhaven In Newhaven Marina:

The Mistress (diver-skipper Raymond Leriche), 10.5m, 10 divers, all electronic gear (tel. 01444 451093; mobile 0973 498078).

Valerie (diver-skipper Al Costas), 9.5m, 8 divers (tel. 0181 857 4551).

RIBS are available for charter. Contact Newhaven Scuba Centre (tel. 01273 612012).

Eastbourne *Catrina* (skipper Roger Wilson), 10.5m, 10 divers, all electronic gear (tel. 01323 766076; boat 0860 421401).

Ice Fox (diver-skipper Zack Matten), 10m, 12 divers, all electronic gear (tel. 01424 434836).

Air and equipment supplies

Most are available during normal working hours and weekends in season, but a telephone check is recommended.

Portsmouth Solent Divers, 122–128 Lake Road, Portsmouth, (tel. 01705 814924). Air to 4,000psi.

Peter Anderson Sports Ltd, 48–50 Elm Grove, Portsmouth, (tel. 01705 820611). Air to 3,000psi.

East Wittering Wittering Divers, 12 Oakfield Road, East Wittering P020 8RP (tel. 01243 672031/ 673494). Air to 4000psi. Nitrox. Equipment and repairs.

Littlehampton Littlehampton Marina, Ferry Road, Littlehampton, (tel. 01903 713553). Air to 3000psi.

Shoreham International Diving and Watersports, 1 New Road, Shoreham-by-Sea, Sussex, BN4 6RA (tel. 01273 455892). Air to 4,000psi. Equipment, repairs, cylinder testing.

Blue Smartie Diving, 68 High Street, Shoreham (tel. 01273 440940). Air to 3500psi. Nitrox. Equipment, repairs.

Brighton Brighton Dive Company, 24 Garnet House, St George's Road (entrance in College Road), Kemptown, Brighton BN2 1EU (tel. 01273 622933). Air to 4,000psi. Equipment, repairs and rental.

Newhaven C and E Sports Centre, 15 Bridge Street, Newhaven (tel. 0273 515450). Air to 3,000psi. Equipment.

Newhaven Scuba Centre, The Yacht Harbour, West Quay, Newhaven (tel. 01273 612012). Air to 4500psi. Nitrox. Equipment, repairs, cylinder testing.

Hastings Sussex Marine, 48 Marina, St Leonards, East Sussex, TN38 0BE (tel. 01424 425882). Air to 4,000psi. Equipment.
Hastings Diving Centre, 6 Marine Court, Marina, St Leonards, East Sussex TN38 0XD (tel. 01424 715006). Air to 4750psi. Nitrox, equipment, repairs, cylinder testing.

Local BSAC branches

Most branches welcome visiting divers and many will let them join branch dives. Visiting divers should therefore carry proof of their qualifications. Places to contact Sussex branches are given below, but current telephone numbers of branch secretaries are available from BSAC HQ (tel. 0151 350 6200).

Billingshurst Branch meets at Crawley Leisure Centre, Crawley on Thursdays at 9pm.

Brighton Branch meets at Prince Regents Pool, Jubilee Street on Wednesdays at 8pm.

Chichester Branch meets at Roman Way Club, Chichester on Tuesdays at 7pm.

Crawley Branch meets at the Horley Anderson Pool, Horley, on Thursdays at 8pm.

Eastbourne Branch meets at the University of Brighton, Gaudick Road, Eastbourne on Wednesdays at 8pm.

South Downs Branch meets at Roedean School, Brighton, on Tuesdays at 7pm.

Sussex Diving Club Branch meets at Balfour Road School, Brighton, on Wednesdays at 7.30pm.

Shoreham Branch and Worthing Branch both meet at the Aquarena pool, Brighton Road, Worthing, on Mondays at 8.30pm.

Conversion table –
seconds to decimals of a minute

Seconds	Decimals of a minute	Seconds	Decimals of a minute	Seconds	Decimals of a minute
1	.02	21	.35	41	.68
2	.03	22	.37	42	.70
3	.05	23	.38	43	.72
4	.07	24	.40	44	.73
5	.08	25	.42	45	.75
6	.10	26	.43	46	.77
7	.12	27	.45	47	.78
8	.13	28	.47	48	.80
9	.15	29	.48	49	.82
10	.17	30	.50	50	.83
11	.18	31	.52	51	.85
12	.20	32	.53	52	.87
13	.22	33	.55	53	.88
14	.23	34	.57	54	.90
15	.25	35	.58	55	.92
16	.27	36	.60	56	.93
17	.28	37	.62	57	.95
18	.30	38	.63	58	.97
19	.32	39	.65	59	.98
20	.33	40	.67	60	1.00

Positions given in this book are shown in degrees, minutes and seconds. This conversion table will enable users of GPS navigation aids to convert the minutes and seconds to minutes and decimals of a minute. The information was kindly provided by the Admiralty Hydrographic Office.

APPENDIX 2:

The Diver's Code of Conduct

Divers must at all times adhere to the BSAC code of conduct. It is reproduced here with the kind permission of the British Sub-Aqua Club, and has been extracted from the BSAC *Safe Diving Practices* booklet, available from BSAC Headquarters.

THE DIVER'S CODE OF CONDUCT

More and more people are taking to the water. Some for recreation; some to earn their living. This code is designed to ensure that divers do not come into conflict with other water users. It is vital that you observe it at all times.

Before leaving home

Contact the nearest British Sub-Aqua Club Branch or the dive operator local to the dive site for their advice. Seek advice from them about the local conditions and regulations.

On the beach, river bank or lakeside

1. Obtain permission, before diving in a harbour or estuary or in private water. Thank those responsible before you leave. Pay harbour dues.

2. Try to avoid overcrowding one site, consider other people on the beach.

3. Park sensibly. Avoid obstructing narrow approach roads. Keep off verges. Pay parking fees and use proper car parks.

4. Don't spread yourselves and your equipment since you may upset other people. Keep launching ramps and slipways clear.

5. Please keep the peace. Don't operate a compressor within earshot of other people – or late at night.

6. Pick up litter. Close gates. Be careful about fires. Avoid any damage to land or crops.

7. Obey special instructions such as National Trust rules, local bye-laws and regulations about camping and caravanning.

8. Remember divers in wetsuits are conspicuous and bad behaviour could ban us from beaches.

In and on the water

1. Mark your dive boats so that your Club can be identified easily. Unmarked boats may become suspect.

2. Ask the harbour-master or local officials where to launch your boat – and do as they say. Tell the Coastguard, or responsible person, where you are going and tell them when you are back.

3. Stay away from buoys, pots, and pot markers. Ask local fishermen where not to dive. Offer to help them recover lost gear.

4. Remember ships have not got brakes, so avoid diving in fairways or areas of heavy surface traffic and observe the "International Regulations for the Prevention of Collisions at Sea".

5. Always fly the diving flag when diving, but not when on the way to, or from, the dive site. Never leave a boat unattended.

6. Do not come in to bathing beaches under power. Use any special approach lanes. Do not disturb any seal or bird colonies with your boats. Watch your wash in crowded anchorages.

7. Whenever possible, divers should use a surface marker buoy.

On conservation

1. Never use a speargun with an aqualung. Never use a speargun in fresh water.

2. Shellfish, such as crabs and lobsters, take several years to grow to maturity; over-collecting in an area soon depletes stocks. Only take mature fish or shellfish and then only what you need for yourself. Never sell your catch or clean it in public or on the beach. Don't display your trophies.

3. Be conservation conscious. Avoid damage to weeds and the sea bed. Do not bring up sea-fans, corals, starfish or sea urchins – in one moment you can destroy years of growth.

4. Take photographs and notes – not specimens. Shoot with a camera not a speargun – spearfishing makes fish shy of divers. Never spearfish wrasse or other inshore species since once an area is depleted of such fish, it may take a long time for them to re-colonise.

On wrecks

1. Do not dive on a designated wreck site. These are indicated on Admiralty Charts and marked by buoys or warning notices on the shore nearby.

2. Do not lift anything which appears to be of historical importance.

3. If you do discover a wreck, do not talk about it. Pinpoint the site, do a rough survey and report it to the BSAC Archaeology Adviser and the Council for Nautical Archaeology who will advise you.

4. If you do not lift anything from the wreck, it is not necessary to report your discovery to the Receiver of Wreck. If you do lift, you must report.

5. If your find is important, you may apply for it to be designated a protected site. Then you can build up a well qualified team with the right credentials and proceed with a systematic survey or excavation under licence without outside interference.

Don't Let Divers Down – Keep To The Diver's Code

The River Rother at low tide. The Windmill Guest House can be seen in the background.

Index

The bold numbers in parentheses are dive site numbers.